ALSO BY LYDIA DAVIS

NOVEL

The End of the Story

STORIES

The Thirteenth Woman and Other Stories
Story and Other Stories
Break It Down
Almost No Memory
Samuel Johnson Is Indignant
Varieties of Disturbance
The Collected Stories of Lydia Davis
Can't and Won't

POETRY

Two American Scenes (with Eliot Weinberger)

SELECTED TRANSLATIONS

Madame Bovary: Provincial Ways by Gustave Flaubert
Swann's Way by Marcel Proust
Death Sentence by Maurice Blanchot
The Madness of the Day by Maurice Blanchot
The Spirit of Mediterranean Places by Michel Butor
Rules of the Game, I: Scratches by Michel Leiris
Rules of the Game, II: Scraps by Michel Leiris
Rules of the Game, III: Fibrils by Michel Leiris
Hélène by Pierre Jean Jouve
Grasses and Trees by A. L. Snijders

ESSAYS ONE

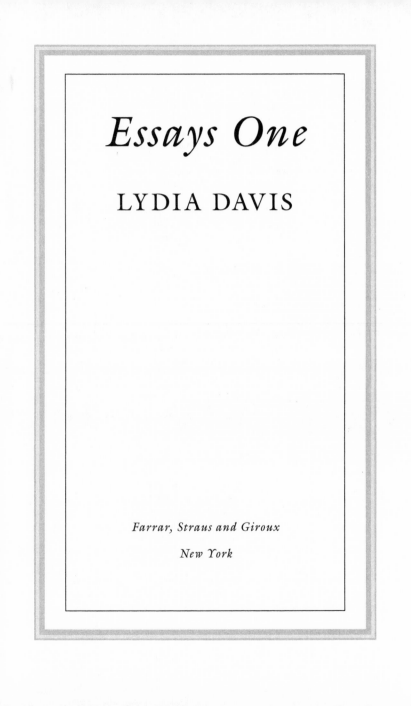

Essays One

LYDIA DAVIS

Farrar, Straus and Giroux

New York

Farrar, Straus and Giroux
120 Broadway, New York 10271

Owing to limitations of space, all acknowledgments for
permission to reprint previously published material
can be found on pages 511–512.

Illustration credits can be found on page 509.

Library of Congress Cataloging-in-Publication Data
Names: Davis, Lydia, 1947– author.
Title: Essays one / Lydia Davis.
Description: First edition. | New York : Farrar, Straus and Giroux,
2019. | Summary: "A selection of essays on writing and reading
by the master short-fiction writer Lydia Davis"—Provided by
publisher.
Identifiers: LCCN 2019020199 | ISBN 9780374148850 (hardcover)
Subjects: LCSH: Reading. | Writing.
Classification: LCC PS3554.A9356 A6 2019 | DDC 814/.54—dc23
LC record available at https://lccn.loc.gov/2019020199

Designed by Jonathan D. Lippincott

Our books may be purchased in bulk for promotional,
educational, or business use. Please contact your local bookseller
or the Macmillan Corporate and Premium Sales Department at
1-800-221-7945, extension 5442, or by e-mail at
MacmillanSpecialMarkets@macmillan.com.

www.fsgbooks.com
www.twitter.com/fsgbooks • www.facebook.com/fsgbooks

1 3 5 7 9 10 8 6 4 2

Contents

Preface

This book came about quite naturally: I thought it was time to collect the pieces of nonfiction I had had occasion to write over the decades and bring them together in one place. Since there were quite a number of them, I then had to decide whether to make one thick volume or two more reasonable ones. I summoned opinions and votes, weighed pros and cons, and, in the end, decided on two. They would reflect, to some extent, two of the main occupations of my life—writing and translating. This is the first book; the second will concentrate more single-mindedly on translation and the experience of reading foreign languages.

What I have collected here are essays, commentaries, reviews, prefaces, observations, analyses, and a few talks. The subject of writing predominates, inevitably, but the subject of translation does make the occasional appearance, as do the visual arts, the writing of history, the figure of Jesus, memoir, and memory. The earliest pieces were written in the late 1970s and early 1980s, the latest within the last year or two. They range in length from my quite long, digressive, and example-laden recommendations for good writing habits down to a response

to the word *gubernatorial* and a summary description
of five favorite short stories.

In reading through and preparing this collection, I
have sometimes made small changes, either minor stylistic revisions or, in a couple of cases, the combining of two
pieces into one. What had been a theoretical question
before I began preparing the collection—will I revise
published pieces or not?—was immediately answered
as I began reading, since, even if most of the published
pieces had already been extensively and closely revised,
I could not leave untouched something that bothered
me, even a little. I felt free, for example, to replace "trolley tracks in them" by "trolley tracks running through
them" if I liked it better, or a plain descriptive title by
one that struck me as more interesting.

I had also asked myself whether I would let an opinion stand if I no longer agreed with it. As it happened,
however, I found that I did not generally disagree with
what I had written years before—whether two years
or forty-some. Once, only, in a review of a translated
book, I was more dismissive of a translator's work than
I would be now, but for quite other reasons I have not
included that review (interesting though the writer was
and is—I highly recommend the novels of the Southern
French author Jean Giono).

THE PRACTICE
OF WRITING

A Beloved Duck Gets Cooked:
Forms and Influences I

The traditional literary forms—the novel, the short story, the poem—although they evolve, do not disappear. But there is a wealth of less traditional forms that writers have adopted over the decades and centuries, forms that are harder to define and less often encountered, either variations on the more familiar, such as the short-short story, or intergeneric—sitting on a line between poetry and prose, or fable and realistic narrative, or essay and fiction, and so on.

I would like to discuss some of these more eccentric forms, and specifically some of the ones I have read and thought about over the years as my own writing has evolved. So this essay includes something about my writing but is predominantly an excuse to study and read from other people's writing, both poetry and prose.

I think of myself as a writer of fiction, but my first books were slim small-press books often shelved in the poetry section, and I am still sometimes called a poet and included in poetry anthologies. It is understandable that there may be some confusion. For instance, my collection of stories titled *Samuel Johnson Is Indignant* contains fifty-six pieces, including what could roughly be described as meditations; parables or fables; an oral history with hiccups; an interrogation about jury duty; a traditional, though brief, story about a family trip; a diary about thyroid disease; excerpts from a bad translation of a poorly written biography of Marie Curie; a fairly traditional narrative about my father and his furnace, though ending in an accidental poem; and, scattered through the book, brief prose pieces of just one or two lines as well as one or two pieces with broken lines.

When I began writing "seriously" and steadily in college, I thought my only choice was the traditional narrative short story. Both my parents had been writers of short stories, and my mother still was. Both of them had had stories published in *The New Yorker*, which loomed large in our life, as some sort of icon, though an icon of exactly what I'm not sure—good writing and editing, urban wit and sophistication? By age twelve, I already felt I was bound to be a writer, and if you were going to be a writer, the choices were limited: first, either poet or prose writer; then, if prose writer, either novelist or short-story writer. I never thought of being a novelist. I wrote poems early on, but to be a poet was somehow not an option. So if, eventually, some of my work comes right up to the line (if there is one) that separates a piece of prose from a poem, and even crosses it, the approach to that line is through the realm of short fiction.

In college, when I told one intelligent friend of mine, with confidence and exuberance, that my ambition was to write short stories and, specifically, to write a short story that would be accepted by *The New Yorker*, he was startled by my certainty. He was also somewhat scornful, and suggested that maybe this should not be the full extent of my ambition. I was so surprised by his reaction that the Manhattan street corner where we were talking is engraved on my memory: Broadway at 114th Street. My fixed ideas had been shaken.

Although I now did not have quite the same confidence in *The New Yorker*, I did not immediately see an obvious alternative to writing short stories, so I continued to work in that form and develop in that direction for the next several years, though the subject matter of the stories gradually moved away from the most conventional. I found the writing difficult; it was pleasurable or exciting only at moments. I worked on one short story for months and months; I spent about two years on another one. I followed the oft-repeated advice, which was to combine invented material and material from my own experience.

My reading might have shown me other possibilities. In addition to a healthy diet of the classic short-story writers, such as Katherine Mansfield, D. H. Lawrence, John Cheever, Hemingway, Updike, and Flannery O'Connor, I was already reading writers who were more unusual formally and imaginatively, such as Beckett, Kafka, Borges, and Isaac Babel.

I was in my early teens when I first laid eyes on a page of Beckett. I was startled. I had come to it from books that included the steamy novels of Mazo de la Roche—though not too steamy to be included in a very proper girls' school library—and the more classic romances of *Jane Eyre* and *Wuthering Heights*, as well as the social panoramas of John Dos Passos, the first writer whose style I consciously noticed and relished. Now here was a book—*Malone Dies*—in which the narrator spent a page describing his pencil, and the first plot development was that he had dropped his pencil. I had never imagined anything like it.

When I look at Beckett now, to try to identify more exactly the qualities that continued to excite my interest as I read his work over the years and did my best to learn from him, I find at least the following:

There was his precise and sonorous use of the Anglo-Saxon vocabulary—especially, in this example, the way he gives a familiar word like *dint* a fresh life by using it in an unfamiliar way: "the flagstone before her door that by dint by dint her little weight has grooved."

There was his use of Anglo-Saxon and alliteration to produce what were almost pieces of Old English verse: "worthy those worn by certain newly dead."

There was his use of complex, almost impossibly tangled, yet correct, syntax for the pleasure of it, though perhaps also as a commentary on composition itself: "Were it not of him to whom it is speaking speaking but of another it would not speak."

There was his deft handling of image and his humor, almost certainly poking fun at more traditional romantic or lyrical writing that I myself quite enjoyed: "the little summer house. A rustic hexahedron."

There was the way he balanced the sonority of rhythm and alliteration with the unexpectedly compassionate depiction of character: "So with what reason remains he reasons and reasons ill."

And lastly, there was his acute psychological analysis, so closely accurate that it became absurd and yet moving at the same time: "Not that Watt felt calm and free and glad, for he did not, and had never done so. But he thought that perhaps he felt calm and free and glad, at least calm and free, or free and glad, or glad and calm, or if not calm and free, or free and glad, or glad and calm, at least calm, or free, or glad, without knowing it." (Here he is no doubt again poking fun at conventional sentimental writing.)

If Beckett interested me more for the way he handled language—the close attention to words, the mining of the richness of English, the ironic distance from prose style, the self-consciousness—and less for the forms in which he wrote, still, as with Joyce, Beckett's example provided a pattern of development through different forms over a lifetime of writing: both these writers started by writing poetry and went on to write short stories, and then novels, and then, in Joyce's case, the most intricately inventive, nearly impenetrable novel *Finnegans Wake*, in Beckett's case the plays and the briefer and increasingly eccentric fictions. Both evolved to a point where they seemed to leave more and more readers behind and write more and more for their own pleasure and interest.

I had the example of writers within the traditional form but abbreviated, as, for instance, Isaac Babel with his condensation, emotional intensity, and richness of imagery, especially in Walter Morison's translation of the *Red Cavalry* stories. One of these, "Crossing into Poland," ends with the thin pregnant woman standing over her dead old father:

> "Good sir," said the Jewess, shaking up the feather bed, "the Poles cut his throat, and he begging them: 'Kill me in the yard so that my daughter shan't see me die.' But they did as suited them. He passed away in this room, thinking of me.—And now I should wish to know," cried the woman with sudden and terrible violence, "I should wish to know where in the whole world you could find another father like my father?"

The ending is abrupt; the story, for all its power, is only a little over two pages long.

I had the example of Grace Paley, who defied conventional pacing and packed every sentence with so much wit, richness of character, and worldly wisdom that the lines were often explosive. Her story "Wants" is, again, all of two pages long. Here is the opening page:

> I saw my ex-husband in the street. I was sitting on the steps of the new library.
>
> Hello, my life, I said. We had once been married for twenty-seven years, so I felt justified.
>
> He said, What? What life? No life of mine.
>
> I said, O.K. I don't argue when there's real disagreement. I got up and went into the library to see how much I owed them.
>
> The librarian said $32 even and you've owed it

for eighteen years. I didn't deny anything. Because I don't understand how time passes. I have had those books. I have often thought of them. The library is only two blocks away.

My ex-husband followed me to the Books Returned desk. He interrupted the librarian, who had more to tell. In many ways, he said, as I look back, I attribute the dissolution of our marriage to the fact that you never invited the Bertrams to dinner.

That's possible, I said. But really, if you remember: first, my father was sick that Friday, then the children were born, then I had those Tuesday-night meetings, then the war began. Then we didn't seem to know them any more. But you're right. I should have had them to dinner.

(Notice, by the way, in this excerpt, how fond she is of short sentences, often following the same pattern, which is the simplest one: subject, verb.)

Yet I was apparently not ready to try the sort of story she was writing. And it took me another decade to see that you could derive the material of a story very largely from your own life, as I suspect she did, or even, though in a selected version, almost *entirely* from your own life, as I later did.

I also had the example of Kafka's very brief *Parables and Paradoxes*, some of which were not so much stories, of course, as they were meditations or logical problems. I studied them closely. Yet I seemed to think that only Kafka, not I or anyone else, could write such odd things.

They all work in slightly different ways. One, for instance, "The Sirens," might be a reinterpretation of a familiar legend:

> These are the seductive voices of the night; the Sirens, too, sang that way. It would be doing them an injustice to think that they wanted to seduce; they knew they had claws and sterile wombs, and they lamented this aloud. They could not help it if their laments sounded so beautiful.

Another, "Leopards in the Temple," might be the creation of, and commentary upon, a ritual:

> Leopards break into the temple and drink to the dregs what is in the sacrificial pitchers; this is repeated over and over again; finally it can be calculated in advance, and it becomes a part of the ceremony.

Another might be the reinterpretation of a moment of history ("Alexander the Great"):

> It is conceivable that Alexander the Great, in spite of the martial successes of his early days, in spite of the excellent army that he had trained, in spite of the power he felt within him to change the world, might have remained standing on the bank of the Hellespont and never have crossed it, and not out of fear, not out of indecision, not out of infirmity of will, but because of the mere weight of his own body.

(Kafka himself, apparently, was inspired by two of his contemporaries or predecessors who wrote in the very short form: the Swiss Robert Walser, also a novelist, whose late writings, almost illegibly tiny, were only recently deciphered; and the Viennese coffeehouse bohemian Peter Altenberg, writing at the turn of the twentieth century.)

For a long time, I did not see Kafka as a model to be emulated, nor other more eccentric or unconventional writers. I did not yet know the work of many writers who later, over the years, became interesting to me or influential: the strange narrative voices and bizarre sensibilities in the stories of the American Jane Bowles or the Brazilian Clarice Lispector or the Swiss Regina Ullmann (whose 1921 collection of stories was not translated into English until 2015, nearly a hundred years after it appeared in German); or the startling and calmly violent, syntactically complex single-paragraph stories of the Austrian Thomas Bernhard's collection *The Voice Imitator*, which I discovered by chance in an airport bookstore; or the tiny chapters of the Brazilian Machado de Assis's novel *Epitaph of a Small Winner*; or the autobiographical paragraph stories of the Spaniard Luis Cernuda; or the many, many small, whimsical tales written in the 1940s, '50s, and '60s, of the Cuban Virgilio Piñera; or, finally, the meditative, semi-autobiographical, very brief stories of the Dutchman A. L. Snijders or the Swiss Peter Bichsel, so appealing to me that I have been translating them for the past five years or so.

But those discoveries were still to come.

At the age of about twenty-six, after having ignored the model of Kafka for so long, I was jolted into taking a new direction, at last, after reading a collection of stories by the contemporary American prose poet Russell Edson.

I had been slogging away at a stubborn story. I had been fighting off my inertia and apathy. I would read, go for a walk, eat. In the midst of this inertia, a friend who had been witnessing it said, "You just sit around all day doing nothing." (I wasn't doing nothing—I was agonizing!) Then I read Russell Edson's book called *The Very Thing That Happens*.

Russell Edson is an unusual writer: you could characterize many of his stories as brief, fantastic, and often funny tales of domestic mayhem involving family members but also, sometimes, their pots and pans, animals, buildings, parts of buildings, and so forth. But some of the pieces are lyrical meditations, or sunnier moral tales. Edson himself calls them poems, sometimes fables. Here is one on the idea of generations ("Waiting for the Signal Man"):

> A woman said to her mother, where is my daughter?
>
> Her mother said, up you and through me and out of grandmother; coming all the way down through all women like a railway train, trailing her brunette hair, which streams back grey into white; waiting for the signal man to raise his light so she can come through.
>
> What she waiting for? said the woman.
>
> For the signal man to raise his light, so she can see to come through.

Here, in "Dead Daughter," is a rather brutal family interaction:

Wake up, I heard something die, said a woman to something else.

Something else was her father. Do not call me something else, he said.

Will it be something dead for breakfast? said the woman.

It is always something dead given by your mother to her husband, said her father, like my dead daughter, dead inside herself; there is nothing living there, no heart, no child.

That is not true, said the daughter, I am in here trying to live, but afraid to come out.

If you're in there oh do come out, we're having a special treat, dead daughter for breakfast, dead daughter for lunch, and dead daughter for supper, in fact dead daughter for the rest of our lives.

And here is a drama involving inanimate objects as well as human beings (When Things Go Wrong):

A woman had just made her bed. A wall leaned down and went to sleep on her bed. So the ceiling decided to go to bed too. The wall and the ceiling began to shove each other. But it was decided that the ceiling had best sleep on the floor. But the floor said, get off of me because I am annoyed with you. And the floor went outside to lie in the grass.

Will you stop it all of you, screamed the woman.

But the rest of the walls yawned and said, we're tired too.

Stop stop stop, she screamed, it is all going wrong, all is wrong wrong wrong.

When her father returned he said, why is my house destroyed?

Because everything went wrong suddenly, screamed the woman.

Why are you screaming and why is my house destroyed? said the father.

I don't know, I don't know, and I am screaming because I am very upset, father, said the woman.

This is very strange, said the father, perhaps I'll walk away and when I return things will be different.

Father, screamed the woman, why do you leave me every time this happens?

Because when I return things will be different, said the father.

Edson opened a path for me for several reasons. One reason was that not every one of his stories succeeded. Some were merely silly. Maybe this had to do with the way Edson went about writing them.

As Natalie Goldberg describes it in her book *Writing Down the Bones*:

He said that he sits down at his typewriter and writes about ten different short pieces at one session. He then comes back later to reread them. Maybe one out of the ten is successful and he keeps that one. He said that if a good first line comes to him, the rest of the piece usually works. Here are some of his first lines:

"A man wants an aeroplane to like him." . . .

"A beloved duck gets cooked by mistake." . . .

"A husband and wife discover that their children are fakes."

"Identical twin old men take turns at being alive."

Some of the stories I found brilliant, but others faltered. Yet the stories that did not quite succeed showed me two things that were helpful to a young writer: they showed more clearly how the stories were put together; and they showed how a writer could try something, fail, try again, partially succeed, and try again. A third thing the stories showed me, both the brilliant ones and the faltering ones, was how you could tap some very difficult emotions and let them burst out in an unexpected, raw, sometimes absurd form—that perhaps, in fact, setting oneself absurd or impossible subjects made it easier for difficult emotions to come forth.

I read this book, and I began writing paragraph-long stories, sometimes just one story on one day, sometimes more.

They, too, arose from different sources and worked in different ways. One, "In a House Besieged," used the landscape where I was living at the time, taking real features of it but putting them together in such a way that the piece sounded like a fable or a fairy tale:

In a house besieged lived a man and a woman. From where they cowered in the kitchen the man and woman heard small explosions. "The wind," said the woman. "Hunters," said the man. "The rain," said the woman. "The army," said the man. The woman wanted to go home, but she was already home, there in the middle of the country in a house besieged.

Another, "The Mother," was entirely made up, but was based on an emotional reality:

> The girl wrote a story. "But how much better it would be if you wrote a novel," said her mother. The girl built a dollhouse. "But how much better if it were a real house," her mother said. The girl made a small pillow for her father. "But wouldn't a quilt be more practical," said her mother. The girl dug a small hole in the garden. "But how much better if you dug a large hole," said her mother. The girl dug a large hole and went to sleep in it. "But how much better if you slept forever," said her mother.

Some of the stories remained unfinished, rough. Some grew to be a page or two long, or longer. These short-short stories, as a group, had a different feel to them from what I had done before—they were bolder, more confident, and more adventurous; they were more of a pleasure to write, and they came more easily. Whereas until this point writing had often felt like hard work, now I began to enjoy it.

One of the longer stories was "Mr. Knockly," which begins: "Last night my aunt burned to death." It was only much later that I realized that this story had very likely been influenced by an Edgar Allan Poe story, "The Man of the Crowd": the main plotline of both stories is the narrator's obsessive pursuit of a man through the streets of a town. And over time I have seen how certain forms, even the forms of nursery rhymes, may impress themselves on us when we hear or read them, and that some of our later work may slip right into these preestablished matrices.

I did not go on to read every one of Russell Edson's books over the years after that. One book was enough—as, often, even a single page of a piece of writing may be enough—to cause a change of direction. I no longer felt that I had to write in accordance with an established, traditional form. After that, although I remained loyal to the traditional narrative short story and revisited it from time to time, I also kept departing from it to try other forms. Sometimes the forms simply occurred to me, and sometimes they were directly inspired by another writer's piece of writing.

About twelve years after I first read Edson, for instance, I was reading a poem by the American poet Bob Perelman on a train going down the coast of California. I was startled—he was incorporating a grammar lesson into his poem! Could one really do that?

Here is the lesson in Perelman's poem, called "Seduced by Analogy," from his collection *To the Reader*:

With afford, agree, and arrange, use the infinitive.
I can't agree to die. With practice,
Imagine, and resist, use the gerund. I practice to live
Is wrong.

A train, or in fact any public transportation, is often a very good place to think and write. After I read this poem, I realized you could teach French in a story. You could write the story in English but incorporate

French words and ideas about language. I began writing
"French Lesson I: *Le Meurtre*" right there on the train,
without any more plan than that:

> See the *vaches* ambling up the hill, head to rump,
> head to rump. Learn what a *vache* is. A *vache*
> is milked in the morning, and milked again in
> the evening, twitching her dung-soaked tail, her
> head in a stanchion. Always start learning your
> foreign language with the names of farm ani-
> mals. Remember that one animal is an *animal*,
> but more than one are *animaux*, ending in *a u
> x*. Do not pronounce the *x*. These *animaux* live
> on a *ferme*.

And the lesson continues, with a short vocabulary list at
the end.

Which is to say that a good poem is bound to offer
you something surprising in the way of language and
thinking, even if some of its meaning eludes you.

The American contemporary Charles Bernstein is another
interesting poet and one of the originators of the so-
called Language School of poetry. Bernstein ventures
into all sorts of new formal territories—he has even written the libretto of an opera based on the work and life of
the critic Walter Benjamin.

One of Bernstein's long sectional poems, "Safe Methods of Business," includes a letter protesting a parking
ticket. In part it reads:

> *The summons charges me with parking at a
> crosswalk on the*

northeast corner of 82nd street and Broadway on
     the evening
of August 17, 1984. The space in question is
east of the crosswalk on 82nd street as indicated
by the yellow lines painted across the street. This space
has been a legal parking space during the over ten
     years I
have lived on the block. Cars are always parked in
     this space
and have continued to (unticketed in several
     observations I
made yesterday and today). Apparently, new
     crosswalk markings
are currently being painted in white on both
     82nd street and
83rd street. At this time, the process is not complete.
When these new lines are finished, several spaces
     may be
eliminated. However, as they looked at the time
     I received
the ticket, they did not appear to override the
     yellow lines
according to which I was clearly in my right to
     park in the space.

I read Bernstein's poem as a poem, de facto, partly
because it has line breaks, partly because it is one section (twenty-six lines long in its entirety) of a more obviously poem-like long poem, and partly because it is
included in a collection of poems and is surrounded by
other poems. Yet how does it work as a poem? Certainly
not by the same rules as the poem by Perelman above.
What it does show is how other factors besides the style,

form, and language of a poem, particularly the context in which we read it, may determine how we receive it—and this in itself can open up new possibilities for a writer.

Perhaps this unusual form of "poem" lodged in my brain somewhere, so that years later a letter of complaint seemed a good form for a story, and I wrote "Letter to a Funeral Parlor," objecting to the use of the word *cremains*. This letter started out as an actual, sincere piece of correspondence and then got carried away by its own language and turned into something too literary to send.

After I wrote it, I realized how many other things I had to complain about and wrote three more: "Letter to a Hotel Manager," in which I objected to the misspelling, on the menu, of *scrod*, the famous Boston fish; "Letter to a Peppermint Candy Company," in which I reported that in the expensive tin of peppermints I had just bought, there were only two-thirds the number of peppermints the company claimed to have put in it; and "Letter to a Frozen Peas Manufacturer," objecting to the artwork on the package.

Some influences reveal themselves only long after the fact, but some are quite conscious. Once, many years ago, I was reading David Foster Wallace's *Brief Interviews with Hideous Men*. It was difficult to read, because the men are truly hideous. But the form is a powerful one—in each interview, we are given the answers at length, but the questions have been left blank. I did not finish reading it, but the form stayed with me. And some time later, after I had had the interesting experience of being on call for jury duty and wanted to write about it, this form felt like the perfect one to use. The content of the story, which is titled "Jury Duty," was taken nearly completely from my own experience, but the story was transformed into fiction by the illusion of the questioner, or examiner.

Here is the opening of the story:

Q.

A. Jury duty.

Q.

A. The night before, we had been quarreling.

Q.

A. The family.

Q.

A. Four of us. Well, one doesn't live at home any-more. But he was home that night. He was leaving the next morning—the same morning I had to go in to the courtroom.

Q.

A. We were all four of us quarreling. Every which way. I was just now trying to figure it out. There are so many different combinations in which four people can quarrel: one on one, two against one, three against one, two against two, etc. I'm sure we were quarreling in just about every combination.

Q.

A. I don't remember now. Funny. Considering how heated it was.

The form is enjoyable because of what you can do with the unspoken questions. Sometimes it's obvious what the question has been. For instance, later in the story we know the questioner has had trouble understanding the name Sojourner Truth—the former slave and women's rights activist—because it has to be repeated several times; but at other points in the story we cannot guess what the questioner has asked: I end the story with the answer "Yes!"—and you will never know what the question was.

Some years ago, during the extended period in which I was working on my translation of Proust's *Swann's Way*, not wanting to stop writing altogether and yet having no time, I tried another form that intrigued me: perhaps because I was spending the days translating such long, complex sentences—though I found this activity engrossing and even exciting—I wanted to see just how brief I could make a piece of writing and still have it mean something.

Perhaps I had also been influenced by a postcard I had kept up on my bulletin board for years. It contained a three-line poem—a translation from the Cheremiss—by the Finnish poet Anselm Hollo:

> *i shouldn't have started these red wool mittens.*
> *they're done now,*
> *but my life is over.*

Even though it's so short, it surprises me each time I read it—which is something I think a good piece of writing should do.

Perhaps, too, the idea for this very brief form was planted in me years ago by some of the entries in Kafka's *Diaries*, which I read very closely when I was in my twenties. For instance, here is one entry, in its entirety:

The picture of dissatisfaction presented by a street, where everyone is perpetually lifting his feet to escape from the place on which he stands.

In just a few words, he offers a different way of seeing a commonplace thing. I wondered if I could write a piece that short—a title and a line or two—that would still have the power to move, or at least startle, or distract, in a way that was not entirely frivolous. I also wanted the piece to stay firmly in the realm of prose.

Here is one, "Lonely," that has some of the rhythms of the Hollo poem:

No one is calling me. I can't check the answering machine because I have been here all this time. If I go out, someone may call while I'm out. Then I can check the answering machine when I come back in.

There are two that are shorter:

HAND
Beyond the hand holding this book that I'm reading, I see another hand lying idle and slightly out of focus—my extra hand.

INDEX ENTRY
Christian, I'm not a

Legend has it that Hemingway once wrote what he called a one-line short story: "For sale: baby shoes, never worn"—an ephemeral variation by someone on the internet reads "For sale: baby crib, never used."

But writers working in very short forms are usually poets. There is Samuel Menashe, who often wrote in four short lines and whose interesting work is too often overlooked:

(UNTITLED)

Pity us
by the sea
on the sands
so briefly

Another poet who is a master of brevity and the concrete is Lorine Niedecker, one of the less well-known poets in the so-called objectivist group that followed a generation or so after Ezra Pound. Here is one of her short, pithy poems, untitled, about a thing that comes back, or might come back, to haunt the poet, having a life and will of its own:

The museum man!
I wish he'd taken Pa's spitbox!
I'm going to take that spitbox out
and bury it in the ground
and put a stone on top.
Because without that stone on top
it would come back.

Then there is an interesting, anarchic poet near Woodstock, New York, known only as Sparrow. Some years ago he became famous—in small circles, anyway—for staging a one-man protest in the reception area of *The New Yorker* for several days, objecting that the magazine published only bland, predictable poetry, rather than offbeat, eccentric poetry such as, in particular, his own. Eventually, in fact, the magazine bought three of his poems and published at least one of them. (Sometimes it pays to be persistent, and to protest.)

Sparrow has written many very small poems, such as the following ("Poem"):

> *This poem replaces*
> *all my previous poems.*

The poems of his that interest me are not lyrical. I like the ones in which he sees things in a different way—as Kafka does in some of his diary entries, as I do in my piece "Hand."

Here's another small poem, "Perfection Wasted":

> *The problem with dying*
> *is you can't be funny anymore,*
> *or charming.*

When I read this, I thought it was an original poem of his, but in fact it is a "translation" of a sonnet by John Updike that appeared in *The New Yorker*. I found it in a group of poems by Sparrow called "Translations from the *New Yorker*." This was in a book of his called *America: A Prophecy: A Sparrow Reader*.

Another translation of his is "Garter Snake." I'll quote Sparrow's translation first, then a little of the original:

> *A snake moved through grass*
> *and I watched.*
> *It looked like an S.*

When it stopped, it was very still.

The grass shook slightly when it moved.

The original, by Eric Ormsby, has a lot more words in it, which is one thing I suppose Sparrow is trying to get away from. Here is the first verse of the original:

The stately ripple of the garter snake
In sinuous procession through the grass
Compelled my eye. It stopped and held its head
High above the lawn, and the delicate curve
Of its slender body formed a letter S—
For "serpent," I assume, as though
Diminutive majesty obliged embodiment.

Further along in the poem, where Sparrow's translation reads "The grass shook slightly when it moved," the original reads:

. . . it gave the rubbled grass
And the dull hollows where its ripple ran
Lithe scintillas of exuberance,
Moving the way a chance felicity
Silvers the whole attention of the mind.

That's the end of the poem. Sparrow's plainer version may not quite succeed as a poem, and some readers will prefer the richer original. But Sparrow's translations raise several interesting questions about writing, and about form in particular—which is what I've been exploring here.

The most pressing question, of course, is one that

would take us, if we pursued it, straight into the realm of translation theory and all its intriguing conundrums: Can you say the same thing in radically different ways? If you write it so differently, are you, in fact, saying the same thing?

2007, 2012

Commentary on One Very Short Story ("In a House Besieged")

First version:

[IN A HOUSE BESIEGED]

In a house beseiged lived a man and a woman, with two dogs and two cats. There were mice there too, but they were not acknowledged. ~~Around the~~ From [where they cowered in] the kitchen the man and woman heard small explosions. "The wind," said the woman. "Hunters," said the man. "Smoke," said the woman. "The army," said the man. The woman wanted to go home, but she was already at home, there in the middle of the country in a house beseiged, in a house that belonged to someone else.

Final version:

IN A HOUSE BESIEGED

In a house besieged lived a man and a woman. From where they cowered in the kitchen the man and woman heard small explosions. "The wind," said the woman. "Hunters," said the man. "The rain," said the woman. "The army," said the man. The woman wanted to go home, but she was already home, there in the middle of the country in a house besieged.

In those days (fall of 1973, age twenty-six, living in the country in France), I would force myself to stay at the desk for a certain number of hours, writing in my notebook whatever came to mind—often descriptions of what I could see or hear, or thoughts or memories—as a way of bringing myself to the point of writing something like a story.

"In a House Besieged" grew directly out of my situation and the descriptions I wrote in the notebook. There were, in fact, hunters and army units in the countryside around the house. So the paragraph in the notebook that directly preceded the first draft of this story reads:

The shots of the hunters this morning (as I lay in bed still trying to order my thoughts): an explosion, a pop: then the echo or reverberation like clouds of smoke washing to the hills and back again. And everything is silent and peaceful until there is another muffled shot.

As for the changes to the story from first draft to final draft, the two cats and two dogs, as well as the mice, were cut. The animals were part of my real situation, but I probably felt that they lessened the ominousness of the story, "domesticated" it, and certainly the bit about acknowledging the mice was chatty and distracting—getting away from the point of the story. The insertion of "where they cowered in" adds explicit drama, whereas if I had said simply "from the kitchen" the drama would be less, especially since *kitchen* has comfortable associations (until one has to cower in it). The change from "smoke" to "rain" replaces something inaudible by something audible. Ending the story on the phrase "in a house besieged," especially if it echoes the title—though the title was added later—is stronger than the rather anticlimactic and irrelevant "in a house that belonged to someone else"; it is confusing and adds new information that is beside the point. Last change: By the time of the final version, I knew how to spell *besieged*.

2014

From Raw Material to Finished Work:
Forms and Influences II

I'm going to start this discussion of forms and influences by returning to some early influences for a couple of reasons. One is to give an example of the sort of traditional fiction I attempted when I was just starting out. The other reason is to describe how two very different stories emerged from the same experience, one early and the other written some forty years later. The experience that inspired all three of these stories took place the summer I turned eighteen, just after graduating from high school.

My parents were living in Buenos Aires. My father had been teaching there and in La Plata since the winter. I went down to join them in June and for two months lived with them in a large apartment they had sublet on the Avenida del Libertador from a British record company executive.

I spent my days practicing the violin, attending dance classes, volunteering in a Catholic orphanage, teaching myself Spanish, going to concerts with my mother, taking walks by myself, and writing in my journal. I know from reading my journal that in the course of my walks I observed the caged chickens in the markets and talked in halting Spanish to butchers and embassy guards, and back at home wrote descriptions of the mist-filled city parks at night and the glimpses, through the windows of private houses, of "gray heads" bent over their tea. I was interested in what was exotic to me—a gypsy girl selling lemons on the sidewalk, the wheels of horse-drawn delivery carts twinkling in the sunlight, a gaucho roasting whole goats in a restaurant window—but I missed my friends and did not always know what to do with myself.

My memories of that time, though sparse and fragmented, remained vivid, and a year later, after my first year of college, I wrote a short story set in the city as I remembered it and depicting the sort of life I thought I could imagine there.

"Ways" was written in the summer of 1966, when I was turning nineteen, for a summer-session fiction workshop at Columbia University. Fiction workshops were much less common in those days, and this was the only one I ever enrolled in, although I did take one creative writing course when I was a senior in college, a few years later. There was no such thing as a creative writing major at Barnard or most other colleges. The idea, at that time, was that if you wanted to "be a writer," you would major in English literature and then, after graduation, most logically, find work as an editor at a publishing house. Or at least that was what I thought would be the progression—what advice or guidance I received, I can't remember now.

I was going to say that I followed quite a different course in the years after college, but, in fact, it's true that after working for a temp agency for a while, I did find a job as an editorial assistant at W. W. Norton & Co. and stayed there a few months, saving as much money as I could. Then I went to live in France, and I didn't work in publishing again.

Here are the first few paragraphs of "Ways," enough to show how traditional it was:

> This afternoon the wind blew in gusts along the street. The women's cheeks warmed with color, their hair tousled, the men spread their woven and fringed scarves over their shoulders. Today was Sunday, the fruit stands boarded up, gratings lowered on all the store fronts. As the afternoon darkened there were only a few breaks in the dusk in each block; a *confitería* on the corner with its glass doors closed, men inside leaning over their tea, their scarves rumpled against their collars, their hands gesturing or cradling their cups in the cold and white light. Here and there along the street trays and tiers of candy flowered from booths between the stores. Curtaining above them hung lines of tickets for the national lottery. The proprietor sat reading a folded newspaper on a stool behind the counter. On the corner across the street from the *confitería* a neon sign glowed down the front of a *parrilla*, where grilled beefsteaks were sold.
>
> The old man crossed over the cobblestones of the street to look in at the *parrilla*. Its white tablecloths glimmered and a few white-jacketed *mozos* stood talking behind the bar. Just after dark: people would not begin arriving until nine. Peering in the window, his eyes sparkled a moment under his heavy eyebrows. Slowly he put his hands

to his collar and turned it up. Away from the window he folded his hands across the soft ends of his shawl, paused a moment, and walked on.

Such a very difficult matter to decide, he began to think. I do not want him in the house with me. He is not quiet like an old man, and he eats and drinks a great deal. He would never be content with a little omelette and vegetable. He frowned and then thought of other things. Should he take tea there on the corner or go on home and have a little *maté*? He walked along slowly and imagined each experience carefully. It comforted him to hold the silver *maté* cup in his palms, to stir the leaves about with the long silver strainer. To sit quiet with his considerations, with his own damp and undisturbed smell, with the noises he was accustomed to, the clanging of elevator gates in the hall beyond the door and an occasional drift of voices, the ticking of a small alarm clock in his room, the other rooms silent. He could sit at the kitchen table with *La Prensa* folded before him and look again at the review of Ricci's first appearance in the city. It was comfortable to suck up the hot bitter drink while he read about the brilliant cadenza that opened the Ginastera concerto, while he remembered the perfect intonation of the violin. Ricci seemed alone there on the edge of the stage, with the orchestra silent behind him. The old man frowned again and rubbed his hands across his eyes; he was ashamed and humiliated when he couldn't stop coughing. He wanted to hear every sequence and every interval, but he wheezed and choked. Three thousand others were quiet. He said angrily to himself, I am an old fool spoiling the music.

I don't remember thinking of Hemingway as one of my influences, but I now see resemblances: the simple language, the repetition, the concrete descriptions, the setting in a foreign, Spanish-speaking place with the foreign names for things.

Here, for comparison, is the opening of "A Clean, Well-Lighted Place," which, even though it is so often anthologized and assigned, has lost none of its effectiveness as a beautifully constructed depiction of a place and three characters. Hemingway's sympathetic portrait of the old man in this story may even have inspired, in part, the old man in my own story. I wonder if it is possible—though this just occurred to me now, as I was looking at the connection to Hemingway—that certain material or settings may trigger a response in a writer that awakens subliminal memories of earlier responses to a significant piece of writing she has studied in the past: that is, the exotic foreign setting of Buenos Aires, the Spanish language, the sight of certain types of men in the street may, taken together, have sparked a synaptic connection in my brain back to the text of "A Clean, Well-Lighted Place":

It was late and every one had left the café except an old man who sat in the shadow the leaves of the tree made against the electric light. In the day time the street was dusty, but at night the dew settled the dust and the old man liked to sit late because he was deaf and now at night it was quiet and he felt the difference. The two waiters inside the café knew that the old man was a little drunk, and while he was a good client they knew that if he became too drunk he would leave without paying, so they kept watch on him.

The differences are apparent, too, of course. In the Hemingway passage there is a more deliberate use of repetition—"The two waiters . . . knew that the old man was . . . drunk, and . . . they knew that if he became too drunk"; there is also the deliberate and eccentric use of repeated "and"s in that paragraph—"and the old man liked to sit late because he was deaf and now at night it was quiet and he felt the difference"; there is a conspicuous lack of commas where another writer might include them; there is also the insistence throughout the story on certain elements of the physical description: the light, the shadows, the leaves and the tree, the dust and the dew, the quiet. The recurrence of the images and the simplicity of the syntax add to the distinctness with which they are impressed on us.

A few years after college, now living in France, I wrote another story inspired by my experiences in Buenos Aires. I need to explain, first, that the apartment my parents were subletting there included the services of a mother-daughter team of live-in cook and maid; as was traditional in a large luxury apartment, their rooms were behind the kitchen. The rent for the apartment, including the cook and the maid, must have been far lower than it would have been in the United States, because this was, I hasten to say, not the way we lived back home—where at first four of us, and then three, lived in a rather cramped though comfortable enough apartment near

Columbia University—galley kitchen, sleeper sofa, no maid, no cook, no terrace.

Although my mother had a certain infatuation with the grand life, and at this time undoubtedly enjoyed throwing parties and taking a long vacation from preparing the family meals, it turned out to be rather more than she had bargained for: she was hardly born to the role of managing servants, having grown up in a family of modest means headed by a thrifty widowed schoolteacher.

The cook in Argentina was a large, confident woman who liked to argue vigorously with my mother. The young maid, her daughter, was sour and angry.

Bewildering and frustrating as it was for my mother, the situation fascinated me for the very reason that it was so unlike our usual way of life. The mother and daughter would disappear through the kitchen door at night, reappear in the morning. I never saw their rooms. There was also a tiny child living with them, a little dark-haired and dark-eyed girl—it was not clear whose child she was. The little girl would creep into my room to watch me practice the violin. The maid, rather simple-minded and always in a temper, would eventually come in search of her, charge into the room, and yank her away by her thin little arm.

Years later, I wrote a story called "The Housemaid." Although the mother and daughter in the story were based on the women in Argentina, the setting of the story was not a Buenos Aires apartment but a large stone manor house of the kind I had in the meantime seen in the Irish countryside, with, in the basement, a wide flagstone corridor and whitewashed storage rooms, and, upstairs, a succession of empty, drafty, high-ceilinged formal rooms. The mother and daughter in the story looked after a lone man named Mr. Martin, with whom the housemaid was, in her own way, in love. The character of Mr. Martin may possibly have been modeled on the British executive who had sublet the apartment in Buenos Aires to my parents. But in his behavior he resembled more closely a strangely silent and gloomy Edgar Allan Poe protagonist—again, perhaps, my choice of character connecting back to what lessons I had absorbed from reading Poe.

Here is the opening of "The Housemaid":

I know I am not pretty. My dark hair is cut short and is so thin it hardly hides my skull. I have a hasty and lopsided way of walking, as though I were crippled in one leg. When I bought my glasses I thought they were elegant—the frames are black and shaped like butterfly wings—but now I have learned how unbecoming they are and am stuck with them, since I have no money to buy new ones. My skin is the color of a toad's belly and my lips are narrow. But I am not nearly as ugly as my mother, who is much older. Her face is small and wrinkled and black like a prune, and her teeth wobble in her mouth. I can hardly bear to sit across from her at dinner and I can tell by the look on her face that she feels the same way about me.

For years we have lived together in the basement. She is the cook; I am the housemaid. We are not good servants, but no one can dismiss us because we are still better than most. My mother's dream is that someday she will save enough money to leave me and live in the country. My dream is nearly the same, except that when I am feeling angry and unhappy I look across the table at her clawlike hands and hope that she will choke to death on her food. Then no one would be there to stop me from going into her closet and breaking open her money box. . . .

Whenever I imagine these things, sitting alone in the kitchen late at night, I am always ill the next day. Then it is my mother herself who nurses me, holding water to my lips and fanning my face with a flyswatter, neglecting her duties in the kitchen, and I struggle to persuade myself that she is not silently gloating over my weakness.

Things have not always been like this. When Mr. Martin lived in the rooms above us, we were happier, though we seldom spoke to one another.

And from the end:

This is only a rented house. My mother and I are included in the rent. People come and go, and every few years there is a new tenant. I should have expected that one day Mr. Martin too would leave.

As I reread the story, I can see that it also expresses a teenage girl's typical ambivalence toward her mother: she may resent her, harbor angry fantasies about her, but then, in times of illness or despair, she often finds herself turning to that same mother for help.

Decades later, after my mother died, I found a folder she had kept documenting all her difficulties with the cook and the maid in Argentina. It included copies of letters she had written to friends, and drafts of letters she had written to the cook—she found it easier, sometimes, to put her ideas in writing than to have a direct conversation, whether her antagonist was the cook or, in fact, her own teenage daughter. I found pieces of paper on which she was trying out individual sentences in Spanish to use in her next confrontation, along with corrections that a Spanish-speaking friend had made.

This found material was both moving to me and funny. As has so often happened, the story I wrote was inspired by a combination of pathos, humor, and the role played by language itself—in this case my mother's attempt to express her desires and difficulties in Spanish.

My approach to using this material was, by now, after all these decades, very different from my approach when I wrote "The Housemaid." In the earlier story, I had more or less followed the advice given to young writers: draw on material with which you are familiar to create fictional characters and a fictional situation with a plotline that arises naturally from the characters and the situation.

This time I did not want first to absorb the material and then to invent a traditional fictional short story, as I had earlier; rather, I wanted to preserve the material largely intact, in its fragmented form. I saw the possibility of a form that would mirror the very intermittent and continuing nature of the battle of wills as it had been. I did not make anything up; I simply rearranged what I found. I say "simply," but of course the arranging was a long process: selecting, ordering, cutting, making little modifications, rereading, deciding how much of the Spanish not to translate, deciding whether to use italics for speech, letting it sit for a while, rearranging it yet again.

I called the story "The Dreadful Mucamas," which was what my mother herself had called the mother and daughter at a certain point, though not to their faces, of course.

The story was written in very short segments, one of the longest coming close to the beginning:

They are very rigid, stubborn women from Bolivia. They resist and sabotage whenever possible.

They came with the apartment. They were bargains because of Adela's low IQ. She is a scatterbrain.

In the beginning, I said to them: *I'm very happy that you can stay, and I am sure that we will get along very well.*

This is an example of the problems we are having. It is a typical incident that has just taken place. I needed to cut a piece of thread and could not find my six-inch scissors. I accosted Adela and told her I could not find my scissors. She protested that she had not seen them. I went with her to the kitchen and asked Luisa if she would cut my thread. She asked me why I did not simply bite it off. I said I could not thread my needle if I bit it off. I asked her please to get some scissors and cut it off—now. She told Adela to look for the scissors of *la Señora Brodie*, and I followed her to the study to see where they were kept. She removed them from a box. At the same time I saw a long, untidy piece of twine attached to the box and asked her why she did not trim off the frayed end while she had the scissors. She shouted that it was impossible. The twine might be needed to tie up the box some time. I admit that I laughed. Then I took the scissors from her and cut it off myself. Adela shrieked. Her mother appeared behind her. I laughed again and now they both shrieked. Then they were quiet.

I have told them: *Please, do not make the toast until we ask for breakfast. We do not like very crisp toast the way the English do.*

I have told them: *Every morning, when I ring the bell, please bring us our mineral water immediately. Afterwards, make the toast and at the same time prepare fresh coffee with milk. We prefer "Franja Blanca" or "Cinta Azul" coffee from Bonafide.*

I spoke pleasantly to Luisa when she came with the mineral water before breakfast. But when I reminded her about the toast, she broke into a tirade—how could I think she would ever let the toast get cold or hard? But it is almost always cold and hard.

We have told them: *We prefer that you always buy "Las Tres Niñas" or "Germa" milk from Kasdorf.*

Adela cannot speak without yelling. I have asked her to speak gently, and to say señora, but she never does. They also speak very loudly to each other in the kitchen.

Often, before I have said three words to her, she
yells at me: *Sí . . . sí, sí, sí . . . !* and leaves the room.
I honestly don't think I can stand it.

I had done something like this before, even quite far
back—using found material and keeping it almost intact. The stories "Lord Royston's Tour" and "Excerpts
from a Life" both consisted of texts by other people
cut and rearranged and put to a very different use. The
first was made from a series of letters written home to
England by an actual young Lord Royston from the exotic places where he was traveling. The second was taken
from an autobiographical book by Shinichi Suzuki that
was required reading for parents of children who were
studying an instrument by the Suzuki method. The element of fiction comes in, in the case of "Lord Royston's
Tour," with the transformation from a collection of
letters into a single continuous narrative, and, in the
case of the Shinichi Suzuki, with the transformation
from straightforward first-person life story to stylized
first-person narrative by fictional character—fictional
because now not quite the same as Suzuki himself. My
intervention, along with the change of form—from continuous narrative to short, titled, almost epigrammatic
sections—in turn alters the personality and approach of
the narrator.

I have also used found material and arranged it,
with minimal rewriting, quite recently, with the stories
I made from anecdotes contained in Gustave Flaubert's
letters—something I will discuss later.

In fact, in addition to those two stories—"The Housemaid" and "The Dreadful Mucamas"—there is a third

story, quite a little one, that was inspired by the situation in Buenos Aires with the cook and the maid. As I looked through the material in the folder, I saw that one particular piece of material might stand alone as a story consisting of only a few lines and a title. Because it is so brief, its effect is very different from that of the coherent, traditional short story "The Housemaid" and also from the fragmented, punctuated, and extended "The Dreadful Mucamas":

THE PROBLEM OF THE VACUUM CLEANER
A priest is about to come visit us—or maybe it is two priests.

But the maid has left the vacuum cleaner in the hall, directly in front of the front door.

I have asked her twice to take it away, but she will not.

I certainly will not.

One of the priests, I know, is the Rector of Patagonia.

Now we move on to another country, another setting, another time, long after the Argentina experience. The intervening years have included college but also periods, longer or shorter, of living in France and Ireland. Now I have returned to the United States to live, and I'm twenty-eight years old. During this particular month or two I am up north, in Canada, staying in a borrowed house. I spend my days in much the same way I spent them in France and in Ireland, sitting at a desk, working not only at a translation job but also at some task I have assigned myself, usually a piece of my own writing but also, in Canada, the intermittent study of German, which has been another constant in my life, though it has no immediate purpose. I sit at a desk and stare out the window from time to time.

I have always kept a notebook by my side when I'm working or trying to work, and it becomes the repository for any stray thought or description that occurs to me—I try to catch every one. In those years I wrote a lot in the notebook because of a certain restlessness: if I was having trouble with a piece of writing—and I usually was—I could at least write something in the notebook. I could at least record in the notebook how much trouble I was having with what I was trying to write. Or I could record an idea for another story, as Kafka did in his notebooks. I might never continue the story, or I might continue it right away or later. The notebook might also contain the germ of an idea that would later find its way into a story without my realizing where the idea came from.

Here is one of those notebook or journal entries, this one dating from 1975, and then two stories that resulted from it many years later. First, the journal entry, which is relatively undistinguished—although I must digress to say that I cared very much whether a journal entry was well written or not, and if I happened to read it over, I would always revise it in small ways until it was as good as it could be, whatever its value. I still do this.

My rather opinionated journal entry is just a couple of long sentences (I have changed the family's name for the sake of discretion):

A concrete mixer has come and gone for the house next door where the Charrays are building a proper wine cellar because fire insurance for their thousands of bottles of good wine is too expensive in the present cellar. They have very good wine and some fine paintings—many of Riopelle's and one of Joan's—but otherwise their taste in clothes and furniture and their whole way of life is dull, mediocre, strictly middle class.

You wouldn't think you could do much with that limited observation, but when I reread it years, or rather decades, later, something about it must have struck me: maybe the judgmental tone—here was this rather unexceptional young person with a strong opinion who felt she was in a position to pass judgment. Perhaps also the idea of the inquisitive neighbor, any neighbor, peering through the window and observing the people next door, perhaps even for a moment living vicariously through the people next door. Perhaps also the absurd extravagance of the situation that produced the activity outside her window—although whether it is absurd or not may depend on one's point of view or situation: in the situation of the young observer with not much money and no career, building a better wine cellar was absurd; but in the context of the successful medical doctor with a high income and a good collection of wine, building a better wine cellar made perfect sense.

Here is the story that resulted, about thirty years later:

REDUCING EXPENSES

This is a problem you might have someday. It's the problem of a couple I know. He's a doctor, I'm not sure what she does. I don't actually know them very well. In fact, I don't know them anymore.

This was years ago. I was bothered by a bulldozer coming and going next door, so I found out what was happening. Their problem was that their fire insurance was very expensive. They wanted to try to lower the insurance premiums. That was a good idea. You don't want any of your regular payments to be too high, or higher than they have to be. For example, you don't want to buy a property with very high taxes, since there will be nothing you can do to lower them and you will always have to pay them. I try to keep that in mind. You could understand this couple's problem even if you didn't have high fire insurance. If you did not have exactly the same problem, someday you might have a similar problem, of regular payments that were going to be too high. Their insurance was high because they owned a large collection of very good wine. The problem was not so much the collection per se but where they were keeping it. They had, actually, thousands of bottles of very good and excellent wine. They were keeping it in their cellar, which was certainly the right thing to do. They had an actual wine cellar. But the problem was, this wine cellar wasn't good enough or big enough. I never saw it, though I once saw another one that was very small. It was the size of a closet, but I was still impressed. But I did taste some of their wine one time. I can't really tell the difference, though, between a bottle of wine that costs $100, or even $30, and a bottle that costs $500. At that dinner they might have been serving wine that cost even more than that. Not for me, especially, but for some of the other guests.

I'm sure that very expensive wines are really wasted on most people, including myself. I was quite young at the time, but even now a very expensive wine would be wasted on me, probably. This couple learned that if they enlarged the wine cellar and improved it in certain other specific ways, their insurance premiums would be lower. They thought this was a good idea, even though it would cost something, initially, to make these improvements. The bulldozer and other machinery and labor that I saw out the window of the place where I was living at the time, which was a house borrowed from a friend who was also a friend of theirs, must have been costing them in the thousands, but I'm sure the money they spent on it was earned back within a few years or even one year by their savings on the premiums. So I can see this was a prudent move on their part. It was a move that anyone could make concerning some other thing, not necessarily a wine cellar. The point is that any improvement that will eventually save money is a good idea. This is long in the past by now. They must have saved quite a lot altogether, over the years, from the changes they made. So many years have gone by, though, that they have probably sold the house by now. Maybe the improved wine cellar raised the price of the house and they earned back even more money. I was not just young but very young when I watched the bulldozer out my window. The noise did not really bother me very much, because there were so many other things bothering me when I tried to work. In fact I probably welcomed the sight of the bulldozer. I was impressed by their wine, and by the good paintings they also owned. They were nice, friendly people, but I didn't think much of their clothes or furniture. I spent a lot of time looking out the window and thinking about them. I don't know what that was worth. It was probably a waste of my time. Now I'm a lot older. But here I am, still thinking about them. There are a lot of other things that I've forgotten, but I haven't forgotten them or their fire insurance. I must have thought I could learn something from them.

The story is one long paragraph. There is a big difference in effect between a single paragraph, especially a long one, and a sequence of two or three paragraphs, even in a short piece. In the case of three paragraphs, the first paragraph is the beginning; the first paragraph break implies that we have settled into the story a bit and now we're going on. After the second paragraph, we take another breath and then go on into the third paragraph and wind down to our conclusion. A series of paragraphs may also imply that the narrator is somewhat organized, somewhat in control. The one unbroken paragraph, on the other hand, can imply more passion and less organization: it can create the illusion that the narrator has launched into this rant or this lecture almost involuntarily and is hardly even aware of it herself. And before she knows it, she's done—she stops short, she runs out of steam. The single paragraph can be more immediate.

As for the narrator of this story, I see her as hapless: either not so smart, or a little scatterbrained, or just disorganized and unproductive, someone who doesn't have a very high opinion of herself in general but who thinks even so that she can make pronouncements and give advice; someone who sits around a lot of the time, contemplates doing things, doesn't do them, has ideas, doesn't carry them through—the character is very clear to me as soon as I start to speak in her voice. She is probably an exaggeration or distortion of the young person I was then, though I see her as older, even in her forties by now.

Generally I resist the label "experimental," which people sometimes reflexively apply to any nontraditional form of fiction or poetry, or to any form that puzzles them, that seems odd or strange. To me, *experimental* implies that the writer had a plan to test some preconceived writing strategy and see if it would work; that what resulted might or might not prove anything, and might or might not be successful. It seems to me both preplanned, deliberate, conceptual, and at the same time rather tentative. Since I generally prefer to start a piece of writing without much of a plan, and not to be sure exactly what I'm doing, I do not consider the stories that result in any way experimental.

But there are exceptions. A second story resulted from that little journal entry, and it could accurately be called experimental: I wanted to see if I could use a finite amount of material to tell the same small story both forward and backward. The first half of it stays quite close to the journal entry, while the second half tells the same story with the content presented in the opposite order.

REVERSIBLE STORY

Necessary Expenditure
A concrete mixer has come and gone from the house next door. Mr. and Mrs. Charray are reno-

vating their wine cellar. They own thousands of bottles of very good wine. For this reason, their fire insurance is very expensive. If they improve their cellar, however, the fire insurance will cost less. They have very good wine and some fine paintings, but their taste in clothes and furniture is strictly lower middle class.

Expenditure Necessary

The Charrays' taste in clothes and furniture is dull, and strictly lower middle class. However, they do own some fine paintings, many by contemporary Canadian and American painters. They also have some good wine. In fact, they own thousands of bottles of very good wine. Because of this, their fire insurance is very expensive. But if they enlarge and otherwise improve their wine cellar, the fire insurance will be less expensive. A concrete mixer has just come and gone from their house, next door.

In discussing the form of "The Dreadful Mucamas," with its short sections, I thought of books I had read early on in my writing life that were written in brief increments. I have already mentioned Kafka's *Diaries*. Of course, Kafka did not conceive of the diaries beforehand as a formal work, but composed them entry by entry; they achieved that form by accumulation. And then, once they existed in that form, and were published, they exerted their influence on succeeding generations of writers as a model of that form.

The two volumes of the *Diaries*, covering only fourteen years, run to more than 660 pages in the edition I have—a great deal of material, and very engaging to delve into. I open at random and find three types of entries on two pages: one type is the abbreviated factual notation, in this case an odd juxtaposition of current events and his own activities (these particular pages were written in 1914, the first year of World War I), thus:

> August 2. Germany has declared war on Russia.—
> Swimming in the afternoon.

Another type of entry is what appears to be a possible story impulsively begun and just as suddenly abandoned:

> July 30. Tired of working in other people's stores, I had opened up a little stationery store of my own. Since my means were limited and I had to pay cash for almost everything——

Yet another type of entry is the more finished opening to a possible story, this one thoroughly characteristic of Kafka in the following ways: its choice of subject matter, confidence, incisiveness, use of repetition, beautifully balanced structure, negativity, paradoxical conclusion, and humor:

> [July 30.] The director of the Progress Insurance Company was always greatly dissatisfied with his employees. Now every director is dissatisfied with his employees; the difference between employees and directors is too vast to be bridged by means of mere commands on the part of the director and mere obedience on the part of the employees. Only mutual hatred can bridge the gap and give the whole enterprise its perfection.

I used to study Kafka's diaries, back in my twenties. They were important to me for several reasons: the quantity of good writing they contained; the insight they gave me into what went on behind the finished pieces of writing—the rough attempts, the more finished attempts, the thoughtfulness, the persistence; and the window they opened into Kafka's mind—his combination of fictional invention and more mundane daily preoccupations, particularly the way his fictions grew organically out of his daily life. And perhaps they were more accessible than the finished work, being so brief, so unfinished.

If Kafka's diaries grew by accumulation and were not originally planned to be a single work, certain other writers such as Blaise Pascal, in his *Pensées*, did intend that form from the outset. Another interesting case is that of the Catalan writer Josep Pla. Starting at the age of twenty-one, for a relatively short period of time, March 1918 to November 1919, he kept a traditional diary. Then, over the next forty-odd years, amid much other writing, he returned to those original entries and expanded on them. In the end, the book, in the edition I have, numbers 638 pages. It retains something of the disjunctiveness, the abrupt changes of subject, of the original diary, but is generously inclusive of long sequential passages of anecdote, commentary, history, moral reflection, and so forth. Among his many other works, *The Gray Notebook* (English translation by Peter Bush), described by one commentator as "an autobiography built of fragments," became arguably his major work.

I discovered Josep Pla only recently, but there is another book by a young writer, based on the entries in his loose-leaf notebook, that I read early on, at about the time it was first published. This one was by an American, Kenneth Gangemi. It is *The Volcanoes from Puebla*, published in 1979, about Gangemi's travels by motorcycle in Mexico. He, too, returned to his notebook for the material out of which to create his book, but this one is constructed as a sequence of alphabetical sections: Acapulco, Aesthete, *Aguas, Alarma!*, Amecameca, Americans Part I, Americans Part II, Anti-Americanism, *Azotea*, Bach, Back in the USA, Bakery, Barber, Beggars, Bicycle, etc. I found it an appealing and stimulating way to organize a book. Gangemi is direct and opinionated, clear, vivid, and informative.

When I think of writing that is in fact truly experimental in the strict sense of the word, I think of writing within an artificially imposed constraint. For some reason, alphabetical constraints come to mind first, and the Gangemi book would count as one of those, though the constraint is very loose, allowing sections of any length and including any number of entries under each letter.

Another book that uses an alphabetical constraint is Walter Abish's *Alphabetical Africa*, with a much more severe limitation: the first chapter can use only words beginning with the letter *a*; the second adds words beginning with *b*; the third adds words beginning with *c*; and so on. In the twenty-sixth chapter, the last one in the first half of the book, Abish can use words beginning with any letter of the alphabet. In the second half of the book, he reverses the process, working his way back down to using only words beginning with *a* in the last chapter.

Then there is an alphabetical poem by David Lehman, a New York City poet of my generation who often works under a constraint—there is, for instance, his book *Daily Mirror*, the result of his challenge to himself to write one poem each day, a challenge that could bear good fruit for any of us.

Lehman's alphabetical poem, "Anna K."—about the character Anna Karenina—from his 2005 book, *When a Woman Loves a Man*, has two parts, both of which work under the constraint of the alphabetical sequence, one letter of the alphabet beginning each word. A second self-imposed constraint is the limitation of just two words to a line:

1.
Anna believed.
Couldn't delay.
Every Friday
grew heroic
infidelity just
knowing love
might never
otherwise present
queenly resplendent
satisfaction trapped
under Vronsky's
wild x-rated
young zap.

2.
Afraid. Betrayed.
Can't divorce.
Envy follows

grim heroine,
inks judgment,
kills lust.
Mercy nowhere.
Opulent pink
quintessence radiates
suicide trip—
unique vacation—
worst Xmas,
yesterday's zero.

And then there is Georges Perec's novel *La Dispari-tion*, written without using the letter *e*. The ingenious English translation, also written without using the letter *e*, is by the Scottish novelist Gilbert Adair and is called *A Void.*

In the English version, Adair, to match Perec's *e*-less parodies of famous French poems, includes *e*-less versions of well-known English-language poems, including the following, of Poe's "The Raven" (here, the "symbol" he refers to is the letter *e*):

"Sybil," said I, "thing of loathing—Sybil, fury in
*   bird's clothing!*
By God's radiant kingdom soothing all man's
*   purgatorial pain,*
Inform this soul laid low with sorrow if upon a
*   distant morrow*
It shall find that symbol for—oh for its too long
*   unjoin'd chain—*
Find that pictographic symbol, missing from its
*   unjoin'd chain."*
*   Quoth that Black Bird, "Not Again." . . .*

*And my Black Bird, still not quitting, still is
    sitting, still is sitting*
*On that pallid bust—still flitting through my
    dolorous domain;*
*But it cannot stop from gazing for it truly finds
    amazing*
*That, by artful paraphrasing, I such rhyming can
    sustain—*
*Notwithstanding my lost symbol I such rhyming
    still sustain—*
                    Though I shan't try it again!

But in the case of the novel by Perec, who has no fewer than four *e*'s in his own name, the deliberate elimination of the *e* was perhaps not just a conceptual antic but had an emotional source and an emotional effect. Absence played a large part in Perec's life: his mother was taken away when he was six years old, and died most probably in Auschwitz; his father had already been killed fighting for the French. It has been suggested that the silent disappearance of the letter *e* from his novel might be emblematic of the experience of the Jews during World War II. (He has also included the Holocaust and life in a concentration camp in his semiautobiographical novel *W, or the Memory of Childhood*, which interweaves two narrative threads: the portrayal of island life under a fictional totalitarian regime; and memories of his own childhood, or fictional memories of what he wishes had been his own childhood.)

Now, to return—from that digression into experimental alphabetical constraints—to the use of found writing, I would like to conclude by talking a little about Gustave

Flaubert's letters and how they became the inspiration for a set of stories.

At a certain point, as I was working on the first draft of my translation of *Madame Bovary*, I decided to read Flaubert's letters from the period during which he was writing the novel. Fortunately for posterity, he had, during that period, a lover with whom he corresponded voluminously, for a time, and to whom he expatiated on, among other things, his progress in writing the novel *Madame Bovary*. His lover, the poet Louise Colet, did not live where he lived, so they had to stay in touch by letter: her home was in Paris, whereas he shared a house with his mother and his little niece in a village outside the city of Rouen. Every so often Flaubert and Colet would meet about halfway in between, in the city of Mantes, and spend a few days together in a hotel. Then they would take their separate trains in opposite directions and return home. Unfortunately for posterity, and particularly for Flaubert researchers, they fell out, and separated, when Flaubert was about two-thirds of the way through the novel. But while he was still writing to Colet, Flaubert described to her in detail which scenes he was working on, and his difficulties and triumphs in the work. (It must be added that he also lavished considerable effort and many pages, over that time, on thoughtful and admiring critiques of her poems and suggestions for revisions.)

I turned to Flaubert's letters for several reasons: simply to get to know him better; to learn what he felt and thought about the work and about his characters; to look for insight into the composition of the novel; and to observe what his style was like when he was writing more spontaneously, without revising, and how it differed from his more polished style.

Some of the material in the letters was not interesting to me—he regularly wrote about literary politics involving personalities most of whom I did not know—but he wrote a good deal about *Madame Bovary* and, in the course of this, revealed his own sympathy for his characters. For instance, he showed a degree of grudging affection for the conniving pharmacist Homais and described how ill he himself had become when working on the scene of Emma Bovary's death from poisoning by arsenic.

As I read along, every now and then I would come across a little story he was telling Louise, something that had happened to him the day before or recently. I enjoyed these little stories, and after a while it occurred to me that they could be extracted from the letters and shaped a little to make freestanding, independent tales. They were a bit lost, or wasted, where they were in the letters. First I extracted the most obviously complete stories, and then, later, I returned to the less obviously complete material to see what I could do with it. I tried to preserve Flaubert's original as much as I could. I did not add anything fictional. I sometimes cut material, or wrote transitions, or made two sentences into one, or vice versa. In one case I combined two separate accounts into one. In another case, I did a little research about a man he mentioned so that I could fill in the story and add a bit of color to it. Often Flaubert would end his anecdote with an exclamation. I kept them. Once, the exclamation was the cryptic "Oh, Shakespeare!" I kept it even though I was not sure what he meant.

Here is one of the earlier stories, "The Cook's Lesson":

Today I have learned a great lesson; our cook was my teacher. She is twenty-five years old and she's French. I discovered, when I asked her, that she *did not know* that Louis-Philippe is no longer king of France and we now have a republic. And yet it has been five years since he left the throne. She said the fact that he is no longer king simply does not interest her in the least—those were her words.

And I think of myself as an intelligent man! But compared to her I'm an imbecile. (96 words)

Here is the original passage, from a letter to Louise Colet dated April 30, 1853:

Today I have learned a great lesson from my cook. This girl, who is 25 years old and is French, did not know that Louis-Philippe was *no longer king of France*, that there was a republic, etc. All that does not interest her (her words). And I think of myself as an intelligent man! But I am no more than a triple imbecile. One should be like that woman. (69 words)

Until I compared them recently, I had forgotten how many little changes I made, without actually changing the content much, or the order in which the ideas unfolded. I did not change Flaubert's exclamation toward the end—"And I think of myself as an intelligent man!" I did look up a fact—the date when Louis-Philippe left the throne—so that I could supply the "five years." It makes a difference to Flaubert's surprise whether the republic has existed for a few months or for five years—and this is something that Flaubert and Louise Colet knew, but that someone reading my version of the story would not otherwise know. I also end the story on the word *imbecile*—a strong ending—rather than Flaubert's milder remark: "One should be like that woman," or, more literally, *C'est comme cette femme qu'il faut être* ("It is like that woman that one ought to be").

When I was on a campus visit not long ago, a French professor looked at both versions of the story and told me she thought I should have kept Flaubert's "etc."—it summed up, she felt, all the ideas that Flaubert would have included in the comment about France now being a republic. I saw her point, and agreed, and also liked the idea that we were giving some time and attention, standing in a rather cavernous auditorium, to such a small word.

Here is another story, "The Washerwomen," which I extracted later from one of Flaubert's letters:

> Yesterday I went back to a village two hours from here that I had visited eleven years ago with good old Orlowski.
>
> Nothing had changed about the houses, or the cliff, or the boats. The women at the washing trough were kneeling in the same position, in the same numbers, and beating their dirty linen in the same blue water.
>
> It was raining a little, like the last time.
>
> It seems, at certain moments, as though the universe has stopped moving, as though everything has turned to stone, and only we are still alive.
>
> How insolent nature is!

In this case, I made very few changes to the original. But one thing I did was to break up Flaubert's single paragraph into many short paragraphs: I sometimes do that just so it will be read more slowly, with a pause between sentences, and so that each sentence will reverberate, have an impact of its own.

So how does this differ from a straight translation of Flaubert's letter? Well, it is not a complete letter, but a part of a letter; it is presented as a story, not a letter; the story is extracted from the letter and to a smaller or greater extent reshaped and rewritten. I would never claim this story as wholly my own: this is a "story from Flaubert"—in other words, created first in his mind from material belonging to his life history.

Maybe there is a little parallel here, something I hadn't thought of before, between my stories from Flaubert—there are thirteen of them now, plus one rant—and Charles and Mary Lamb's *Tales from Shakespeare*, written in 1807. You may or may not be aware of that book, but it was standard reading for well over a hundred years and is still considered a classic. In it, the brother-and-sister team of Charles and Mary Lamb retold the stories of all the Shakespeare plays, interweaving their own language with Shakespeare's, in a form that was easier for schoolchildren—and for grown-ups, for that matter—to understand. What the authors said about their work could equally well apply to my adaptations of Flaubert's stories:

> His words are used whenever it seemed possible to bring them in; and in whatever has been added to give them the regular form of a connected story, diligent care has been taken to select such words as might least interrupt the effect of the beautiful English tongue [here, read French tongue] in which he wrote: therefore, words introduced into

our language since his time have been as far as possible avoided.

The stories as written by the Lambs did not replace the plays, but they were certainly an aid to reading them or seeing them performed. My Flaubert stories aren't wholly mine, and they don't replace Flaubert's letters: when the stories Flaubert tells are encountered in the context of the letters, their meaning shifts a little or a lot—which is evidence, yet again, of the importance of context.

2012

A Note on the Word *Gubernatorial*

Gubernatorial: Even though I have never used it in a story, and probably never will, this word has always fascinated and pleased me because of its odd divergence from its noun, *governor*. Why did the noun and the adjective develop in different directions? The adjective is actually closer to the origin of both, which was the Latin *gubernator*, "governor," and *gubernare*, "to steer." The original, primary meaning of "to govern" was "to steer." In fact, there is a maritime word in French, *gouvernail*, that means "rudder," or "helm"—what we need to steer a boat. The Latin *gubernator* evolved into the Old French *gouverneur* and hence, eventually, into our English *governor*—our governor is one who steers the metaphorical ship of state. (The Latin also evolved into the Spanish *gobernador*—keeping the *b*—and the Italian *governatore*.)

But of course it is all more complicated, as the development of language always is: the English word *gubernator*, meaning "ruler," was also in use starting in the 1520s, though it was rare—and so was *gubernatrix*, meaning a female ruler. *Gubernator* disappeared from use and *governor* remained. I do not know why our adjective did not evolve in the same way as our noun. Why did it not turn into *governatorial* or *governorial*? Simply because it was not spoken as often?

I have always enjoyed pronouncing *gubernatorial*, as though its rather crude sound, incorporating two voiced plosives and the word "goober," is concealing its more elegant, softer, silkier cousin, "govern." *Gubernatorial* swings us closer to our Spanish friends, *governor* to our Italian. During the U.S. presidency of Jimmy Carter, former governor of Georgia, there was much talk of his association with the cultivation of peanuts (colloquially known as "goobers"); thus, *goober-natorial*, as applied to the office of the governor of the Peanut State, was doubly appropriate.

2011

VISUAL ARTISTS:
JOAN MITCHELL

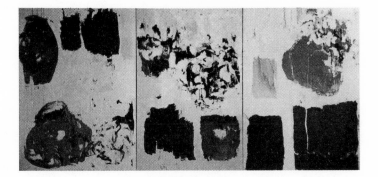

Previous page: *Les Bluets* (1973, 110.5 × 228.25 in.)

Joan Mitchell and *Les Bluets*, 1973

According to Deirdre Bair's biography of Samuel Beckett, he saw Joan Mitchell, at least on first acquaintance, as a younger version of his close friend Bram van Velde. To him she expressed the same relentless quest for the void that he found in the older man's painting. Her manner of speaking was economical, and just as Beckett was unable and unwilling to discuss his writings, she refused to explain or justify her art. She was also, like him, a prodigious drinker. And for a time, according to Klaus Kertess's study, *Joan Mitchell*, the two were close friends.

In Kertess's opinion, however, what Mitchell was seeking was not "the void," but a reconciliation or perhaps comprehension, in the full sense of the word, of the various dualities or paradoxes in her life: joy and rage, vastness and containment, chaos and order, the furious intimacy of her closest personal relationships and the happiness of her relationship to nature; her place, within her chosen French landscape, in an American tradition "of a somber, nature-bound aloneness"; the urban versus the natural elements in her landscapes; her resilience in the face of severe physical disability and her "inordinate fear of death"; the intense physical invitations of her canvases and her gestures of brutal, self-protective rejection in personal encounters, even with relative strangers—what Kertess calls "preemptive strikes." Perhaps the prevailing paradox of her work, however, was the fact that although she sought, even to the end, to go beyond the limits of what she had already done as an artist, she remained, during the forty-odd years of her painting life, resolutely within her self-imposed limits as an abstract expressionist painter. With close focus, with single-minded concentration, through periods in which abstract expressionism fell out of favor, through periods when, as Kertess says, "the hand was being withdrawn from action," Mitchell "continued on her chosen path."

The question of why one artist will evolve and change within relatively narrow limits while another will move from one expressive form to another is just one of many Kertess raises: paired nouns juxtapose themselves and demand consideration or reconsideration as they figure in Mitchell's work—order and disorder, mess and clarity; dark paint in a rosy canvas; dark paint and dark mood, black as a joyous color, white as a dark color. And another question that comes up when we look at Mitchell's life and work: Why, indeed, do some artists and writers need to leave their native lands in order to paint the childhood landscape or write about it (Beckett, Joyce) while others do not (William Carlos Williams, Charles Olson, Mitchell's close friend Frank O'Hara)? "I carry my landscape around with me" was something Mitchell said more than once, though not, of course, as any sort of explanation.

I am not even certain that Mitchell's *Les Bluets* (The Cornflowers) was the actual painting I saw on that particular day, but I'm going to say it was. What I saw was a very large white-and-blue painting by Joan Mitchell in her studio more than forty-five years ago, and that is the one I am thinking of.

To get closer to the actual experience of seeing the painting, I first confirm or revise some of my memories of visiting her where she lived at Vétheuil, of her strong personality (I witnessed some of the "preemptive strikes" that Kertess mentions, but witnessed also her generosity and warm welcome), of my life in Paris. Then I remember more, more than I need to, about where I was living, and how I worked at my writing, pushing myself relentlessly to do better and more, with moments of pleasure but often a hounding sense of obligation, a fear that if I did not work terribly hard something would catch up with me—perhaps the possibility that I did not need to be doing this.

I would take the train out of the city, with its closed spaces, its darkness, to the village of Vétheuil, sixty-nine kilometers to the north. A blue gate at street level opened to a climb on foot to the house, to a terrace before the front door. The view from the hilltop, if I turned back before going in, was of a landscape managed and orderly: poplars by the winding river, and a village on the far bank. The grounds, the rooms in the house, and the mealtimes were also orderly, though I did not give much thought, then, to the value of order. Monet had once lived here, though at the base of the hill, in what was now the cook's and gardener's cottage. His first wife, Camille, was buried in a cemetery beyond the garden. (Mitchell's early influences had included Matisse and Van Gogh, but not, she said, Monet.)

On one visit I walked out to Joan Mitchell's studio to look at a painting. I don't know if this was the first time I had gone into her studio. I liked the painting very much, in my naive way, and thought there was no problem with the way I looked at it. It was what it was, shapes and colors, white and blue. Then I was told by Joan or someone else that it referred to the landscape here in Vétheuil, specifically to the cornflowers. Whatever I had known or not known about painting before, this was a surprise to me, even a shock. Apparently I had not known before that an abstract painting could contain references to concrete, objective, identifiable subject matter. Two things happened at once: the painting abruptly went beyond itself, lost its isolation, acquired a relationship to fields, to flowers; and it changed from something I understood into something I did not understand, a mystery, a problem.

Later I could try to figure it out: there had to be visual clues in the picture. Were all, or only some, of the elements in it clues? If the lighter, scattered, or broken areas of blue referred to cornflowers, what did the blocks of darker blue refer to, and the opulent white? (Kertess discusses how that color in Mitchell's paintings functioned in different ways at different times, ranging from "interactive," to atmospheric, to nurturing, to "perilous," "deathly," "smothering," and finally to "haunting.") Or were all the elements clues but some of them to private, unknowable subjects? Was this a representation of an emotional response to cornflowers, or to a memory of cornflowers?

I like to understand things and tend to ask questions of myself or another person until there is nothing left that I do not understand. At the time, in the midst of a period when I was training myself so hard in another kind of representation and seeing more and more clearly into the subtler workings of my language, I was confronted with this experience of opacity.

I had had other striking experiences of incomprehension, of opacity, the most extended being the first weeks I spent, at age seven, in an Austrian classroom listening to the German language before I began to understand it. Years later, when translating the French texts of Maurice Blanchot into English, I struggled so hard with the meaning of certain complex sentences that I was sure I felt this struggle physiologically inside my brain—the little currents of electricity sparked, traveled, leaped forward against the problem, fell back, leaped again from a different side, failed. But the experience of incomprehension in front of Joan Mitchell's painting caught me unprepared, in its novel form—no words, but three panels of blue and white.

Eventually I began to find answers to my questions, but they were not complete answers, and after a time I did not feel the need for complete answers, because I saw that part of the force of the painting was that it continued to elude explanation. I became willing to allow aspects of the painting to remain mysterious, and I became willing to allow aspects of other problems to remain unsolved as well, and it was this new tolerance for, and then satisfaction in, the unexplained and unsolved that marked a change in me.

Even now, just by remaining so mysteriously fixed in my memory, the painting poses a question that, once again, remains even after I have attempted to answer it, and that is not How does the painting work? but How does the memory of the painting work?

1996, 1997, 2017

WRITERS

John Ashbery's Translation of Rimbaud's *Illuminations*

Some associations with the name Rimbaud are familiar: the highly romantic photograph of the seventeen-year-old French poet taken a few months after he first settled in Paris, already the resolutely bohemian artist, with his pale eyes, distant gaze, thatch of hair, carelessly rumpled clothes; the startling, much-interpreted declaration *Je est un autre* ("I is another" or "I is someone else"); the fact that he produced a masterly, innovative, and influential body of work while still in his teens; that he stopped writing around age twenty-one and never went back to it; that he engaged thereafter in various, sometimes mysterious commercial and mystical enterprises in far-flung locations, including a period of gunrunning in Africa and, perhaps even stranger, an attempt to enlist in the U.S. Navy. He died of cancer in a Marseilles hospital, still young, having in effect compressed what for others would have been a long lifetime of artistic revolution and exotic adventure into just thirty-seven years.

A deepened and more detailed familiarity with the legend does not disappoint: he is one of those exceptional individuals whose very existence is hard to account for, whose development was meteoric, and whose accomplishments continue to dazzle.

Arthur Rimbaud was born in 1854 in Charleville, a town in the northeast of France close to the Belgian border, to a sour-tempered, repressively pious mother and a mostly absent army-officer father who disappeared for good when Rimbaud was six. He excelled in school, reading voraciously and retentively, and regularly carried off most of his grade's year-end prizes in every subject. Early poems were written not just in French but sometimes in Latin and Greek and included a fanciful rendering of a math assignment and a sixty-line ode dedicated (and sent) to the young son of Napoleon III.

At the age of just fifteen, Rimbaud had announced in a letter that he intended to create an entirely new kind of poetry, written in an entirely new language, through a "rational derangement of all the senses," and when, not yet seventeen, he made his first successful escape to Paris, funded by the older poet Paul Verlaine, he came prepared to change the world, or at least literature. He was immediately a colorful figure: the filthy, lice-infested, intermittently bewitching young rebel with notably large hands and feet, whose mission required scandalizing the conventional-minded and defying moral codes not only through his verse but also through his rude, self-destructive, and anarchical behavior; the brilliantly skillful and versatile poet not only of the occasional sentimental subject (orphans receiving gifts on New Year's Day) but also of lovely scatological verse; the child-faced innovator whose literary development evolved from poem to poem at lightning speed. (This determined young roué would no doubt be horrified to learn that in his hometown there is now a Rimbaud Museum, housed in an old water mill.)

In Paris, he became close friends and soon lovers—openly gay behavior being very much a part of his project of self-exploration and defiance of society—with Verlaine, whose own poetry Rimbaud had already admired from a distance. He appreciated, among its other qualities, its transgression of traditional formal constraints, such as, shockingly, bridging the caesura in the alexandrine line. Their stormy relationship, which extended into Belgium and England and lasted a surprising length of time, was richly productive literarily on both sides.

It is therefore no surprise that Rimbaud has been the perfect subject, for 150 years now, of sanctification, vilification, multiple rival exegeses, obfuscation, memoirs that rely on often faulty recollection—all of which has generated, of course, many times the few hundred pages left by the poet himself in the form of letters, juvenilia, more than eighty individual poems, including the hundred-line "The Drunken Boat," written when he was still sixteen, and the nine-section confessional and self-condemnatory prose sequence *A Season in Hell*, besides what was close to his last work, the sequence of mostly prose poems called *Illuminations*.

If the dating of all the poems in this last work cannot be verified precisely, neither can their proper order or the circumstances leading to their publication. We are told by the rather unreliable Verlaine that in 1875, upon the latter's release from prison—he had shot Rimbaud in the arm in a Brussels hotel room—the younger poet handed him a pile of loose pages and asked him to find a publisher for them. After passing through several hands, the sequence appeared in the magazine *La Vogue* ten years later, in 1886, having been prepared for publication by Félix Fénéon (journalist, publisher, and author of the bizarre collection of police-blotter-generated newspaper

fillers published as *Novels in Three Lines* by New York
Review Books in 2007, in a translation by Luc Sante).

When asked many years later, Fénéon could not remember whether the order was his own or whether he
had preserved the order in which he received them—
though since he did not receive them directly from
Rimbaud, that order was not necessarily the author's.
The work was greeted at the time with some laudatory
reviews, though not many copies were bought.

Formally, *Illuminations*—the title may refer to engraved illustrations, to epiphanies or flashes of insight, or
to the productions of the poet-seer who has transformed
himself into pure light—consists of forty-three poems
ranging from a few lines to works of several sections
covering two or three pages; some are in large blocks
of justified type, some in paragraphs so brief they are
virtually two-line stanzas on the page. (In one instance,
a single comma, placed at the end of the paragraph,
magically turns it into a strophe.) Only three poems
have broken lines.

Despite the uncertainty of its dates of composition,
Illuminations is quite clearly a work written after Rimbaud's most defiant and scurrilous phase had passed. It
does not contain the explicit playful or lyrical obscenity
of earlier times; rather, it has a subtler incandescent or
ecstatic range of congruous and incongruous, urban
and pastoral imagery, and historical and mythological
reference often grounded in near-recognizable autobiographical narrative. A wealth of images—mineral, in-
dustrial, theatrical, royal, natural, and of childhood
days—develops by leaps of immediate personal association rather than by sequential or narrative logic, employing the techniques of surrealism decades before it existed

as a movement. The poems shift in tone and register from the matter-of-fact to the highly rhetorical ("O world!"), the statements from the simple ("the hand of the countryside on my shoulder") to the more abstruse ("He is affection and the present since he opened the house to foaming winter and the hum of summer"), while always departing from and returning to a concrete, sensory world. The more narrative poems—faux reminiscences, exhortations, modern fairy tales—are punctuated by verse consisting almost solely of exclamatory lists of sentence fragments, what sound like celebrations of repeated amazement, contributing to create what John Ashbery, in his brief but enlightening preface to the translation, calls "the crystalline jumble of Rimbaud's *Illuminations*, like a disordered collection of magic lantern slides, each an 'intense and rapid dream,' in his words."

Ashbery has said that he first read Rimbaud when he was sixteen, and that he took to heart the young poet's declaration that "you must be absolutely modern"—absolute modernity being, as Ashbery describes it in his preface, "the acknowledging of the simultaneity of all of life, the condition that nourishes poetry at every second." When Rimbaud's mother asked of *A Season in Hell*, "What does it mean?"—a question that is still asked of his poetry, and is regularly asked of Ashbery's, too—Rimbaud would not give more of an answer than "It means what it says, literally and in every sense."

If Rimbaud anticipated the surrealists by decades, Ashbery is said to have gone beyond them and defied even their rules and logic. Yet, though more than 150 years have intervened since Rimbaud's first declaration of independence, many readers in our own age, too, still prefer a coherence of imagery, a sameness of tone, a readable sequential message, even, ultimately, what amounts to a prose narrative broken into lines. Enough others, however, find the "crystalline jumble" intellectually and emotionally revitalizing and say, Yes, please do interrupt the reverie you have created for us to allow an intrusion of Popeye!

Besides his early absorption of Rimbaud's work, John Ashbery brings to this translation a long and deep familiarity with French life, language, culture (particularly artistic and literary culture), and the experience of having translated many other French works over the years— by Pierre Reverdy, Raymond Roussel, Max Jacob, Pierre Martory (as well as at least one detective novel under the re-assorted nom de plume Jonas Berry). These translations are part of a larger body of work of Ashbery's that has served to offer us—his largely monolingual Anglophone readership—access to poets of another culture, either foreign or earlier in time. (Notable, for instance, is his keenly investigatory, instructive, and engrossing *Other Traditions*, the six Norton Lectures that open our eyes to the work of John Clare, Laura Riding, and others.)

In his meticulously faithful yet nimbly inventive translation, Ashbery's approach has been to stay close to the original, following the line of the sentence, retaining the order of ideas and images, reproducing even eccentric or inconsistent punctuation. He shifts away from the closest translation only where necessary, and there is plenty of room within this close adherence for vibrant and less obvious English word choices. One of the pleasures of the translation, for instance, is the concise, mildly archaic Anglo-Saxon vocabulary that he occasionally deploys— "hued" for *teinte* and "clad" for *revêtus*, "chattels" for *possessions*—or a more particular or flavorful English for a more general or blander French: "posh" for *riches*, "hum of summer" for *rumeurs de l'été*, "trembling" for *mouvante*.

Even a simple problem reveals his practiced ease with handling English. In one section of "Childhood," there occurs the following portrayal of would-be tranquility: "I rest my elbows on the table, the lamp lights up these newspapers that I'm a fool for rereading, these books of no interest." The two words *sans intérêt* ("without interest") allow for surprisingly many solutions, as one can see from a quick sampling of previous translations. Yet these other choices are either less rhythmical than the French—"uninteresting," "empty of interest"—or do not retain the subtlety of the French: "mediocre," "boring," "idiotic." Ashbery's "books of no interest" is quietly matter-of-fact and dismissive, like the French; rhythmically satisfying; and placed, liked the original, at the end of the sentence.

It takes one sort of linguistic sensitivity to stay close to the original in a pleasing way, another to bring a certain inventiveness to one's choices without being unfaithful. Ashbery's ingenuity is evident at many moments in the book, and an especially lovely example occurs in the same poem: he has translated *Qu'on me loue enfin ce tombeau, blanchi à la chaux* as "Let someone finally rent me this tomb, whited with quicklime." Here, his "whited with quicklime" (rather than "whitewashed," the choice of all the other translations I found) at once exploits the possibilities of assonance and introduces the echo of the King James "whited sepulchre" without betraying the meaning of the original.

The translations of some of the poems in this book have appeared previously in literary journals one by one over the past two years or so—evidently done slowly over time, as translations ought to be, especially of poems, and especially of these poems, given their extreme compression, their tonal and stylistic shifts, their liberating importance in the history of poetry. We are fortunate that John Ashbery has turned his attention to a text he knows so well, and brought to it such care and imaginative resourcefulness.

2011

Young Pynchon

The books I'm thinking about today, of Thomas Pynchon's, are the smaller, earlier ones: *The Crying of Lot 49* and *Slow Learner*, the collection of stories written when he was very young—four when he was still in college. I am curious to see how he writes particularly when he is just beginning, rawly instilled with his influences and full of a heady sense of a smart college boy's power over language. All of these stories were published in magazines—one in *The Kenyon Review* and one in *The Saturday Evening Post*—and he is indeed a very impressive writer for that age. The stories are well structured; the characters are present, if not very fully realized or deeply sympathetic; the details believable; and the vocabulary rich, wide-ranging, and well used. The characters are mostly men and boys, with occasional appearances in secondary roles by such females as "co-eds," mothers, "chicks," and "brown-haired beauties." The situations for several of the stories draw upon life in the army and/or the navy, while the last one centers on a gang of schoolboy practical jokers. The language is casually tough: "lousy," etc. There are the tics of a young writer, such as an overuse of explanatory verbs in dialogue—something that carries over, too, into *Crying* ("remembered Oedipa," "squinted Di Presso," "allowed Di Presso," "Metzger explained")—and there are skilled epithets and descriptions ("When he spoke it was with a precise, dry Beacon Hill accent"), colorful names, and economical dialogue ("He went over to where Picnic was eating and said, 'Guess what.' 'I figured,' Picnic said").

What is interesting is the complex position of the author/narrator in relation to the book, characters, language itself, and reader at this stage in Pynchon's writing career. With both books, he is working in the traditional mode: author adopts persona of narrator (third person omniscient) narrating in a certain tone and vocabulary the events of a collection of characters. In the stories, the author/narrator stays more in the background, less noticeable for his verbal flair; the illusion of some sort of familiar but alternative reality is maintained. In *The Crying of Lot 49* he comes more to the fore, and we are constantly aware of the clever narrator and, through or behind him, the playful author, partly because of the easy mix of highly educated vocabulary ("annular corridor," "radial aisles," "moue") with pop-cultural references (Road Runner), and especially because of his clever punning in the naming of his characters: we know we are not being asked to believe in a woman named Oedipa Maas or a man named Stanley Koteks, and our attention is distracted from the story to the artifice and artificer. What is shared by the two books is a sense of tight control by the author over the characters, the language, the book, and probably the reader. Sometimes the control is achieved through his mastery of a graceful prose style or an appealing notion ("Creaking, or echoing, or left as dark-ribbed sneaker-prints in a fine layer of damp, the footsteps of the Junta carried them into King Yrjö's house, past pier glasses that gave them back their images dark and faded, as if some part were being kept as the price of admission"): here is control by persuasion. Sometimes, on the other hand, the young author goes beyond eloquence to a kind of hyper-eloquence that becomes a display of power over language itself that perhaps borders on control by coercion.

I chose to read the stories before reading the introduction by Pynchon himself (beyond the first sentences explaining how old the stories were: they were more than twenty years old at the time they were collected, and that publication is now twenty years in the past, so we are looking at stories well back in time). The introduction is fairly substantial and perhaps preempts our own reaction to the stories if we read it first, as perhaps it is meant to. Because of the existence of such an extensive introduction, in fact, we have, in this book, the author explicitly in the foreground as well as implicitly in the background, behind the narrator. If we wonder about the dominance of male characters in the stories, the men being powerful doers, the women mostly decorative and/ or useful to the men (the coed serving food, the ballet dancer with frostbitten toes), which tends to some degree to exclude or daunt a fully sympathetic female readership, Pynchon himself explains it in part by naming the very male roster of some of his influences in those days: Eliot, Hemingway, Kerouac, Saul Bellow, Herbert Gold, Philip Roth, Norman Mailer.

If we look for more than mere competence or even skill in these young stories, if we look for the fresh experience or the transcendent image that holds promise for the future of the young writer, we are regularly rewarded, as in this image from the last story in his collection, "The Secret Integration": "Each lot was only fifty by a hundred feet, nowhere near the size of the old Gilded Age estates, real ones, that surrounded the old town the way creatures in dreams surround your bed."

A rather appealing specimen of early Pynchon, "The Secret Integration" was first published in *The Saturday Evening Post* more than forty years ago (one year after *V.* appeared) and places its gang of schoolboy jokesters in a setting rich in possibilities for the childish imagination: an old town with a new development, a sprawling estate with a derelict mansion, a natural landscape open to exploration, a downtown complete with a seedy hotel. In a deftly described scene, the boys coast on their bikes down a long hill in the early evening toward the hotel, "leaving behind two pages of arithmetic homework and a chapter of science" as well as "a lousy movie, some romantic comedy" on TV. Because all the televisions in town receive only one channel, the boys, as they fly by, can follow the progress of the movie from house to house, through doors and windows "still open for the dark's first coolness," as it advances.

In his introduction to *Slow Learner*, Pynchon remarks rather diffidently that he likes more than he dislikes the story. In fact, it is so likable that one envies the boys their comfortable society and the fields, streams, street corners, and alleyways of their games. Their collaboration and apportioning of assignments is charming—develop an arsenal for sabotaging the railroad, enlist malcontent first-graders for destroying the boys' latrine, infiltrate PTA meetings. The elaborateness of their schemes is impressive, as are some of their successes, and the animation of the central character, Grover, the boy genius, particularly savory, with his enormous vocabulary, fund of information, and flights of hilarity.

The pranks they plan are potentially devastating to the community, yet, as Pynchon lets us know, the boys would never actually take "any clear or irreversible step" because "everybody on the school board, and the railroad, and the PTA and paper mill had to be somebody's mother or father, whether really or as a member of a category; and there was a point at which the reflex to their covering warmth, protection, effectiveness against bad dreams, bruised heads and simple loneliness took over and made worthwhile anger with them impossible." There is a quiet lyrical humanity in this story, an almost unapologetic gentleness, inviting and inclusive, that contrasts with the weightier complex pessimism and bravado of the later novels, in which perhaps it is more difficult for the characters to go home and be comforted at the end of the day.

2005

The Story Is the Thing: Lucia Berlin's
A Manual for Cleaning Women

Lucia Berlin's stories are electric; they buzz and crackle as the live wires touch. And in response, the reader's mind, too, beguiled, enraptured, comes alive, all synapses firing. This is the way we like to be when we're reading—using our brains, feeling our hearts beat.

Part of the vibrancy of Lucia Berlin's prose is in the pacing—sometimes fluent and calm, balanced, ambling and easy; and sometimes staccato, notational, speedy. Part of it is in her specific naming of things: Piggly Wiggly (a supermarket), Beenie-Weenie Wonder (a strange culinary creation), Big Mama panty hose (a way to tell us how large the narrator is). It is in the dialogue. What are those exclamations? "Jesus wept." "Well, I'm blamed!" The characterizations—the boss of the switchboard operators says she can tell when it's close to quitting time by the behavior of Thelma: "Your wig gets crooked and you start talking dirty."

And there is the language itself, word by word. Lucia Berlin is always listening, hearing. Her sensitivity to the sounds of the language is always awake, and we, too, savor the rhythms of the syllables, or the perfect coincidence of sound and sense. Another switchboard operator, this one angry, moves "with much slamming and slapping of her things." At another moment, in a different story, Berlin describes the cries of the "gawky raucous crows." In a letter she wrote to me from Colorado in 2000, the language was just as vital: "Branches heavy with snow break and crack against my roof and the wind shakes the walls. Snug though, like being in a good sturdy boat, a scow or a tug." (Hear those monosyllables, and that rhyme.)

Her stories are also full of surprises: unexpected phrases, insights, turns of events, and humor, as in "So Long," whose narrator is living in Mexico and speaking mostly Spanish, and comments a little sadly, "Of course I have a self here, and a new family, new cats, new jokes. But I keep trying to remember who I was in English."

In "Panteón de Dolores," the narrator, as child, is contending with a difficult mother—as she will in several more stories:

> One night after he had gone home she came in, to the bedroom where I slept with her. She kept on drinking and crying and scribbling, literally scribbling, in her diary.
>
> "Are you okay?" I finally asked her, and she slapped me.

In "Dear Conchi," the narrator is a wry, smart college student:

> Ella, my roommate . . . I wish we got along better. Her mother mails her her Kotex from Oklahoma every month. She's a drama major. God, how

can she ever play Lady Macbeth if she can't relax about a little blood?

Or the surprise can come in a simile—and her stories are rich in similes:

In "A Manual for Cleaning Women," she writes, "Once he told me he loved me because I was like San Pablo Avenue."

She goes right on to another, even more surprising comparison: "He was like the Berkeley dump."

And she is just as lyrical describing a dump (whether in Berkeley or in Chile) as she is describing a field of wildflowers:

> I wish there was a bus to the dump. We went there when we got homesick for New Mexico. It is stark and windy and gulls soar like nighthawks in the desert. You can see the sky all around you and above you. Garbage trucks thunder through dust-billowing roads. Gray dinosaurs.

Always embedding the stories in a real physical world is just this kind of concrete physical imagery: the trucks "thunder," the dust "billows." Sometimes the imagery is beautiful; at other times, it is not beautiful but intensely palpable: we experience each story not only with our intellects and our hearts but also through our senses. The smell of the history teacher, her sweat and mildewed clothing, in "Good and Bad." Or, in another story, "the sinking soft tarmac . . . the dirt and sage." The cranes flying up "with the sound of shuffling cards." The "Caliche dust and oleander." The "wild sunflowers and purple weed" in yet another story; and crowds of poplars, planted years before in better times, thriving in a slum. She was always watching, even if only out the window (when it became hard for her to move): in that same letter to me from Boulder, magpies "dive-bomb" for the apple pulp—"quick flashes of aqua and black against the snow."

A description can start out romantic—"the *parroquia* in Veracruz, palm trees, lanterns in the moonlight"—but the romanticism is cut, as in real life, by the realistic Flaubertian detail, so sharply observed by her: "dogs and cats among the dancers' polished shoes." A writer's embrace of the world is all the more evident when she sees the ordinary along with the extraordinary, the commonplace or the ugly along with the beautiful.

She credits her mother, or one of her narrators does, with teaching her that observant eye:

> We have remembered . . . your way of looking, never missing a thing. You gave us that. Looking.
>
> Not listening though. You'd give us maybe five minutes, to tell you about something, and then you'd say, "Enough."

The mother stayed in her bedroom drinking. The grandfather stayed in his bedroom drinking. The girl heard the separate gurgling of their bottles from the porch where she slept. This was in a story, but maybe also in reality—or the story is an exaggeration of the reality, so acutely witnessed, so funny, that even as we feel the pain of it, we have that paradoxical pleasure in the way it is told, and the pleasure is greater than the pain.

Lucia Berlin based many of her stories on events in her own life. One of her sons said, after her death, "Ma wrote true stories, not necessarily autobiographical, but close enough for horseshoes."

Although people nowadays in literary circles talk, as though it were a new thing, about the form of fiction known in France as *auto-fiction* ("self-fiction"), the narration of one's own life, lifted almost unchanged from the reality, selected and judiciously, artfully told, Lucia Berlin has been doing this, or a version of this, as far as I can see, from the beginning, back in the 1960s. Her son went on to say, "Our family stories and memories have been slowly reshaped, embellished and edited to the extent that I'm not sure what really happened all the time. Lucia said this didn't matter: the story is the thing."

For the sake of balance, or color, she changed whatever she had to, in shaping her stories—details of events and descriptions, chronology. She admitted to exaggerating. One of her narrators says, "I exaggerate a lot and I get fiction and reality mixed up, but I don't actually ever lie."

Certainly she invented. For example, Alastair Johnston, the publisher of one of her early, small-press collections, reports the following conversation he had with her: "I love that description of your aunt at the airport," he said to her, "how you sank into her great body like a chaise." Her answer was: "The truth is . . . no one met me. I thought of that image the other day and as I was writing that story just worked it in." In fact, some of her stories were entirely made up, as she explains in an interview. A person could not think he knew her just because he had read her stories.

Her life was rich and full of incident, and the material she took from it for her stories was colorful, dramatic, and wide-ranging. The places she and her family lived in her childhood and youth were determined by her father—where he worked in her early years, then his going off to serve in World War II, and then his job when he returned from the war. Thus, she was born in Alaska and grew up first in mining camps in the west of the United States; then lived with her mother's family in El Paso while her father was gone; then was transplanted south into a very different life in Chile, one of wealth and privilege, which is portrayed in her stories about a teenage girl in Santiago, about Catholic school there, about political turbulence, yacht clubs, dressmakers, slums, revolution. As an adult she continued to lead a restless life, geographically, living in Mexico, Arizona, New Mexico, New York City; one of her sons remembers moving about every nine months as a child. Later in her life she taught in Boulder, Colorado, and at the very end of it she moved closer to her sons, to Los Angeles.

She writes about her sons—she had four—and the jobs she worked to support them, often on her own. Or, we should say, she writes about a woman with four sons, and jobs like her jobs—cleaning woman, ER nurse, hospital ward clerk, hospital switchboard operator, teacher.

She lived in so many places, experienced so much—it was enough to fill several lives. We have, most of us, known at least some part of what she went through: children in trouble, a rapturous love affair; or early molestation, struggles with addiction, a difficult illness or disability, an unexpected bond with a sibling; or a tedious job, difficult fellow workers, a demanding boss; or a deceitful friend; not to speak of awe in the presence of the natural world—Hereford cattle knee-deep in Indian paintbrush, a field of bluebonnets, a pink rocket flower growing in the alley behind a hospital. Because we have

known some part of it, or something like it, we are right
there with her as she takes us through it.

Things actually happen in the stories—a whole mouth-
ful of teeth gets pulled at once; a little girl gets expelled
from school for striking a nun; an old man dies in a
mountaintop cabin, his goats and his dog in bed with
him; the history teacher with her mildewed sweater is
dismissed for being a Communist—"That's all it took.
Three words to my father. She was fired sometime that
weekend and we never saw her again."

Is this why it is almost impossible to stop reading a
story of Lucia Berlin's once you begin? Is it because
things keep happening? Is it also the narrating voice, so
engaging, so companionable? Along with the economy,
the pacing, the imagery, the clarity? These stories make
you forget what you were doing, where you are, and even
who you are.

"Wait," begins one story. "Let me explain . . ." It is
a voice close to Lucia's own, though never identical. Her
wit and her irony flow through the stories and overflow
in her letters, too: "She is taking her medication," she
told me once, in 2002, about a friend, "which makes a
big difference! What did people do before Prozac? Beat
up horses I guess."

Beat up horses. Where did that come from? The past
was maybe as alive in her mind as were other cultures,
other languages, politics, human foibles; the range of her
reference so rich and even exotic that switchboard operators lean into their boards like milkmaids leaning into
their cows; or a friend comes to the door, "her black
hair . . . up in tin rollers, like a kabuki headdress."

The past—I read this paragraph from "Panteón de

Dolores" a few times, with relish, with wonder, before I
realized what she was doing:

> One night it was bitterly cold, Ben and Keith
> were sleeping with me, in snowsuits. The shutters
> banged in the wind, shutters as old as Herman
> Melville. It was Sunday so there were no cars. Be-
> low in the streets the sailmaker passed, in a horse-
> drawn cart. Clop clop. Sleet hissed cold against
> the windows and Max called. Hello, he said. I'm
> right around the corner in a phone booth.
>
> He came with roses, a bottle of brandy, and
> four tickets to Acapulco. I woke up the boys and
> we left.

They were living in lower Manhattan, at a time when
the heat would be turned off at the end of the working
day if you lived in a loft. Maybe the shutters really were
as old as Herman Melville, since in some parts of Manhattan buildings did date from the 1860s, back then,
more of them than now, though now, too. Though it
could be that she is exaggerating again—a beautiful exaggeration, if so, a beautiful flourish. She goes on: "It
was Sunday so there were no cars." That sounded realistic, so, then, I was fooled by the sailmaker and the
horse-drawn cart, which came next—I believed it and accepted it, and only realized after another reading that
she must have jumped back effortlessly into Melville's
time again. The "Clop clop," too, is something she likes
to do—waste no words, add a detail in note form. The
sleet hissing took me in there, within those walls, and
then the action accelerated and we were suddenly on our
way to Acapulco.

This is exhilarating writing.

Another story begins with a typically straightforward and informative statement that I can easily believe is drawn directly from Berlin's own life: "I've worked in hospitals for years now and if there's one thing I've learned it's that the sicker the patients are the less noise they make. That's why I ignore the patient intercom." Reading that, I'm reminded of the stories of William Carlos Williams when he wrote as the family doctor he was—his directness, his frank and knowledgeable details of medical conditions and treatment, his objective reporting. Even more than Williams, she also saw Chekhov (another doctor) as a model and teacher. In fact, she says in a letter to her friend and fellow writer Stephen Emerson that what gives life to their work is their physician's detachment, combined with compassion. She goes on to mention their use of specific detail and their economy—"No words are written that aren't necessary." Detachment, compassion, specific detail, and economy—and we are well on the way to identifying some of the most important things in good writing. But there is always a little more to say.

How does she do it? It's that we never know quite what is going to come next. Nothing is predictable. And yet everything is also natural, true to life, true to our expectations of psychology and emotion.

At the end of "Dr. H. A. Moynihan," the narrator's mother seems to soften a bit toward her drunk, mean, bigoted old father: "'He did a good job,' my mother said." This is the tail end of the story, and so we think—having been trained by all our years of reading stories—that now the mother will relent; people in troubled families can be reconciled, at least for a while. But when the daughter asks, "You don't still hate him, do you Mama?" the answer, brutally honest, and in some way satisfying, is "Oh, yes . . . Yes I do."

Berlin is unflinching, pulls no punches, and yet the brutality of life is always tempered by her compassion for human frailty, the wit and intelligence of that narrating voice, and her gentle humor.

In a story called "Silence," the narrator says: "I don't mind telling people awful things if I can make them funny." (Though some things, she adds, just weren't funny.)

Sometimes the comedy is broad, as in "Sex Appeal," where the pretty cousin Bella Lynn sets off in an airplane toward what she hopes will be a Hollywood career, her bust enhanced by an inflatable bra—but when the airplane reaches cruising altitude, the bra explodes. Usually the humor is more understated, a natural part of the narrative conversation—for instance, about the difficulty of buying alcoholic beverages in Boulder: "The liquor stores are gigantic Target-size nightmares. You could die from DTs just trying to find the Jim Beam aisle." She goes on to inform us that "the best town is Albuquerque, where the liquor stores have drive-through windows, so you don't even have to get out of your pajamas."

As in life, comedy can occur in the midst of tragedy: the younger sister, dying of cancer, wails, "I'll never see donkeys again!" and both sisters eventually laugh and laugh, but the poignant exclamation stays with you. Death has become so immediate—no more donkeys, no more of so many things.

Did she learn her fantastic ability to tell a story from the storytellers she grew up with? Or was she always attracted to storytellers, did she seek them out, learn from them? Both, no doubt. She had a natural feel for the form, the structure of a story. Natural? What I mean is that a story of hers has a balanced, solid structure and yet moves with such an illusion of naturalness from one subject to another, or, in some stories, from present into past— even within a sentence, as in the following:

> I worked mechanically at my desk, answering phones, calling for oxygen and lab techs, drifting away into warm waves of pussywillows and sweet peas and trout pools. The pulleys and riggings of the mine at night, after the first snow. Queen Anne's lace against the starry sky.

And then, her endings. In so many stories, Wham! comes the end, at once surprising and yet inevitable, resulting organically from the material of the story. In "Mama," the younger sister finds a way to sympathize, finally, with the difficult mother, but the last few words of the older sister, the narrator—talking to herself, now, or to us—take us by surprise: "Me . . . I have no mercy."

How did a story come into being, for Lucia Berlin? Johnston has a possible answer: "She would start with something as simple as the line of a jaw, or a yellow mimosa." She herself goes on to say: "But the image has to connect to a specific intense experience." Elsewhere, in a letter to August Kleinzahler, she describes how she goes forward: "I *get* started, & then it's just like writing this to you, only more legible." Some part of her mind, at the same time, must always have been in control of the shape and sequence of the story, and the end of it.

She said the story had to be real—whatever that meant

for her. I think it meant not contrived, not incidental or gratuitous: it had to be deeply felt, emotionally important. She told a student of hers that the story he had written was too clever—don't try to be clever, she said. She once typeset one of her own stories in hot metal on a linotype machine, and after three days of work threw all the slugs back into the melting pot, because, she said, the story was "false."

What about the difficulty of the (real) material?

"Silence" is a story she tells about some of the real events she also mentions more briefly to Kleinzahler in a kind of pained shorthand ("Fight with Hope devastating"). In the story, the narrator's uncle John, who is an alcoholic, is driving drunk with his little niece in the truck. He hits a boy and a dog, injuring both, the dog badly, and doesn't stop. Lucia Berlin says, of the incident, to Kleinzahler: "The disillusion when he hit the kid and the dog was Awful for me." The story, when she turns it into fiction, has the same incident, and the same pain, but there is a resolution of sorts. The narrator knows Uncle John later in his life, when, in a happy marriage, he is mild, gentle, and no longer drinking. Her last words, in the story, are "Of course by this time I had realized all the reasons why he couldn't stop the truck, because by this time I was an alcoholic."

About handling the difficult material, she comments: "Somehow there must occur the most imperceptible alteration of reality. A transformation, not a distortion of the truth. The story itself becomes the truth, not just for the writer but for the reader. In any good piece of writing it is not an identification with a situation, but this recognition of truth that is thrilling."

A transformation, not a distortion of the truth.

—————

I have known Lucia Berlin's work for over thirty years—
ever since I acquired the slim, beige 1981 Turtle Island
paperback called *Angels Laundromat*. By the time of
her third collection, I had come to know her personally,
from a distance, though I can't remember how. There
on the flyleaf of the beautiful *Safe & Sound* (Poltroon
Press, 1988) is her inscription. We never did meet face-
to-face, though we nearly did once.

Her publications eventually moved out of the small-
press world and into the medium-press world of Black
Sparrow and then, later, of Godine. One of her collections won the American Book Award. But even with that
recognition, and hosts of dedicated fans, she had not
yet found the wide readership she should have had by
then.

I had always thought another story of hers included a
mother and her children out picking the first wild asparagus of early spring, but I have found it only, so far, in
another letter she wrote to me. I had sent her a description of asparagus by Proust. She replied:

Only ones I ever saw growing were the thin crayon-
green wild ones. In New Mexico, where we lived
outside of Albuquerque, by the river. One day in
spring they'd be up beneath the cotton woods.
About six inches tall, just right to snap off. My four
sons and I would gather dozens, while down the
river would be Granma Price and her boys, up
river all of the Waggoners. No one ever seemed
to see them as one or two inch high, only at the
perfect height. One of the boys would run in and

shout "Asparagus!" just as somebody was doing the same at the Prices' and Waggoners'.

I have always had faith that the best writers will rise to the top, like cream, sooner or later, and will become as well-known as they should be—their work talked about, quoted, taught, performed, filmed, set to music, anthologized. Perhaps now, Lucia Berlin will begin to gain the attention she deserves.

In closing, I could quote almost any part of any story of hers for contemplation, for enjoyment, but here is one last favorite:

So what is marriage anyway? I never figured it out. And now it is death I don't understand.

2016

A Close Look at Two Books
by Rae Armantrout

I. *Precedence* (1985)

I begin with a close look at one poem:

HOME FEDERAL

A merchant is
probing for us
with his chintz curtain
effect.

•

"Ha, ha, you missed me,"
a dead person says.

•

There's the bank's
Colonial balcony
where no one has
ever stood.

"Home Federal" is a compact, clear poem, three stanzas that may or may not cluster around the bank or savings and loan referred to in the title: a bank probes for us, if its special conveniences are not usually chintz curtains, and a bank manager is a dubious sort of merchant; the dead person may be pleased to be out of reach of the enticements of merchants and bank managers; the balcony is almost certainly the balcony of this same bank or savings and loan, but also recalls the many other inaccessible balconies and blind windows and unused doors of American (federal) civic architecture, built to be symbolic as well as functional space.

The poem opens with a chintz curtain at a window and closes with an un-stepped-on balcony, an illusion of a home beckoning but remaining stubbornly nonutilitarian as a living space. There are three characters in the poem—a merchant, a dead person, and "no one"—or three stages of being: living (though a merchant), dead, and not there.

The title, "Home Federal," is presumably part of the name of the bank, probably a savings bank or loan company. But truncated and isolated in its position as title, it reaches out for other contexts as well—which is what Rae Armantrout's words often do, excised from their more usual context, held up for scrutiny. Just several associations—and it's interesting to see how one poet's tone will determine one set of associations and another's will another, how Robert Frost's associations around the word "home" could never be shared by Armantrout—might be "home free" in "all-ee all-ee home free"; "home on the range"; "home" in the real estate dealer's "lovely home"; while "federal" can seem adjectival, qualifying "home" so that we say "home federal" as we would say "Prometheus Unbound," referring more or less to a home in federal America. None of this imagery is out of place in Armantrout's work, which draws fully from the well of America and all it has to offer—the American childhood, the American family, the American holiday, the American landscape, the American city, the American culture, American television, and the American language.

But "home" has also become overridingly ironic, especially once we know Armantrout's subjects and tone; it appears to be so simple a concept and in fact applies to such an extremely problematic complex of ideals and emotions—and some of the power of Armantrout's work lies in the fact that she offers this sort of problematic idea without trying to explain it or draw any conclusions from it, so that it remains alive.

The word "home" appears with the same force and irony in the first line of "Double," the first poem in *Precedence*: "So these are the hills of home." And here, it is the little word "So" that does all the work toward the way we hear "home." Without it, the irony might drop away and the line might open a different kind of book, with a different tone, one that would say, as Armantrout does not say, that the world is a clear, explicable thing to which we all react with shared and acceptable emotions: "These are the hills of home."

In fact, "so" is an excellent word with which to open a book as permeated as this one by the three meanings of "so" that we see in that line: the positing "so," meaning "in such a way"—"so do we live our lives," "so is the landscape and the culture"; the climactic and slightly judgmental "so"—"So this is the little son I've been hearing about," "So this is where you grew up," "So these are the hills of home"; and the concluding "so"— "So this was what it all came to in the end."

The word "effect," when standing by itself and coming after the careful merchant with his chintz, has the same power to ring associations as the word "home" divorced from its more comfortable contexts: we see all possible merchants, agents, managers—workers of a certain level in the American workforce—striving after a special "effect," as so much of American commercial activity depends on response to "effect" as much as response to real need.

Armantrout's use of the phrase "chintz curtain" is slightly different: here she is not freshly creating the ironic overtone, as she does in the words "home," "federal," and "effect," but counting on our familiarity with chintz curtains as a hackneyed symbol of hominess and then putting them in the hands of an artful bank manager (or other merchant). But since they don't really belong in his hands—he and his type are not the bosomy housewife associated with chintz curtains in the cliché—he becomes ridiculous in his dislocation and isolation, as do many of Armantrout's characters.

The word "merchant" itself, with its slightly archaic ring—"merchants' guild," *The Merchant of Venice*—here, with a hint of mockery, endowing a twentieth-century artful bank manager with the title of a member of the Hanseatic League, identifies his more generic function, makes him also in some sense an absurd historical figure, so that, for us, the man in the window and the word "merchant" borrow from each other an enhanced life.

A couple of other incongruities create space around the word or image, or dislocate it so that we see it from a different angle:

"probing"—a word taken from the vocabulary of medicine, and implying delicacy and skill. The slightly ridiculous merchant has the hands of a physician. We think of all the misplaced, wasted skills in the world of American commerce.

and "Ha, ha, you missed me!"—the language of children, with overtones of meanness and rivalry, but spoken by "a dead person" (a descriptor that could also be heard as childish). The enticements of this homey, Hanseatic banker can at least be avoided by children, because they are unsophisticated, and by the dead, because they are not here anymore, no longer consumers.

Why "there's the"? Why that construction, in the last verse—"There's the bank's / Colonial balcony"? Nothing in Armantrout's work is not placed with extreme deliberation, with a view to its "effect," just as, in her hands, even or especially the most unpicturesque words, like "there" and "so," become carriers of a wonderful burden of meaning. "There's the" can be read in both of two ways, depending on where we let the accent fall: the poet is at once showing us certain particular features of the town—there's the library's rough stone facing, there's Woolworth's red sign, there's the bank's Colonial balcony—and listing some damning evidence about America, or America's commercialism, or commercialism in general, or architecture, of which the bank's Colonial balcony where no one has ever stood is the strongest.

I say the three verses may or may not cluster because although they seem to want to cluster around the bank, they are forcibly kept apart not only by spaces on the page but also by printer's marks serving as asterisks, as though too much surface continuity would obscure the imagery, obscure the voice, just as too much familiar context would obscure what this banker or this bank really is, just as the term "bank manager" rather than "merchant" would also obscure what this man is, and just as too much familiar context for the words themselves, in general, would obscure their force and vitality. So often, in fact, Armantrout's poems have seemed to be built word by word rather than phrase by phrase, or rather, by now, in this book, phrase by phrase rather than sentence by sentence; they seem to be pieces of language skillfully extracted from the surrounding world and the surrounding language and set by themselves on the page as though experimentally, to see what electrical interaction will take place with other isolated words or phrases. Armantrout plays the role of the passionately questing, methodical, intelligent, well-informed, yet bemused scientist at arm's length from her experiments, at an ironic distance from what she sees, as though once she begins to understand and then reorganize, for her own greater understanding, fragments of her surrounding world and language, the only reasonable attitude available to her is an attitude of irony.

The logical or narrative continuity has often gone underground and flows there like a water table. Though some poems are tidily laid out, all there on the page— "Postcards," "Traveling Through the Yard," "Compound," "Sigh"—in many more, richer and more provocative with their single words and phrases glittering in their empty spaces, we work hard at making the connections for ourselves, leaping the intervals (or, like Goofy in "Single Most," running across the synapses, hooting in mock terror).

Some of the fragments taken from the surrounding language are fragments of speech, the speech of characters who usually appear in these pages and the pages of Armantrout's earlier books frozen in the midst of performing some "typical" piece of action that renders them isolated and pathetic because so bound to the performance of the inevitable: most overtly, for example, there is the "man in / the eye clinic / rubbing his / eye"; in her collection *Extremities*, a mother reading, "with angry intensity," "When the Frost is on the Punkin"; also in that book, "the crone" with a "white corsage" who is

reading *Thunder at Sunset*; and in *Precedence*, an African American man in a Union Jack T-shirt yelling, "Do
you have any idea *what I mean*?"

When people speak, and also when speech appears
in the poems unattached to any speaking character, the
speech, too, is isolated, spotlighted, and has the plaintive
sound of speech that has been used so many times before, in so many other conversations, usually arguments
(one of our most crucial forms of conversation), that it
is not really our own and suggests, again, how we are
trapped into performing in situations that many others
have performed in before us: "Do you have any idea
what I mean?" Then, from "Entries: look," where they
punctuate—though not always directly related to other
material—the several pages of the poem, "IS THAT
YOU?" "ARE YOU SICK OF ME?" "DON'T LOOK
AT ME LIKE THAT!" "WHAT DO YOU WANT?"

Then, finally, from "The Music," "I can't seem to
get comfortable." Taken with the line before it, "On
every bar the music shifts," it can apply specifically to the
music, characterizing it or characterizing a reaction to
it; taken with several more lines that come before it, the
sense of it is still larger:

> *I want to leave someplace out!*
> *To know the world must mean to know how to get*
>   *through.*
>
> *On every bar the music shifts.*
> *"I can't seem to get comfortable."*

"I can't seem to get comfortable" is also the last line of
the last poem in the book, so that not only the first and
last *poems* in the book but also the first and last *lines* in

the book, taken together, frame the book or sum it up quite aptly. They also identify, symbolically, one major aspect of Rae Armantrout's position as expressed in her work: "So these are the hills of home . . . 'I can't seem to get comfortable.'"

1986

II. "Why Stop with a Barnacle?": *Made to Seem* (1995)

> I think I used to be more "surreal"—though I was only referencing what I saw.
>   —Rae Armantrout, 2017

In her letters and other communications, as in her work, she is brief, concise; each word is essential, nothing merely decorative, though in her poems she writes about the decorative in our streets, in our minds, in our culture. Brevity, probably the brevity of distillation, is inherent in her work: the poems themselves are usually not long, the stanzas a few lines, the lines short, often three words, and links are often missing, or merely implied, and a reader makes the links herself, possibly her own inventions. This is work that requires a reader to use his mind; and since Rae Armantrout's mind is an active, explicit participant in the poem, often, the reader's mind actively engages with her mind, on the page. She has taken nothing for granted, every idea is tested and tried, off the page and on the page, as every word and arrangement of words is tested and tried. Her reactions, like her wit, are often quick, but her quickness is informed by long, patient thought and work on and off the page.

No, there is no such thing as glibness about her. Glibness is a town thousands of miles away from San Diego. As is Easy Sophistication, Empty Lyricism, World-Weariness, Facile Sententiousness, Idle Chatter. This is not to say she is solemn.

Chevron's
exemplary rectangles

Humor is not merely within reach but is mixed into the very substance, the flesh, of all her interesting ideas, her observations of our strange society:

Here I protest
the corny names
of destinations like "Dreamland."
Still, at dawn it's clear
the seedy club
is, in fact, the state of being—

What does this ingredient of humor do? Is the humor a charge of intense emotion in a form we can tolerate and even enjoy? It is often a humor of incongruity.

In my communications to her, though to no one else, I tend to put certain words into quotation marks, as for instance "society," "we," "poetry," "happiness." Why to Rae in particular, and what do the quotation marks do?

They draw attention to a word; they acknowledge the "received" meaning of the word; they also indicate an awareness of complexities of meaning or contradictions often ignored by the common usage of the word.

My own heightened awareness of the words I am using when I communicate with Rae must be partly in response to her great alertness; and my distancing from received notions may be in response to her own ironic distance from everything, including herself: with my quotation marks I am stepping back to join her in the place where she stands to view the world.

What is her subject, then? Contemporary society or culture? Partly, or maybe always, or regularly recurring, but this society or culture in relation to other subjects. In each poem of this brilliantly exact, never obvious collection, a modicum of hard-won understanding is achieved, or at least a good question is asked about the oddities of daily life, the lessons of television, an urban Southern Californian landscape in which nature appears almost as unpredictable and paradoxical as the barely noticing humans who dangle "spontaneous abortions" from rearview mirrors, embarrassed singing crabs, and gloating Green Giants, as well as friends, family, semantics, jobs, trees, teleology, things we see or learn on television, responsibility, animals, dreams, other plants besides trees—here is a son, a mother, a student, Daffy Duck, here is honeysuckle, a barnacle.

Why stop with a barnacle?

What are the plants in *Made to Seem*, for instance? Two junipers, one palm (p. 8); "slap-happy fronds" (p. 9); the honeysuckle (p. 16); pine, grass (p. 27).

The mother
dreams her thoughts

have parted company
and become innocent:

pine, grass and wind.

In this piece of "Spans," how pleasing the language is just here (I stop a moment to admire): "parted company" with its slightly antiquated flavor; the simplicity of "become innocent"; and the skillful line break that gives a teasing ambiguity to the line "dreams her thoughts." But of course not just the language is arresting, but the whole idea contained in these lines: thoughts parting company and thereby becoming innocent, as though in our minds, habitually, our thoughts cluster and connive in a way less than innocent. And what's a separated thought as opposed to a congregating thought anyway? Surrounding all this, there is the beguiling idea of dreaming about one's thoughts as subjects, as characters.

Which reminds me how the satisfaction of reading her work comes from several sources at once: the ear, the eye, and the mind. Under the lens she turns on everything, the refractive lens, a bland world loses its blandness. I see differently because of the way she sees; and I see more clearly. Or, to put it the other way around, I see more clearly because of the way she sees; and I see differently.

To go on with the search for plant life: eucalyptus (p. 30):

Here eucalyptus
leaves dandle,

redundant but syncopated.

(Observe the nice rhythm and alliteration in "dandle, / redundant.")

"Fields of lilies" (p. 33); "Leaf still / fibrillating on the vine" (p. 38); jacaranda (p. 41); "Outside it was the same as before, scrawny palms and oleanders, their long leaves, ostensible fingers, not pointing, but tumbling in place—plants someone might call exotic if anybody called—and the same birds and hours, presumably, slipping in and out of view" (p. 48)—this from the opening of "Turn of Events," a prose poem.

How much is conveyed with that one word "presumably": a ladylike, discriminating word; critical, high heels in the grass; issuing from the vocabulary of the philosopher, doubting, questioning; from the scientist—are these in fact the same birds, or different birds?

"Ostensible," "if anybody called." So often she looks for location, sequence, logic, ascertainable facts, and finds that everything is temporary, or conditional, or out of sequence, contradicted, contradicted again, in the face of the questioning "I": things qualified often, often coming up against opposing forces (of contradiction or qualification).

She reads philosophy, she reads psychology, she reads science, and what she observes is the everyday, the ordinary, "our" behavior: she tries to make sense of it all, or tries to verify that there is no sense in it; she seeks answers, or at least more questions.

(She is modest; she admits to what she hasn't read and doesn't know. But she is not falsely modest. And she will not let mere politeness get in the way of the truth. If she thinks I am wrong about some of this, or not entirely right, she will tell me.)

Continuing the search: cabbages (p. 49). Or, rather,

cabbages (suddenly looking, in *italics*, like an unfamiliar vegetable, named in Arabic, say, in a Moroccan market):

> *Forever drawing water through a maze of*
> cabbages?

Junipers and palms again (p. 51), "a spate of slick, / heart-shaped leaves" (p. 57), bamboo (p. 58, last page). The bamboo takes part in a comment about writing that, as usual with her work, gives one something to think about for more than a little while:

> *Coarse splay*
> *of bamboo*
> *from the gullies,*
> *I write,*
> *as if I'd been expecting*
> *folds of lace.*

Which makes me think of another spot in the book where she comments specifically, as she writes, about the act of writing, something she doesn't do very often. From "The Known":

> *A dog's bark whooshes by, looming large on the*
>   *night-*
> *time or suddenly anonymous street. I could be*
>   *disqualified*
> *for writing, "suddenly"—or could have been*
>   *"if the*
> *truth were known." It's the job of the poem to find*
> *homes for all these noises.*

A nice notion, homes for noises; and what comes before poses several more questions for thought—or layers of questions, which is a way of composing that builds up the complexity (and thus the richness) of her work.

Hunting through the book like this, I find fewer plants than I expected, and more "abstract ideas": from which I conclude that a few plant forms very particularly and distinctly mentioned must make the impression of many plant forms; and this much abstraction still does not leave the impression of abstract verse, but, magically, of very concrete verse—lively and sensual.

But the plant life is not some romantic host: it is what manages to survive or is manipulated in a Southern Californian urban landscape: It is plant life in relation, again, to our society—a flowering vine, probably accidental, growing over an ugly man-made structure:

> *A honeysuckle,*
> *thrown like an arm*
> *around a chain-link fence*

And what strange beauty she creates out of a mixed situation, a situation (for the plants and animals) that could be said to be dismal. Beauty that comes not only from the particularity of her observing eye—the honeysuckle, the eucalyptus—but from the equal particularity of her language, marrying visual detail with strong, pleasing sound: twitching, sync, fronds.

She uses any available vocabulary with equal aplomb. She uses the language of everyday overheard speech:

> *"Well, look who . . ."*

though she then takes it to a conclusion that requires some mental agility from us in order to "understand" it:

> *"Well, look who missed*
> *the fleeting moment,"*
>
> *Green Giant gloats*

She uses the languages of stylistics and music: "redundant but syncopated." (She demands that we "hear" with our eye the syncopation of a leaf.)

She uses jargon happily, for instance the jargon of "our" nuclear industry, the simplest of words but already fraught, before she picks them up, with a burden of many-colored agony—

> *. . . protective gear . . .*

and puts them in the service of a scene that shows a comforting image of a past, simpler way of life (what Mother does once a week in the morning, as it used to be) with the broadest comic possibilities:

> *There's someone familiar*
> *in a beauty shop,*
>
> *wearing protective gear*

Her comedy depends in part on surprise, the unexpected. But then everything in her verse, comic or not, is fresh, surprising, unpredictable. Not only is her humor often a humor of incongruity: incongruity is a recurring characteristic of the poems generally.

The language of math (here, geometry) has a natural and easy place in her work, too. This from "Turn of Events," which involves a woman going into a house and out again onto a porch and standing on the porch:

Shape was the only evidence. She went back in.
She should think about how the house was built
or how it was paid for. How a feeling can have a
shape for so long, say an oblong, with sun falling
in a series of rhomboids on its wooden strips. It
would have an orientation.

And beyond the questions of vocabularies, more generally how she can gather in and deploy language in more classical fashion for rhetorical effect when she wishes, as in the last stanza of the book:

Mine was about
escaping Death though
Death was stylized, somehow,
even stylish. So was I!
So I was hidden
among fashionable allies.

Observe the handling of repetition or echo: "Death though / Death," "stylized, somehow, / even stylish," "So was I! / So I was." The faux naivete of the exclamation point. The humor—dark, as often—of this linking of death and style. And the faux innocence, more generally, of the telling of this dream, which acts as a foil to that dark humor. So much is done with a single exclamation point (as, above, with a selective use of italics).

And it seems that the longer I look, the more I

discover: it strikes me only now, for instance, probably as I read the word "bamboo" yet one more time, how Armantrout's poems sometimes hearken to sensibilities to the west of her California home (though "Eastern" to us) in their tone or their approach; how there is an unexpected obeisance in her work to a different tradition, in the delicacy with which evocations of natural features punctuate her expressions of human emotion. How surprised we are, as we have been surprised before by other things in the work, that from a marriage of the U.S. Navy (her father) and a fundamentalist kind of Christian faith (her mother) come, now, these shades of Matsuo Bashō!

1995, 1999

Small but Perfectly Formed:
Five Favorite Short Stories

"Dante and the Lobster," by Samuel Beckett. Anything by Beckett, of course, but particularly this story, for the deadly (and deadpan) precision and accuracy of its conclusion: "Well, thought Belacqua, it's a quick death, God help us all," followed by "It is not."

Again, almost any story by Grace Paley because of her brilliantly dense style, her economy, her humor, and the generous reach of her spirit. "Wants" is all of two pages, involving an ex-husband and a library fine of $32, family life, and antiwar activism.

Flannery O'Connor's "Everything That Rises Must Converge" for its cleverness, its wry integration of the colloquial speech of its characters (the naively bigoted mother and the martyred son), its cutting humor and deft portraiture.

Isaac Babel's "You Must Know Everything": The boy spends Saturday with his old grandmother in her stifling apartment, studying and taking his lessons under her watchful eye—it was when I studied this one with a class that I realized how skillfully the scene is presented in ever more amplified detail, bringing us wholly into that afternoon.

Franz Kafka's "The Burrow," because of the confident and convincing narrative voice of its obsessed narrator, who begins: "I have completed the construction of my burrow and it seems to be successful." Kafka fully inhabits his characters and presents them with a realism that makes them, though they are impossible, believable.

2010

VISUAL ARTISTS:
JOSEPH CORNELL

Previous page: *Aviary (Parrot Music Box)*
(c. 1945, 18.625 × 16.1875 × 5 in.)

The Impetus Was Delight:
A Response by Analogy to
the Work of Joseph Cornell

In the home of the Baker Carpet Cleaning family, the box with many compartments containing the mother's heteroclite collection, waterfalls, plants, a plethora of furniture, vases, clocks, lamps, birds appearing and reappearing in motifs in the furniture and china as though alive, rapid heartbeats, Florida room, California room, Florida mug with flamingos,

the Philosophy of Fire, and the two coincided, in a moment as magical for me as,

as,

a television inset in a stone wall, a niche for a vase in a stone wall, a safe behind the back of the niche, a secret switch, a gas fireplace inset in a stone wall, objects valued for themselves, not to enhance or furnish the interior of the home but the opposite, the house extended to make room for the objects, the house too small for the objects, objects everywhere, crowded in, packed in, in a corner of an enclosed porch were many small and large china dogs, one china dog life-size next to a real dog, the real dog fat as a barrel, she has complicatedly conserved them as simply as she can, these elements of her experience, so specific, the heart of their value or the reason for their value often invisible to the general eye, the story of their finding often and readily told explaining their value,

and so long as I have these surprises, omens, five turkey vultures in a bare tree early in the morning before their first disturbance,

like a doll's house furnished or overfurnished, filled or overfilled, the family home of Baker Carpet Cleaning, which has been in business forty years, eight hundred lamps, vases, copper pots and pans, Teddy Roosevelt's grandfather clock,

from the Psalm of David throughout, *let their way be dark and slippery, they have hid for me their net in a pit,*

flocks of starlings passing overhead at dusk with only a *luft luft* sound of their wings,

light GIANT BLUE candles, *behold how good and how pleasant it is,*

profusion within a frame, profusion within the bounds of the house of the Baker Carpet Cleaning family,

a book, too, within the bounds of the covers, the box of the book, the content of the book, which is the fruit of concentration, condensation, of heteroclite elements,

The Master Book of Candle Burning,

the invited guests are customers of the carpet cleaning company, those who have had their carpets excellently cleaned by them during the past year, they come into the house shyly, it is always unusual but it is especially beautiful at Christmastime, because

of all the Christmas decorations and the special arrange-
ments of the mother, who has fashioned little snowy
scenes involving miniature fir trees and figures skating
in circles on glass lakes, penguins or little men and
women, who do not stop going round and round while
the guests walk through and pause to sit at a table and
talk and eat cake, or sit at the bar and eat chips and nuts
and drink an alcoholic drink, the guests are dressed nicely,
it is Sunday,

followers of the Philosophy of Fire, in the
Bibliography Man and His Motives, Popular Amuse-
ments and Superstitions of the Highlanders of Scotland,

how can *I* burn candles, neologists and others
who should be in a position to know,

the house is a
single-storied ranch house among other ranch houses
on small plots on a street called Pine Street, one would
never guess what is within the house, immediately inside the front door is Teddy Roosevelt's grandfather
clock the star attraction and following it the ebony room,
ebony table, ebony cabinets, little sculptures of ebony,
value is high in $$$ but those $$$ are for reasons of
historical interest and fine workmanship,

in Scotland to
ward off witches, *among the Pharisees by a newborn baby*,
fire temples on a hill top and the faithful worshiped in
the open air, and licked up the water that was in the
trench, many people keep a vigil light burning constantly
in their homes, *all things were made by him and without
him was not anything made that was made*, Sunday is
yellow, Monday white, Tuesday red, Wednesday purple,
Thursday blue, Friday green, Saturday black, In the

Shadow of the Bush, she rakes out the fire and drenches it with water, she then cuts off her hair, a crossed condition, Weed of Misfortune Brand Candle, Confusion Brand Oil, White Power Brand Candle, Domination Brand Oil, *they are as stubble before the wind and as chaff that the storm carrieth away*, sputtering candle a prediction of misfortune,

the mother Baker's offering of an array of sumptuous dessert foods, cheesecake, chocolate cake, small foamy pies, chocolate candies, coming in a state of perfection magically from her kitchen, plate after plate for only a handful of guests, just now, one family of three of large stature, one family of three of smaller stature, one old couple dressed in their Sunday best, and this is Sunday, later a pair of men,

if two leaves of Basil are placed upon a candle and burn away quietly the marriage will be happy, manufacturers of automobiles, cosmetics, dresses, etc. use colors which *please* and *soothe*, this *leaning toward* a color, Astral Colors, these would be your PRIMARY CANDLES, available in authentic Astral colors,

kitchen looking out on the dining table on which sits the valuable Tiffany lamp, to the right is the copper collection hanging against the fieldstone wall,

Gold (Yellow) the Color of Attraction, Magnetic, Hypnotic, Captivating, Drawing, Fascinating, Persuasive, Charming, Alluring, Cheerfulness, applications for Fire Worship based upon research by no less an authority than W. S. Blackman, in this era of modern homes it is not practical to utilize open altar fires, to Learn the Truth, to Relieve Pressure by an Enemy, some time ago I heard of the account of a young woman who felt pangs of Fear, she had so many doubts about her ability to keep a job, to keep her husband's love, she felt that she was being harassed by unseen, hidden forces,

the guests do not know one another, they are introduced and sometimes talk to one another, but are not expected to talk and are free to stand and eat desserts with their forks off a small plate or to keep wandering, without eating, there is a billiard table around in back of the stone hearth, a secretary desk, an escritoire, near an ebony-black serving man, a meridienne, banquette, pouf, ottoman, ear, stile, cross rail, stretcher, cross stretcher, crinoline stretcher, cornice, top rail, diamond point, hanging stile, bracket base, frieze, frame stile, the value is in their being what they are, not in their meanings, door panel, peg, chiffonier, column, bobeche, globe, tureen,

every cause has its effect, the blackness of night offsets the light of day, certain cults of mad adventurers who attempted to rule the people, these religious racketeers, the infamous Black Mass, degraded nature and base hideousness, for example, muddy brown-green, greenish yellow, purple red, very dark brown, midnight blue, black, etc., all such Magic is based on the Law of Sympathy,

ran a needle through his head, or where the heart would be located in reality, take wax from a deserted bee's comb, if a hunter drives a nail into the foot print of an animal, a dirt highway winding twelve miles, when his feet were wrapped in his coat he was WALKING ON HIS OWN PROPERTY,

it is in the mother's house that you will see all these things that the mother recognized as wonderful, worth so many thousands or hundreds of dollars, at first appearing to be plain items of little value, now recognized as magnificent, among the hosts of low-priced items at a flea market or yard sale, a low-value vase, a low-value lamp, and then a fine ebony carving, and then the grandfather clock of Teddy Roosevelt, which is the star attraction,

out of his holy hill, Selah, the lifter up of my head, thou has smitten all my enemies upon the cheek bone, thou hast broken the teeth of the ungodly,

ninety percent have amatory difficulties, try this, a small supply of Frankincense and Myrrh, one candle of each color should be lighted each morning before going to look for a job, the law of Moses permitted altars of either clay and earth or of stone, ALWAYS USE VEGETABLE OIL CANDLES,

the energy and intensity of these two Bakers, mother and son, their glistening eyes, their enthusiasm leading and serving the varieties of guests who walk with respect from room to room, slow, gingerly, eyes stopping at each packed cabinet, a clock-lined, clock-topped chest, an inlaid chest, a room full of ebony, the father before his death was the builder, the father built walls of stone, made a fountain to run down the wall of the old living room, the first living room, then the mother wanted a larger fountain, and the father built another living room onto the back, right around the backyard barbecue fireplace, and turned that into a hearth, and built a larger fountain now surrounded by a host of illuminated plants beyond an ebony wild pig, an ebony boar discovered at a flea market when the mother spied the one tusk sticking out

from under a truck, the boar was offered for $50, worth
so many hundreds of $$$ now,

the first man is of the
earth earthy, as is the earthy, such are they also that are
earthy, as we know, there is but one true Altar, and that
is our HEART, *his hands full of sweet incense beaten small,*
and bring it within the vail, the mercy seat that is upon the
testimony,

an exaggeration of any house for ordinary liv-
ing though they do live here, or rather she, just she lives
here now, so many seats, so many cupboards, more than
one living room, so much glass, crystal, so many cups,
dishes, vases, plants, pictures, sofas, chairs, tables, what-
nots, drawers, splayed legs, knobs, aprons, drop leaves,
crosspieces, pins, butt hinges, clocks, cockleshells, cabri-
ole legs, acanthus leaves, palmettes, splats, volutes, arm
stumps, S-scrolls, carpets, around every corner more,
eye stopped and resting here, there, high, low,

set aside a
place in the home that is quiet, attic, basement, playroom,
bedroom, spare room, and within it create a beautiful
altar of which you can be proud, many people believe
that all that is necessary is to procure a candle of the
right color and light it and then every dream and wish
will come true, it is not as easy as all that, FIERY WALL
of PROTECTION Brand OIL, DOVE's BLOOD
Brand OIL, BIBLE Brand OIL, COMPELLING Brand
OIL, INFLAMMATORY CONFUSION Brand OIL,
dressed with Uncrossing Brand Oil, 30 minutes each
evening before retiring, the use of SYMBOL candles
is strictly an American custom prevalent in certain of
our Southern States but now also found in Detroit,
Philadelphia, St. Louis and many cities and towns be-

tween, molded in the shape of an animal—such as a cat or lion, in order to understand the symbolism involved it is necessary to go to the Dark Continent, strange and weird rites of African Medicine Men, the accomplishments of these individuals, the story of the brutal Congo trader, the native workmen, unable to endure it longer, sent one of their number, the idol in question was still on the dresser but THE HEAD HAD BEEN SNAPPED OFF!,

the mother saw the value of them within their form apparently of low value, bergère, cabriolet, recamier, canapé, settee, club chair, chesterfield, the mother went with a girlfriend to the field of stones to find the right stones and bring them home, they made many trips at dawn, and the father built, the mother and father went to the old buildings in the city as they were being torn down and went inside to buy pieces of the old buildings, an ironwork partition,

a neutral tone the color of pale coffee is said to be the most desirable, Confusion Brand Oil, each day a chapter of the Song of Solomon will be read with *all* candles burning,

although war is perhaps the most ungodlike expression of the human race and is in itself an irreligious activity, during Time of War, in short, he is King to his Queen in the Kingdom of his Home, but when a man is called to war there is a definite let down, those remaining behind turn their faces heavenward seeking Calmness and Dynamic Power, those who follow the Philosophy of Fire have delved deep into historical archives, half forgotten practices of the Ancient Zoroastrians, though a nominally peaceful people, did have their wars, he would guide his spirit to Paradise, where it would forever be engaged in the conflict with evil and the ultimate victory of Ahura-Mazda,

what she thinks is valuable, what may be valuable and what may be worthless, cheap, ugly, or may be valuable, worth a great deal, beautiful, or may be valuable only to her and her family because they are her creation, the skaters on the mirror-pond skating above a motor-driven magnet, or what is valuable to more than one, to many, to the world,

two inches daily in direction of arrows, repeat until satisfied, TO STOP SLANDER, Candle of Petitioner, before retiring until satisfied, FIERY WALL of Protection, Mandrake root in a saucer or incense burner, *thou shalt break them with a rod of iron, thou shalt dash them in pieces like a potter's vessel,* if the Success deals with MONEY use GREEN Candle or WEALTHY WAY, FORTUNATE DREAMS Lavender or Beneficial Dream,

in the center is placed a GIANT EVERLASTING TYPE CANDLE, an even larger candle is available that weighs 13 pounds and burns for TWO YEARS, CONQUERING Glory Brand Oil, the following verses are read either by the soldier or by someone whom he designates, *fight against them that fight against me, let their way be dark and slippery, they have hid for me their net in a pit which without cause they have digged, neither let them wink with the eye that hate me without cause, against them that are quiet in the land, the precious ointment upon the head that ran down upon the beard, that went down to the skirts of his garments,*

for about 500 days (or nearly 1 year), some tantalizing vision of some happier hunting ground, the novitiate will at first stumble upon many obstacles unless he or she first acquaints himself with certain fundamentals of the Art, the Rituals can be a delightful occasion or a confused muddle, a hopeless waste of time,

no deviation was permitted, it is now realized that they must be modified and adapted to meet the needs of individuals living in a fast moving world, the Zoroastrians could not go out to a corner store, available from reliable Supply Houses, SPARK of SUSPICION Brand Candle (Brown), RADIANT HEALTH (Red), WEALTHY WAY (Green), GLOW of ATTRACTION (Gold or Yellow), BENEFICIAL DREAM (Lavender), SATAN-BE-GONE (Orchid), LADY LUCK (Gold), WEED of MISFORTUNE (Black), when you order from your dealer always give your date of birth and let him select your Astral Candle for you, with such branded candles you just cannot go wrong, of the HAND FIXED type, many people start each *new* ritual for each *new* purpose with an entirely *new* set of candles and this truly is the most logical procedure to follow for it insures an altar of outstanding beauty and dignity, for if a used Blue candle which had been dressed with a particular oil were re-used later for another purpose *the symbolism would be lost* because of the improper dressing, purchase one of the Basic Candle Burning kits,

Darkest Africa, missing things of a most personal nature, Dame Fortune seemed to frown upon his every activity, a rival had taken the things, robes worn by ancient priests, etc., in this position was placed a clipped piece of sock, glove, shirt, hair, tooth brush bristles, evil influence dominates the scene, Master of his own Destiny, said to give off depressing vibrations,

TO BRING CONFUSION OR
TO EXERT PRESSURE ON ONE'S ENEMIES,
Midnight Blue Inflammatory Confusion Brand Can-
dles, move candles closer to the center each day, WHEN
TWO ARE IN LOVE WITH THE SAME PERSON
AND THE STUDENT WISHES TO ELIMINATE
THE RIVAL, Glow of Attraction Brand Candle, a fa-
vorable combination of vibrations, symbolically speaking,
when two people are after the same job, Green Crown
of Success Brand Candle dressed with Crown of Success
Brand Oil instead of the Glow of Attraction Brand
Candle, to be read: the 93rd Psalm,

platter, rim bowl,
creamer, ramekin, pepper pot, saltcellar, gravy boat,
pitcher, jug, blade, bolster, ferrule, point, slot, prong,
root,

your author has dug deeply, everything new in
it is old and everything old in it is new (animal fat
excepted),

a folly like Hearst Castle, like the Winchester
House, this can be a highly subjective (personal) business
& yet a means of attempting expression of communication, water running down the wall, a couch formed of
concrete,

these seven fundamental rules are simple and
easy to follow, the more progressive individual may create
his own particular symbolism,

early and late the appre-
ciation of the acquirer was the desired reward,

each guest
is given a pretty-colored gift bag upon departing containing a white unglazed ceramic cupid for an adult, a
bright chrome car for a child,

from the yard to the porch to the kitchen, said Joseph, don't think we're working on my work, fixing lunch, raking, banking, running to town, Bohack's, after a while they took their lunch and tea breaks together,

they enjoy a wide sale among reliable Supply Houses, so noble a custom, TO SETTLE A DISTURBED CONDITION IN THE HOME, Peaceful Home Brand, *and he shall be like a tree planted by the rivers of water*,

first o'week coming upon an abandoned house with no keep out signs, it is on a main artery but protected by a hedge unlike the side (open) approach, a smashed-up commonplace affair but an intriguing challenge, not one of the older places,

TO OBTAIN MONEY, *mine own familiar friend which did eat of my bread hath lifted up his heel against me*, TO WIN THE LOVE OF MAN OR WOMAN, in position X may be placed a photo of the loved one if one is available, a mixture of Frankincense and Myrrh may be burned, TO CONQUER FEAR, Crucible of Courage Brand Candle, Psalm 31 in its entirety, *be thou my strong rock, for an house of defense to save me, pull me out of the net that they have laid, thou hast considered my trouble, thou hast set my feet in a large room, I am in trouble, I was a reproach, I am forgotten as a dead man out of mind, thou shalt keep them secretly in a pavilion, and the proud doer*,

sit with Joseph in the backyard, many times he would eat a meal consisting entirely of desserts, I know these things, but it is not necessary to know them to enjoy the postcard,

Rockefeller Center, Christian Science,

TO CHANGE ONE'S LUCK, Astral Candle of person who is object of wrath, Spark of Suspicion candle dressed with Domination Brand Oil, ORCHID Candle or Satan-be-Gone candle dressed with Uncrossing Brand Oil, Conquering Glory candles,

collecting loved or desired things and putting them together in some kind of order within a frame, or excess, or jumble, lumber room,

disregard position A as this applies to Exercise 17 only, each evening for 15 days or until satisfied,

time and again, beehive forests and thimble gardens, as skillful as he was, the recipients, he did not share the accepted conception of the limitations of time, the past for him was not something that continuously receded, it was as available as the present, home poor heart,

p o o r heart, marvelous and ordinary, available in 14 colors, note the two-color effect and speckles, available in authentic colors, TO HEAL AN UNHAPPY MARRIAGE, Astral Candle of husband dressed, Astral Candle of wife dressed, Fire of Love candle, should be moved two inches daily in direction of arrows, the Song of Solomon, TO OVERCOME A BAD HABIT, to symbolize the bad habit undressed, *for he shall pluck my feet out of the net,*

in his yard bunny statues wandered, organic matter moved itself along but he tended to the decay of organic matter, pound cake was brought to harden in the sun, pears became softer and softer and more liquid by the day, it does not pay, it was not intended to pay,

it was not intended to pay, its air, full of

music, is a fog that turns from brown to yellow, from yellow to white, sunrise and sunset,

his hours, compounded of foreign woods, the impetus was delight, gifts without the recipient's knowing their origins,

Red Candles or Radiant Health dressed with Crucible of Courage Oil, TO LEARN THE TRUTH, TO BRING CONFUSION TO ANOTHER WHO IS THOUGHT TO HAVE CAUSED UNFAVORABLE VIBRATIONS, *let them be turned backward, let them be turned back for a reward of their shame that say, Aha, aha,* TO BREAK UP A LOVE AFFAIR, *and he heard me out of his holy hill,* BLACK Crucifix Candles dressed with XX Double Cross Brand Oil, Red Candle UNDRESSED to symbolize sterility or barrenness, DO NOT move candle 4, *thou hast broken the teeth of the ungodly,* TO SOOTHE AND QUIET THE NERVES, Astral Candle of person in nervous condition, *the enemies of the Lord shall be as the fat of lambs, they shall consume, into smoke shall they consume away,* the Psalm should be read slowly and with careful attention and should be accompanied by a state of calm meditation, *the steps of a good man are ordered by the Lord, and he delighteth in his way*

2001

THE PRACTICE
OF WRITING (2)

Sources, Revision, Order, and Endings:
Forms and Influences III

When I was starting out as a writer, I thought, not knowing any better, that I would be a writer of traditional short stories, though I didn't put it quite that way. As my writing developed, I began departing from this form, and I have departed further and further, as the years have gone by, but I have revisited it now and then because it is a solid and trustworthy form. One example of this return to a more traditional form is a story called "The Walk," written about twelve years ago.

"The Walk" is set in Oxford, England, during and after a literary conference on translation—this would be typical, very acceptable subject matter for a *New Yorker* short story, for instance. The main characters are a translator, modeled on myself, and a critic, who is a composite of a couple of people I know. Much of the action is taken from real events at the time of a real translation conference in Oxford, and some elements in it are fictional. (One of the turning points in my development as a writer was the realization that I could, with great satisfaction, write fictional stories that were accounts of actual events, only thinly disguised.)

The main action in this story is simply a walk taken

by the two principal characters. The central drama—not highly dramatic—is the narrator's perception that there is a resemblance between the walk that she takes with the critic and a passage in her translation of Proust's *Swann's Way*. At another, more conventionally dramatic moment in the story, the narrator nearly sets off a fire alarm in the building where she is staying. In reality, the main character in the actual situation—I myself—*did* set off the fire alarm. But to recount this episode as it actually happened, with all the students evacuated onto the lawn, some in their bathrobes with wet hair, etc., myself apologizing profusely, would have completely overbalanced the story in the wrong direction. As it is, then, this is a highly intellectual, even rarefied story.

As is almost always true of any story, this one was born of not just one thing but several. First of all, as I said, there is my ongoing love of the traditional form of short story, so that every now and then, when the opportunity presents itself, I like to reproduce it, though usually with some less traditional variations. I am, in a way, adopting even the traditional voice in which such a story is told, entering the persona of a certain kind of typical narrator, as in what follows, the quite traditional opening:

A translator and a critic happened to be together in the great university town of Oxford, having been invited to take part in a conference on translation. The conference occupied all of one Saturday, and that evening they had dinner alone together, though not entirely by choice. Everyone else who had participated in the conference or attended it had departed, even the organizers. Only they had chosen to stay a second night in the rooms provided for them in the college in which the conference had taken place, a down-at-heels building with stained carpets in the hallways, a smell of mildew in the guest rooms, and creaking iron bedsteads.

(Originally I had not named the town at any point in the story, because I prefer not to put place names on places, but then, considering that among other things the narrator of the story is looking for the home of the famous editor of the *Oxford English Dictionary*, this began to seem unnecessarily coy.)

So, first, there was that abiding wish to write a traditional story, and therefore I was on the lookout, though I did not know it, for an appropriate subject. Second, I was moved by the physical beauty of Oxford as I had experienced it, especially at evening—the beauty of the buildings, with their varied architecture, in the evening light—and therefore wanted to describe the place. Third, I had for some years been interested in the story of the creation of the *Oxford English Dictionary*, which took place right there. In a wonderful book called *Caught in the Web of Words*, Elisabeth Murray, the granddaughter of the editor, James Murray, recounts how he worked; I was curious about the creation of the dictionary not only because of a general interest in philology, reference books, and people obsessed with language but also because of the human story, the fact that the man had involved his many children in the project, working in a little house in their backyard—and not only his children but also various correspondents from around the world, including incarcerated criminals, who would send him words and quotations containing the words. Fourth, I was moved to frustration by one critic's remarks about my translation of *Swann's Way*, and it was mildly enjoyable to give expression to some of my reactions in the guise of fiction. Fifth, I was pleased and amused by the actual event of the walk, which paralleled or alluded to the walk in *Swann's Way* itself, and I wanted to reproduce that in the story. This coincidence was probably the starting point of the story, what sparked it.

I was going to say that the desire was there from the beginning to include an element that would not have been allowed into a completely conventional short story, and that was the quoting of an extensive passage from Proust's novel in not just one but two translated versions that to a casual reader would appear to be almost identical. But, really, I did not plan that from the beginning; it happened as I was writing.

Before I go on to talk about a completely different kind of story and its origin, I'd like to digress to quote two statements about the emotion common to inspiration itself, since what I've been talking about and will go on to talk about is inspiration—what makes a piece of writing come into being.

The first quotation is actually about the impulse to translate, which I see as very closely related to the impulse to write something original. I have gradually, over the years, come to see the close parallel: that, just as I want to capture something outside myself in a piece of original writing, when I want to translate something I also want to capture it, in this case to reproduce it in English.

Clare Cavanagh, the translator of Czesław Miłosz

and Wisława Szymborska, has written an essay about translation called "The Art of Losing: Polish Poetry and Translation" which she closes with the following statement:

> Of course translating poetry is impossible: all the best things are. But the impulse that drives one to try is not so far removed, I think, from the force that sends the lyric poet out time after time to master the world in a few lines of verse. You see a wonderful thing in front of you, and you want it. You try reading it over and over, you see if you can memorize it, or copy it out line by line. And nothing works; it's still there. So if it doesn't already exist in English, you turn to translation; you try remaking it in your own language, in your own words, in the vain hope of getting it once and for all, of finally making it your own. And sometimes you even feel, for a while at least, for a day or two or even a couple of weeks, that you've got it, it's worked, the poem's yours. But then you turn back to the poem itself at some point, and you have to hit your head against the wall and laugh: it's still there.

Contrast this with a passage from *Swann's Way* in which Proust describes what it is like for the young Marcel to want to capture in writing something that moves him:

> Then, quite apart from all these literary preoccupations and not connected to them in any way, suddenly a roof, a glimmer of sun on a stone,

the smell of the road would stop me because of a particular pleasure they gave me, and also because they seemed to be concealing, beyond what I could see, something which they were inviting me to come take and which despite my efforts I could not manage to discover. Since I felt that it could be found within them, I would stay there, motionless, looking, breathing, trying to go with my thoughts beyond the image or the smell. And if I had to catch up with my grandfather, continue on my way, I would try to find them again by closing my eyes; I would concentrate on recalling precisely the line of the roof, the shade of the stone which, without my being able to understand why, had seemed to me so full, so ready to open, to yield me the thing for which they themselves were merely a cover.

And, in fact, as I copied out this passage, I saw a connection here that I hadn't seen when I chose to quote it, between Proust's examples of a roof and a glimmer of sun on a stone and my being moved by the physical beauty of Oxford—because that was part of the beauty of the city for me, the way the sun as it lowered in the sky toward sunset shone with a warm, honey-colored light on the roofs of the town and the stones of the buildings and the cobblestone streets.

To go from Proust's more sublime sort of inspiration to a more ridiculous one, perhaps—although, as I think about it, even though the subject matter is less sublime, the impulse feels the same: here is material that you relish, that you want to devour, somehow. The story was born of a group email I read. "Nancy

Brown Will Be in Town" is about a woman returning to a community in order to prepare to move away for good.

NANCY BROWN WILL BE IN TOWN

Nancy Brown will be in town. She will be in town to sell her things. Nancy Brown is moving far away. She would like to sell her queen mattress.

Do we want her queen mattress? Do we want her ottoman? Do we want her bath items?

It is time to say goodbye to Nancy Brown.

We have enjoyed her friendship. We have enjoyed her tennis lessons.

Before I show you the email that inspired this story, I thought it might be interesting to quote an earlier version and explain how I revised it:

NANCY BROWN

Nancy Brown will be in town. We are told that Nancy Brown will be in town. We are told that Nancy Brown wants to sell her mattress. Do we want to buy Nancy Brown's queen mattress? Do we want her ottoman? Do we want her bath items?

If she will be in town, why is she selling her things? Oh, she is only coming back to town to sell her things. She will soon be leaving town again. She will not be coming back. It is time to say goodbye to Nancy Brown.

We have enjoyed her tennis lessons. We have enjoyed her friendship.

1. First, the title: "Nancy Brown" is okay, I like the name, but "Nancy Brown Will Be in Town" is even

nicer, and I don't mind repeating the title in the first line—something often done in poems, less often done in prose.

2. You could probably hear that the earlier version was wordier, overall. Too wordy. It was 106 words as opposed to 72 in the final version. I like repetitions, but the earlier version included repetitions that didn't move the piece forward much. It included thinking through questions and answers that could be cut back in the first little paragraph.

3. I also removed the implied middleman when I took out "We are told."

4. Now, the last revision is the most interesting, to me: I changed—actually, reversed—the order of the last two sentences. Instead of "We have enjoyed her tennis lessons. We have enjoyed her friendship," I now have "We have enjoyed her friendship. We have enjoyed her tennis lessons." The first order was more "logical" or traditional. It is often true that we think more conventionally *first*, as though reflexively, and after that we may think more adventurously and more inventively. The first, logical order placed the less important, more particular "tennis lessons" first; the more important, and more general, "friendship" second—as though moving outward from the particular to end on an appropriately general note. And yet the reversed order was actually more interesting to me: the more familiar, and expected, "friendship" first; the more surprising, even absurd "tennis lessons" second, so that the piece, which is, after all, somewhat absurd, ends on an absurd note.

As for the original email, it was the subject line, of course, that caught my attention: "Darcy Brown will be in town." The sender was either aware or unaware of the felicity of the rhyme and the charm of it. Then, the body of the email:

> For those of you who have enjoyed Darcy Brown's tennis lessons, cardio tennis classes, or friendship, she'll be in town at the end of the week for about a week and a half. She'd love to see or hear from you.
>
> She is also getting rid of some items that she has in storage:
> 1 Queen mattress
> 1 Single mattress—box spring—frame
> 1 Surfboard Table
> 1 Scan Chair and ottoman
> 5 boxes of Kitchen and Bath items
> etc.

What allowed me to see this email as a possible, slightly absurd piece of writing was probably, first, the charm and the singsong lyricism of the subject line, and then the unexpectedness of the email, since I didn't know Darcy Brown. I don't know Darcy Brown, and yet I am suddenly drawn, intimately, into the world of Darcy Brown. Again, so much depends on context. Here, since I didn't know her, I reacted—as though the email had been directed at me personally—by asking myself: Why do *I* care if Darcy Brown is moving away, and why would *I* want Darcy Brown's queen mattress? I read down the list of her possessions and I was not so interested—as a writer—in the "Single mattress—box spring—frame," but then I was struck by "ottoman." I like the word *ottoman*—which reminds me of the Ottoman Empire and sounds so very elevated for a piece of furniture. So I wanted to keep that in my story. And then we come to the "Bath items"—why would I want this stranger's bath items?

Maybe I'm also struck by the sender's including three things in the first sentence as though they were of equivalent value: "For those of you who have enjoyed Darcy Brown's tennis lessons, cardio tennis lessons, or friendship"—another reason to reverse the order of the last line of my piece, so that "friendship" is not climactic or conclusive.

I also changed the woman Brown's real first name (disguised here), which I liked, to Nancy, just to give a little protection to the real woman, though her name was common enough. Nancy Brown was also the name of someone I knew as a teenager—who at some point, incidentally, also changed her own name, to one much more exotic.

From the question of order at the end of "Nancy Brown Will Be in Town," I'd like to talk a little more about the importance of order in general.

A question I'm sometimes asked is: When do you know a piece is finished? Instead of addressing exactly that interesting question, I'll address the writing of the very last lines of a piece, or, rather, I'll give a partial answer to that question by saying that sometimes the piece as a whole may be more or less complete, but the very last lines are weak and need fixing, so it isn't quite finished. I will go into a little detail about that in a moment, but first I want to say something about order within a line or a sentence.

Order is very important, order in a list of any kind.

You may have the elements you want in a list, within a sentence, but in an order that is arbitrary or a bit jumbled. The reader receives the content that you have offered, but doesn't receive it in the best possible order, in an order that falls neatly into place in his or her mind: click, click, click.

I'll give an example of a very good order in a list, so that you'll see what I mean.

The quotation is taken from Thomas Jefferson's Declaration of Independence, and I found it in a book that should perhaps become a young—or, in fact, any—writer's bible, or should at least be firmly in place on a shelf of reference books (and I know some of us have abandoned actual shelves of actual reference books, but I think we should keep this one handy): Virginia Tufte's *Artful Sentences: Syntax as Style*. I've assigned this book to classes a few times now; some do adopt it as their bible. Others find it too difficult or frustrating. But it is worth it. It is full of wonderful quotations, and what Tufte is in effect doing is showing you all the various sentence constructions or fragment constructions that can go to create effective, moving style. She shows them all, systematically, and analyzes how they work, through a wonderful variety of quotations that may lead you to authors you never knew. She takes the mystery out of eloquence, I could say, by showing you how the magic works. I have said to classes: If you read this book from cover to cover, really absorbing and thinking about every example, you will be a better writer. That is certainly true, though it is true of quite a few other books, too, such as the complete works of Shakespeare.

The Jefferson sentence reads:

He has plundered our seas, ravaged our Coasts, burnt our towns, and destroyed the lives of our people.

("He" refers to the enemy, King George III of England.)

Tufte points out, apropos of the order in this list, (1) how the verbs, by their sequence, illustrate the increasing violence of the action. And if you look at the example again, you will see another pattern that is in place at the same time: (2) the violence is moving from out on the water in to the coast, into the towns, and then into the very lives of the people. There is one more pattern to be detected, which is that (3) the list, or series, is parallel in structure, consisting of verb-noun pairs, except for the last, which is a little longer than the preceding ones. The extra syllables at the end let us down gently by giving us a few more beats—a three-accented phrase—instead of abruptly, with a two-accented phrase. This is rhetoric, persuasion, eloquence. Jefferson could have given the list in a careless or arbitrary order, and without the parallel structure, and although the content might have been the same, the effect would not have been as powerful, enhanced by the two or, really, three patterns that can be heard, or felt, in the sentence.

I believe, by the way, that a close, conscious analysis of the best writing—the sort of analysis we've just done of this one rather short sentence, and that Tufte does throughout her book—will teach you in a useful way about writing well, not only on a conscious level but also on a subconscious or subliminal level, as the good patterns are imprinted in your brain. But you do have to bring patience to it.

———

Don't worry about the order of your lists as you are writing your first draft, when you shouldn't worry about much except getting your story or poem down on paper. But in later drafts, look carefully at your lists to make sure they are in the best order, whatever pattern it may be that will determine that order, whether from less violent to more violent, from past to present, from more particular to more general, from sea onto land, from few syllables to many, from short phrases to longer, etc.

Here is another example of order in a list, or series, but this time the order would seem to be incorrect.

I know the beginnings of quite a few poems by heart—and memorizing good poems, or fragments of them, is another thing I recommend for improving your writing. One of these poems is Shakespeare's sonnet 73. It's about old age, beginning with a comparison of old age to autumn:

> *That time of year thou mayst in me behold*
> *When yellow leaves, or none, or few, do hang*
> *Upon those boughs which shake against the cold,*
> *Bare ruined choirs where late the sweet birds*
>   *sang.*

I can now recite these lines accurately, but for a long time I had a problem with the second line. I recited it in the wrong order. I said: "When yellow leaves, or few, or none, do hang." By saying it wrong, I was giving that list the more logical progression in time, from leaves that are still there but have turned yellow, to few leaves (most having fallen off), to no leaves at all—the way it usually happens in nature. And yet the counterintuitive order is more interesting, and reflects the poet's mind at work: he is seeing yellow leaves, then no leaves at all, then he is conceding that a few may remain. Now I relish the "out of order" order of that line when I say it.

Similarly, as I said, in an earlier version of "Nancy Brown Will Be in Town" I ended with two sentences that followed the more "natural" order and then saw that because of the character of the piece, which is somewhat absurd, I should reverse that order and end on a stranger note: "We will miss her friendship. We will miss her tennis lessons," as though actually—come to think of it!—we may value her tennis lessons more than her friendship. It is a better order not only because it is more absurd but also because it is more surprising. Subtly, or less subtly, you always want to surprise a reader. You certainly don't want the reader to predict exactly where you're about to go. Or if you do—there are always exceptions—you want to put that expectation to good use.

I will describe two more revisions I made to improve an ending.

The first is in the story called "A Man from Her Past." Here is the whole of it:

A MAN FROM HER PAST

I think Mother is flirting with a man from her past who is not Father. I say to myself: Mother ought not to have improper relations with this man "Franz"! "Franz" is a European. I say she should not see this man improperly while Father is away! But I am confusing an old reality with a new reality: Father will not be returning home. He will be staying on at Vernon Hall. As for Mother, she is ninety-four years old. How can there be improper relations with a woman of ninety-four? Yet my confusion must be this: though her body is old, her capacity for betrayal is still young and fresh.

In an earlier version, the last sentence read: "Yet my confusion must be this: her capacity for subversion and betrayal is quite young and fresh, if her body is not." In the earlier version, the content of the ending is more or less the same, but the way the ending is written needs to be tightened up and the order changed. The very last word, *not*, with the implied "young"—"not young"—is weak here, certainly not as strong and clear as the word *old*. But even if I replaced *not* by *old*—"if her body is old," the order is wrong. We already know she is old, her body is old, so in the very last words I'm not offering any new information.

In the earlier version, the new information, the narrator's revelation, is given first, then the familiar information—that her body is old—is given second, and concludes the piece, which is anticlimactic. Whereas when the familiar information is given first—that her body is old—that is all right, especially because it is preceded by the word *though*—"though her body is old"—signaling to the reader that after this familiar information, something else will be coming. And when it comes, it is surprising: "her capacity for betrayal is still young and fresh." First of all, I have tightened up the clause by taking out *subversion and* as well as *quite*. (And you should always be on the lookout for qualifying words like *quite* and *rather* and *very*—you probably could benefit by taking them out.) I have prepared, earlier in the story, for this idea of betrayal by saying that she is flirting. But then, at the very end, come the words *young and fresh*, which are surprising because they are usually associated with something more positive. And so with these words comes a new concept: that betrayal, or the capacity for betrayal, can be young and fresh, and that something we don't consider a good thing, like betrayal, can be qualified with adjectives that are usually positive.

In this case, it was a simple matter of reversing two elements so that the known came first and the more surprising came second—which more or less follows a piece of advice I remember from my adolescence, when I was attempting to write a poem in rhymed couplets and I was told: Always put the stronger rhyme second. That often works well, not only with rhymed couplets but also with elements in a sentence or sentences in a paragraph or paragraphs in a story. (And I hope you noticed the parallel structure in that last sentence, as well as the progression of the list from smaller units to larger.) So consider the order when you are revising the very last words of a piece of writing: consider changing the order to end with the more surprising or stronger element.

Before I go on to the last example of the order of an ending, I'd like to quote some perhaps helpful advice about endings from a *New Yorker* article by John McPhee on his strategies for structuring a long piece of nonfiction. He earlier makes another helpful—to me, anyway—observation that in seeking a structure for a piece, he has often found himself with the choice of organizing it chronologically *or* thematically, and that the pull of the chronological has usually been stronger.

Now, about endings, here is what he says, close to the end of this essay:

> William Shawn [longtime editor of *The New Yorker*] once told me that my pieces were a little strange because they seemed to have three or four endings. That surely is a result of preoccupation with structure. In any case, it may have led to an experience I have sometimes had in the struggle for satisfaction at the end.
>
> Look back upstream. If you have come to your planned ending and it doesn't seem to be working, run your eye up the page and the page before that. You may see that your best ending is somewhere in there, that you were finished before you thought you were.

To go on to the somewhat similar situation in which the previous *sentence* or sentence *fragment* is the one you should end on, I will talk about the last two lines in my poem "Head, Heart." But first I will say something about how it came to be—and here we're back to inspirations or influences—via Old English poetry and Gerard Manley Hopkins.

I'm calling "Head, Heart" a poem because it was written to be a poem, unlike other poem-like pieces I have written. One example of these other poem-like pieces would be "The Fly," four lines long:

THE FLY

At the back of the bus,
inside the bathroom,
this very small illegal passenger,
on its way to Boston.

This piece started out as a prose piece and is still intended as a prose piece, of sorts, but ends up looking like a poem because it has line breaks. I added line breaks in order to control the pace and rhythm with which it was read. I thought of it not as a song, but as a matter-of-fact statement. I'll point out something about the function and importance of the title here, too, which is almost always true of the very shortest pieces: the title is essential to place the reader before the beginning of the piece. I name what I'm writing about, so that the reader knows what it is before going on to see the creature in a different light—as a passenger with a destination.

Another kind of poem-like piece is the piece that is written to be a poem but is a poem in prose, and so looks like prose with justified lines, as in the case of "Traveling with Mother," in prose with justified lines and arranged in six numbered sections, each having two groups of prose lines. Each group of prose lines, I could say, functions in the same way as a single line in a more conventional-looking poem with line breaks.

I will quote just the beginning of "Traveling with Mother," sections 1 and 2, which are quite prosy in syntax and vocabulary, rather than poetic:

TRAVELING WITH MOTHER

1

The bus said "Buffalo" on the front, after all, not "Cleveland." The backpack was from the Sierra Club, not the Audubon Society.

They had said that the bus with "Cleveland" on the front would be the right bus, even though I wasn't going to Cleveland.

2

The backpack I had brought with me for this was a very sturdy one. It was even stronger than it needed to be.

I practiced many answers to their possible question about what I was carrying in my backpack. I was going to say, "It is sand for potting plants" or "It is for an aromatherapy cushion." I would also have told the truth. But they did not search the luggage this time.

So, all this justified prose, with fairly prosaic content—backpacks, Sierra Club, Cleveland—doesn't necessarily look like a poem, but in my mind it is intended as a poem, whereas, as I said, "The Fly" was not intended as a poem but looks like a poem. In this case, I'm thinking of, or defining, a poem as a song—more ceremonious, more rhythmical, more punctuated than prose. Although in this case, again, the prose in "Traveling with Mother" is rather flat, the long lines, for me, cry out into the spaces around them, maybe because each statement is somehow broken off. The narrator or reciter must keep stopping.

Now I'd like to turn from that prosy, nonlyrical poem to the quite lyrical, "singing" poems of Gerard Manley Hopkins. When I was striving hardest, in my twenties, to learn to write well, I liked to read Kafka's diaries to see the work and the thinking that went on behind his finished writing, and also the rough drafts or the false starts and the unfinished pieces. Similarly, while I was engaged on my translation of *Madame Bovary*, about five years ago, I liked to read Flaubert's letters for the same reason.

There was also a time when I liked to delve into Gerard Manley Hopkins's journals and read, especially, his detailed and thorough descriptions of natural things— the movement of eddies of water in a brook, for instance. This journal writing of his was done in a compensatory sort of way during the seven years in which he did not allow himself to write poetry, having become convinced that it conflicted with his devotion to religion—he had recently converted to Catholicism and eventually entered the Jesuit order and was ordained a priest. (Similarly, the objectivist poet George Oppen, an American of the twentieth century, stopped writing poetry—in his case for more than twenty years—because he, too, felt that it conflicted with his discipline, though his discipline was not religious belief but political activism and for a while the programs of communism.) It is fascinating to see how the extensive and detailed descriptions in Hopkins's journals become concentrated into the economical images in his finished poems.

The poem "Pied Beauty," well-known to many, can be summarized as a poem in praise of God for all the great variety, complexity, and changeability of the physical world he has created, in contrast to the unchanging beauty of God himself:

PIED BEAUTY

Glory be to God for dappled things—
  For skies of couple-colour as a brinded cow;
    For rose-moles all in stipple upon trout that
    swim;
Fresh-firecoal chestnut-falls; finches' wings;
  Landscape plotted and pieced—fold, fallow, and
  plough;
    And áll trádes, their gear and tackle and trim.

All things counter, original, spare, strange;
  Whatever is fickle, freckled (who knows how?)
    With swift, slow; sweet, sour; adazzle, dim;
He fathers-forth whose beauty is past change:
                    Praise him.

Here's another well-known poem by Hopkins:

SPRING AND FALL: TO A YOUNG CHILD

Márgarét, áre you grieving
Over Goldengrove unleaving?
Leáves, like the things of man, you
With your fresh thoughts care for, can you?
Ah! ás the heart grows older
It will come to such sights colder
By and by, nor spare a sigh
Though worlds of wanwood leafmeal lie;
And yet you wíll weep and know why.
Now no matter, child, the name:
Sórrow's spríngs áre the same.

Nor mouth had, no nor mind, expressed
What heart heard of, ghost guessed:
It is the blight man was born for,
It is Margaret you mourn for.

An explicator at an online site (David Coomler at the site Hokku) goes through the poem in a cogent, sensible manner—his commentary is enjoyable to read, though this is not an especially difficult poem. I happened upon his site because I was looking for the meaning of *wanwood*, which he interpreted to mean just what the word if separated into two words would mean: *wan*, meaning "pale" (i.e., fading, dying), and *wood*, meaning "woods" or "forest." He had some good things to say about *leafmeal*:

> "*Leafmeal*," as Hopkins uses it here, is a very inter-esting term, formed by using the Old English word *mael*, meaning a "measure" of something. When used as a suffix, it means something is happening "measure by measure," that is, gradually, like say-ing a field of grain was cleared "sheafmeal," that is, "sheaf by sheaf." So here Hopkins is saying that all the autumn forests lie "leafmeal," that is, fall-ing and piling up leaf by leaf, countless scattered leaves. "*Meal*" of course also means grain ground fine—as in "cornmeal"—so we have an undertone in this word of the leaves gradually falling apart as they decay—transforming from leaves to soil.

But when he came to the end, he expressed an opin-ion that I disagreed with, as to whether or not a couple of lines were "poetic" or not. Here are the last four lines of the poem again:

> *Nor mouth had, no nor mind, expressed*
> *What heart heard of, ghost guessed:*
> *It is the blight man was born for,*
> *It is Margaret you mourn for.*

I had *particularly* always liked the first two of these lines, especially the first one:

> *Nor mouth had, no nor mind, expressed*
> *What heart heard of, ghost guessed:*

But the commentator, Coomler, says that he feels these lines are left for the reader to "somewhat laboriously unravel" and that they "are not very poetic in their complexity."

Another site suggests that the most beautiful line in the poem is "Though worlds of wanwood leafmeal lie"—the *w* and *l* sounds, the assonance of *leafmeal* and the alliteration of *leafmeal lie*. What we have here are simply two different ideas—not mutually exclusive—of what constitutes a beautiful line of poetry.

There are reasons why I like the more difficult lines: First and most obvious, there is the parallel alliteration: "Nor mouth . . . nor mind" in the first line; and then the one-syllable words and alliteration of "heart heard . . . ghost guessed" in the second (*ghost* here meaning "spirit"). Then there is the compression of the whole, created in the following way: through the inversion of "Nor mouth had," the elision of the article *the* in "Nor mouth," the jamming-together of the words "no nor mind" without the usual comma punctuation. Besides the compression, there is the vehemence of the *no*, along with the bluntness, the almost animal reference of the word *mouth* to indicate the organ of expression: "Nor mouth had, no nor mind, expressed" rather than something more refined such as "Your lips [or tongue] had not expressed this thought; nay, your mind not even entertained it."

The effect, to my ear, anyway, of this compression and bluntness was to make the lines convey more emotion, as though they had been wrested from the speaker almost by force.

I had thought that the alliteration and compression of Old English poetry might have led to the form of my poem "Head, Heart," but the more I look at these two poems by Hopkins, the more I think that perhaps they, too, had an influence—particularly his use of alliteration so extreme that it calls attention to itself, which nicely breaks another sometimes-repeated rule, which is that your deployment of rhetorical techniques should not be so overt that it distracts from what you're saying.

And in fact, the connection I see between Anglo-Saxon poetry and the verse of Gerard Manley Hopkins is not accidental, since, as I learn when I read more about Hopkins, he himself became fascinated with the older rhythmic structure of Anglo-Saxon poetry.

I would have to go back and do some studying to talk properly about the characteristics of Old English poetry—that is, poetry written in Old English, or Anglo-Saxon, between the seventh century and a few decades after the Norman Conquest of England, which occurred in 1066. (This date is one that should be remembered especially by writers in English, because it is after this date that the French language was aggressively introduced into the existing languages of England; the Norman Conquest resulted in our having the wonderful doubled vocabulary that we have in English: *subterranean* and *underground*, *hearty* and *cordial*, *omnipotent* and *almighty*.) But what I can say is that it makes heavy use of alliteration within each line and also breaks each line into two parts, with a caesura—the technical term in poetry for a pause.

Here are just a few lines from the beginning of a poem called "The Battle of Brunanburh." It is the earliest poem contained in the *Anglo-Saxon Chronicle*, and it dates from 937. It celebrates the victory of King Aethelstan over the Scots and the Norse. I don't know how to pronounce Old English very well, but I found a good YouTube reading of this poem by Michael D. C. Drout, a professor at Wheaton College and specialist in Anglo-Saxon and medieval literature, which I recommend. I have put some pronunciations in brackets next to the word.

> feld dænnede
> *The field flowed*
> secga [sedgea] swate   siðþan sunne up
> *with blood of   warriors from sun up*
> on morgentid [teed],   mære [ma-] tungol,
> *in the morning,   glorious star*
> glad ofer grundas,   godes candel beorht,
> *glided over the earth   God's bright candle,*
> eces [aitches] drihtnes [drrik],   oð sio æþele gesceaft
> *eternal lord,   till that noble creation*
> sah to setle.
> *sank to its seat.*

Old English rhythms and word-sounds may lie somewhere in the distant or not-so-distant past behind my choices in "Head, Heart," and so may Hopkins's rhythms and word-sounds, as the Anglo-Saxon rhythms lay somewhere behind Hopkins's rhythms. I also see the word and line choices of "Head, Heart" as being in a way deliberately somewhat awkward, and I am interested in writing that is eloquent yet awkward, or awkward yet eloquent, as in the Hopkins lines that included "Nor mouth had, no nor mind." The awkwardness implying that the writer was too moved to be more elegant. However, I didn't plan this before I started the poem—or even think of it after I had finished. The deliberate awkwardness was an instinctive move.

Here is an earlier version of the poem:

HEAD, HEART

Heart is disturbed.
Head is trying to help heart "deal" with this.
Head tells heart how it is, again:
Here is life, here is death, you will lose the ones you
  love. They will all go. We will all go. Even the
  earth will go, one day.
Heart feels better, then.
Now heart feels worse again. The words of head do
  not remain long in the ears of heart.
Heart is so new to this.
I want them back, says heart.
Help, head. Help heart. You are all heart has.

And here is the final version, for comparison:

HEAD, HEART

Heart weeps.
Head tries to help heart.

Head tells heart how it is, again:
You will lose the ones you love. They will all go. But
*   even the earth will go, someday.*
Heart feels better, then.
But the words of head do not remain long in the
*   ears of heart.*
Heart is so new to this.
I want them back, says heart.
Head is all heart has.
Help, head. Help heart.

The opening line of the final version is plainer and actually more Anglo-Saxon: "weeps" as opposed to "is disturbed." The second line is also plainer and less contemporary in its language: "Head tries to help heart"—all of these being Anglo-Saxon-derived words. As opposed to the wordier and more contemporary "Head is trying to help heart 'deal' with this." Although that line is completely Anglo-Saxon too, "deal with" is a contemporary expression. There is also a shift of tense. In the earlier version, the first two lines establish the situation with the use of the verb *to be* as an auxiliary with an adjective and a present participle—"is disturbed . . . is trying"—then in the third line comes the action: "Head tells heart." In the later version, the verbs express action from the beginning: "Heart weeps / Head tries . . . / Head tells." It is also blunter and therefore, to my ears anyway, more emotional.

The revised version has been cut throughout—more than one-fifth of the material is gone. And I have reversed the last sentences so that the stronger sentences come last, in a single line: Instead of "Help, head. Help heart. You are all heart has," the last lines now read: "Head is all heart has. / Help, head. Help heart." It ends, also, with two commands.

Do work hard on the very last words—they can sometimes make all the difference as to whether or not a story or poem seems finished.

2013

Revising One Sentence

This morning I walk around the house feeling happy and I'm struck by what I'm doing. Actually, I'm struck by only one gesture I happen to make, but that one gesture inspires me to write a sentence describing what I have just been doing. This is usually an effective approach in writing because one striking element can be the culmination of a series of more familiar elements that would not stand on their own.

So I go to my notebook, which is lying open beside my "official" work—a typed and nearly finished story that needs three or four changes. My notebook always lies beside my "official" work because I write in it most when I am supposed to be doing something else. So today I write down a sentence about what I have just been doing. I write it in the third person. I write about myself sometimes in the third person and sometimes in the first. Thinking about it now, I realize what determines this: If it matters that *I*'m the one doing something, if *I* am truly the subject, then I write in the first person. If it does not matter who is doing it but I'm simply interested that a person is doing this, then I write in the third person—that is, I'm using myself as a source of material and I'm more comfortable writing in the third person because then I (the writing I) don't get in the way of the character that may evolve from this action. (Sometimes, the "I" has tended to become a "he" in the stories—the "he" being a slightly overweight, feminine sort of man, gentle, androgynous. More recently, the "I" usually becomes a "she.")

So I write it down and then immediately revise it. In revised form it reads: "She walks around the house balancing on the balls of her feet, sometimes whistling and singing, sometimes talking to herself, sometimes stopping dead in a fencing position." Today I have revised this sentence immediately; sometimes I do and sometimes I don't. Maybe it depends on how interested I am in what I write down, or maybe I don't revise it if the writing is so simple or brief that it comes out exactly right the first time. Today it isn't quite right and I must be interested because I revise it: I want it to be exactly right. I will work on it until it is exactly right, whether or not the observation is important and whether or not I think I'll ever "use" it. In fact, I don't often use notebook entries in a story unless the entry turns into the story (as was the case, for instance, with "Liminal: The Little Man" in *Break It Down*, and many others).

I don't generally use these entries because my stories tend to be written in one uninterrupted "breath" and they usually don't work if I start piecing them together. Then why do I revise the notebook entries? I'm not sure, but I will guess. For one thing, it is hard for me to let a sentence stand if I see something wrong with it. Even when I'm writing a grocery list it is hard for me not to correct a misspelling. For another, I tend to follow my instinct in writing—I don't question my impulses. So if I want to revise, I don't tell myself there is no point in revising. I follow my instinct: there may be a reason for my doing something, a reason that I don't understand at the moment but that will become clear later on. There may come a day when I will use one or more of these separate notebook entries in a larger written work. I may turn back a few years in the notebook, read an entry, and see how it could become something larger. And if it is poorly written, if it is left unrevised, I will have more trouble seeing what it wants to be.

There is also the constant practice I get from revising notebook entries. And it may be that what I have worked out in the final version of one notebook entry will inspire another sentence in a new story without my even realizing it. Or maybe the notebook is a place to practice not only writing but also thinking. After all, when you revise a sentence you are revising not only the words of the sentence but also the *thought* in the sentence. And more generally, by getting a certain description exactly right, I am sharpening the acuteness of my observation as well as my ability to handle the language. So there are many ways to justify working hard on one sentence in a notebook, a sentence that you may never use. But most of all, as I said, I follow my impulses in writing (in the notebook) without asking whether what I am doing is sensible, efficient, even moral, etc. I do it because I like to or want to—which is where everything in writing should begin anyway. (As for the question of morality—I won't *publish* something if it seems to me morally wrong to publish it, but the act of exploration that is writing is very different from the finality and public-ness of publishing. Writing is still private until it is made public.)

The notebook is also where I write stories. Every story I write begins in the notebook and in fact is usually written entirely in the notebook. There is a good reason for that, though it took me a while to realize it: in the notebook nothing has to be permanent or good. Here I have complete freedom and so I am not afraid. You can't write well—you probably can't do anything well—if you feel cornered. I am not afraid because what I write in here doesn't have to become a story, but if it wants to, it will. In some sense, I don't deliberately set out to write stories anymore. I used to, and I started them on clean sheets of typing paper in the typewriter (this was actually at the time when I took my one writing workshop, which was with Grace Paley—I must have felt more professional working this way). Now the stories force themselves on me. It took years for this to happen, and I'm not sure how I got it to happen, except by pushing myself—if the stories weren't occurring to me, then I sat down and thought them up and wrote them no matter how uncomfortable and forced that felt and despite the fact that the stories were not entirely satisfactory to me.

First I wrote long stories because I thought a story had to be long. My characters were based on people I did not know very much about, and sometimes I guessed right about human nature. At least the settings were sometimes good, because I knew the settings well. Then I realized I did not have to write long stories—in fact I could write in whatever way I wanted, and for a while I pushed myself out of a dry spell by writing two paragraph-long stories every day. Most of them were not wonderful, but a few were good, and that was enough. For a while after that, I wrote only very short stories in short, neat sentences.

Eventually I didn't have to search for ideas; a story would impose itself on me or well up in me—now I feel I *must* write the story, I must get rid of it. Nabokov said he never set out to write a novel but to get rid of it. Maybe the notebook is also, for me, a place to get rid of everything, and the more exactly I put it down the more completely I get rid of it. Some sentences want to be stories right away. The latest one that grew immediately into a story—still in rough form at the moment—was "It took the Queen of England to make my mother stop criticizing my sister." This happens to be true.

Sometimes the notebook entry becomes a story; in other cases, it is nothing more than a sentence or a few sentences and will never be more, or not for the foreseeable future; and sometimes it seems to want to be a story and I go back to it from time to time, but it won't grow. It may be just too limited (or too absurd) to make a developed story, even though it is striking. Or maybe I haven't quite got the idea yet, and I'm trying to develop the story in the wrong direction.

Speaking of not being afraid when you write, I see that I have evolved quite involuntarily two habits that make me not afraid. One is the habit of starting every story in the notebook, where it is under no pressure to be a story; the other is that quite often I do what I did today: I sit in front of the typed pages of a story that is nearly finished and that I am not trying to finish, and instead of working on it, I begin another story in my notebook and write that out until nothing more occurs to me. It is easier to do that—to begin a story—when that is not what I had planned to do. My unconscious, or whatever part of the brain works hardest in writing something new, is very relaxed and comfortable because there is a clear-cut task to go back to when I have nothing more to add, for the moment, to the new story.

Meanwhile the typed story just sits there. The same thing may happen the next day. Sometimes I have four or five, or more, stories in progress at once. It is nice to feel that there is too much to work on rather than nothing at all—the blank page. Some stories, not quite finished, may get pushed out of the way in all this activity and may be forgotten for a while—even months. But sooner or later I come back to them and finish them, and it does not hurt them to let this time pass. I see them more clearly.

On the day I'm talking about, my plan had been to finish the last story of a collection of stories. I did work on it for a while, then I noticed my behavior walking through the house, then I recorded what I was doing, then I stopped to think how the process of writing and revision worked for me, and then I decided to write down this description of it.

Of course, there is much more to say about notebooks. Many writers have kept notebooks. Kafka kept a notebook full of ideas for stories, beginnings of stories, complete stories, accounts of evenings he spent with friends in cafés, and then also complaints about his family, landlady, neighbors, etc. His complaints about his neighbors' real noises on the other side of the wall became written fantasies about unreal people on the other side of the wall. A writer's notebook becomes a record, or the objectification of a mind. There were painters, like Delacroix, who kept wonderful notebooks. And then there were writers who never published anything else but their notebooks, like the eighteenth-century Frenchman Joseph Joubert.

What follows is the way in which that sentence was revised:

HOW ONE SENTENCE MAY BE REVISED

Final version:

She walks around the house balancing on the balls of her feet, sometimes whistling and singing, sometimes talking to herself, sometimes stopping dead in a fencing position.

Here's how it evolved from first sentences and phrases to last:

She is likely to walk around the house lightly on the balls of her feet . . . (bad rhyme here: *likely/ lightly*)

She walks . . .

  . . . around the house slowly . . . (doesn't suggest happiness)

  . . . around the house slowly but delicately . . . (too much explanation)

  . . . around the house slowly, carefully . . . (not strong enough)

  . . . around the house slowly, carefully, balancing on the balls of her feet . . . (too wordy)

  . . . around the house slowly balancing on the balls of her feet . . . (good, I like it. then later I think *too much* and take out *slowly*; now the first part of the sentence is finished)

sometimes whistling, sometimes singing, sometimes talking to herself, sometimes . . . (no.
too many *sometimes*)

sometimes whistling and singing, (no. can't do
both at once)

sometimes whistling or singing (no. sounds too
deliberate)

sometimes whistling and singing (okay after all,
can be one after the other)

sometimes stopping dead and assuming a fencing position (no. too many *-ing*s in there. but
I know I have to end with *fencing position*—
it's the culminating, striking image; it's what
made me write the sentence down in the first
place. it's also a strong phrase, and the word
position is a strong word)

sometimes stopping dead in a fencing position
(cutting solved the *-ing* problem)

1982, 2002, 2004

Found Material, Syntax, Brevity, and the Beauty of Awkward Prose: Forms and Influences IV

In this essay I will continue several topics from earlier discussions, including the origins of some of my stories, using found material or appropriating, complex and simple syntax, brevity in pieces of writing, and the beauty of awkward prose. I'll start by talking about another poem of mine—one actually written, or arranged, to be a poem with broken lines—that uses found material from an email, this time an email from a stranger, in other words not meant for me personally.

1. Another email-inspired piece: "Hello Dear"

HELLO DEAR

Hello dear,
do you remember
how we communicated with you?

Long ago you could not see,
but I am Marina—with Russia.
Do you remember me?

I am writing this mail to you
with heavy tears in my eyes
and great sorrow in my heart.
Come to my page.

I want you please to consider me
with so much full heartily.
Please—let us talk.

I'm waiting!

I was drawn to this material by the awkward language and the lyricism of it—some deliberate and some accidental—and its inadvertent pathos. I have searched for the original email to see how I changed it, but I could not find it. (I am somewhat irrationally afraid of keeping scam mail, for fear of infection.) But I remember moving phrases around, inserting line breaks, and no doubt cutting.

I enjoy awkward nonprofessional writing and incorrect language use partly because of the unexpected combinations that simply wouldn't be produced by the brain of a practiced writer of English—such as "with so much full heartily"—or, if attempted, might not be as good.

2. Modified found material: dream pieces

Another adventure in the use of found material resulted in a long series of what I have called dream pieces, amounting to about twenty-eight in all, at latest count. In this case, the raw material was, mostly, my own dreams and those of friends, as well as some waking experiences of ours that resembled dreams.

Dreams are strange phenomena: You try to tell someone your dream in the morning, and he's usually pretty bored. That is because there is a radical difference between your experience of your dream and his experience of hearing about it. To you, the experience was real, as it was happening, and often you reacted with the full depth of feeling to the dream experience that you would have brought to a waking experience. You were sitting with your mother, who, though in reality dead, was alive again. Or you were in love with some lovely man who also loved you. Or you were at the top of a cliff with—really—no way down and you were terrified. Etc. But to your listener, these experiences were all thin and colorless, simply because they weren't real.

I recently learned that a part of the brain is in fact "turned off" while you're dreaming, a part whose name I can't remember; this is the part that would have told you that what you were experiencing couldn't be true. This part of your brain is actually inoperative, and that's why you believe that you are talking to your deceased mother, or that your twenty-four-year-old son is only eleven and is already smoking, or that a rather dim-witted gym teacher has instructed his team of basketball players to keep their eyes shut while they're throwing and catching the ball so that they don't risk hurting them.

Dreams have been used to predict the future; they have been used in psychotherapy to expose psychological trauma; they have been used as the starting point for making a piece of art, as when Coleridge dreamed of Kubla Khan. I had not been particularly interested in my dreams before as possible subjects for writing, only as occasionally fantastic entertainment.

The dream pieces started from a conjunction of at least two things: a book I had read some time before and an uncannily dreamlike experience I had while out driving. (Often—or maybe always—it is the conjunction of at least two things that inspires a form or an individual piece of writing, another example being my story "Jury Duty," which arose from my actual experience of jury duty and my interest in the form of David Foster Wallace's *Brief Interviews with Hideous Men.*)

I had some time ago read a book by the French surrealist and ethnographer Michel Leiris called, in the English translation by Richard Sieburth, *Nights as Day, Days as Night.* This book was a collection of the more interesting dreams Leiris had recorded over forty years. The surrealists, of course, were very interested in the potential of dreams, since their project was to use irrationality to disrupt reality and its conventions.

What was particularly interesting about Michel Leiris's book was that besides collecting all of his interesting dreams, he also mixed them in with accounts of waking experiences that resembled dreams. He seemed to be demonstrating how fine the line was between the irrationality of the dramas that take place while one is asleep and the weirdness of events in everyday waking life, some events being obviously strange even as they happen and others including elements of strangeness that can be isolated in a piece of writing by excluding the more familiar aspects of the experience. In other words, the account of the waking experience can be written in such a way as to include only the strange elements and leave out the elements that might have "normalized" it in the telling.

I'll quote three of the shortest of Leiris's dream accounts, all working in slightly different ways. The first is almost no more than an image:

NOVEMBER 20–21, 1923

Racing across fields, in pursuit of my thoughts. The sun low on the horizon, and my feet in the furrows of the plowed earth. The bicycle so graceful, so light I hop on it for greater speed.

The second is longer, more typically dreamlike, still sounding like the report of a dream, but now also like a tiny story:

APRIL 12–13, 1923

One evening, upon entering my room, I see myself sitting on my bed. With a single punch, I annihilate the phantom who has stolen my appearance. At this point my mother appears at a door while her double, a perfect replica of the model, enters through a facing door. I scream very loudly, but my brother turns up unexpectedly, also accompanied by his double who orders me to be quiet, claiming I will frighten my mother.

And finally, one that Leiris dreamed nearly forty years later and that to me sounds like a complete little story:

NOVEMBER 6–7, 1960

"Charity! Charity!" I am wandering through the streets of an unfamiliar neighborhood, trying to catch a small dog who bears the name of this theological virtue. He was given to me by a baker; I was careless enough to walk him without a leash, and he ran away. A butcher (or some other shopkeeper) has already had a good laugh hearing me call after the dog that he has just watched race by. Shouting at the top of my lungs like some incensed beggar, I could very well be taken for a village idiot or for an escaped lunatic whom the police will swiftly move to arrest. Who cares. I go on shouting as loudly as I can, not only because I am so mortified at the loss of the little dog but also because I am drunk with the sound of my own voice: "Charity! Charity!"

I have talked before about surprises in a short piece, and surprises in general, and how you should in some way keep surprising the reader, not be predictable. In this little dream of Leiris's, the opening, the name of the dog, is a surprise, as is the image of this man wandering the streets calling "Charity!" New information is constantly added in the piece. And after repeating more familiar information—that he regrets the loss of the dog—it ends with yet another piece of new information—that he is drunk with the sound of his own voice.

The image of the narrator wandering the streets like a lunatic reminds me of an image that has stayed with me for a long time: the French Marxist philosopher Louis Althusser went through periods of mental instability and during one such period, toward the end of his life, murdered his wife (this was in 1980). After his release from the psychiatric hospital, he used to wander the streets of Paris shouting: "I am the great Althusser!" What interests me about this is that he was indeed, if not great, at least important. A person wandering the streets shouting something that is not delusional can still be described as a bit of a lunatic.

To return to Leiris and his dream pieces, what interested me first was not so much, in fact, how to narrate a dream, though I liked the idea of giving the shape of a little story to the sometimes sprawling and incoherent narrative of an actual dream, by selecting from it. I was more interested in how to narrate a waking experience as though it had been a dream. And then, I was interested in combining actual dreams and waking experiences intermingled in the same group so as to blur the line between waking and sleeping. As I said above, I used not only my own dreams and waking experiences but those of friends, too.

As for the writing of these pieces, I had to figure out what it was about the narration of a dream that made it sound like a dream, and then work to make the piece fit those requirements. For one thing, the material had to include some element of the irrational or the surreal, to a greater or lesser extent. For another, it had to be told in a dream narrative style, meaning: in short sentences (mimicking our style as we grope to remember or reproduce a dream); with some (optional) element of uncertainty; maybe with some mystery as to the identities of people and places; sometimes or always with strong and striking imagery. And it had to be just long enough to sound like a complete dream experience.

These two are actual dreams, though I was half awake in the first:

AWAKE IN THE NIGHT

I can't go to sleep, in this hotel room in this strange city. It is very late, two in the morning, then three, then four. I am lying in the dark. What is the problem? Oh, maybe I am missing him, the person I sleep next to. Then I hear a door shut somewhere nearby. Another guest has come in, very late. Now I have the answer. I will go to this person's room and get in bed next to him, and then I will be able to sleep.

DINNER

I am still in bed when friends of ours arrive at the house for dinner. My bed is in the kitchen. I get up to see what I can make for them. I find three or four packages of hamburger in the refrigerator, some partly used and some untouched. I think I can put all the hamburger together and make a meatloaf. This would take an hour, but nothing else occurs to me. I go back to bed for a while to think about it.

And this last was a real-life experience told as a dream:

IN THE TRAIN STATION

The train station is very crowded. People are walking in every direction at once, though some are standing still. A Tibetan Buddhist monk with shaved head and long wine-colored robe is in the crowd, looking worried. I am standing still, watching him. I have plenty of time before my train leaves, because I have just missed a train. The monk sees me watching him. He comes up to me and tells me he is looking for Track 3. I know where the tracks are. I show him the way.

3. Drastically shortened dream pieces

Some of the pieces that I wrote intending them to be dream pieces were, in their final versions, too short to feel like dream narrations. I liked them, but I no longer considered them dream pieces. Here is a literary one:

CAN'T AND WON'T

I was recently denied a writing prize because, they said, I was *lazy*. What they meant by *lazy* was that I used too many contractions: for instance, I would not write out in full the words *cannot* and *will not*, but instead contracted them to *can't* and *won't*.

Another that became too short was "Ph.D." The original material for this piece was the recurring anxiety dream of a friend of mine who, in the dream, believed that because she had failed to take one important exam, though she had done all the other required work—the coursework and the thesis—she had in fact never been awarded her Ph.D. In its original version, that dream was fully recounted, including the missed exam. Then I cut the piece more and more until in its final form it reads, simply:

PH.D.

All these years I thought I had a Ph.D.
But I do not have a Ph.D.

(In truth, she did earn her Ph.D. at NYU, her thesis—the
result of long and extremely meticulous editing—being
The Collected Poems of Paul Blackburn.)

4. From dream accounts to Bernhard stories

At the time when I was working on the dream pieces,
I discovered a very helpful book by Thomas Bernhard
that presented me with yet another model for a tightly
organized and written very short story, ensuring that
the dream pieces would be not solely dependent on the
impact of the dream material for their effect, but fully
developed and integrated and well-structured pieces in
themselves, though approached in this new way, coming
from the perspective of seeing life as material for dream
pieces.

I discovered the Bernhard book between flights in
O'Hare Airport. I had a lot of time to kill, came upon a
surprisingly good bookstore there in the airport, and
went in. Instead of browsing idly through the fiction
section, which was quite large, I decided, in one of those
impulses of slightly fanatical orderliness that we all have
from time to time, to proceed alphabetically, starting
with the very first book in the *A* section and looking at
every title. When I was just a short way into the *B*s, I
was astonished to discover a book by Thomas Bernhard
that I had never heard of and that couldn't have been
better suited to me just then.

5. Thomas Bernhard as novelist

Thomas Bernhard (1931–1989) was a rather misanthropic
and vitriolic Austrian writer, mainly a novelist, the au-

thor of *Concrete*, *Old Masters*, *The Loser*, *Gargoyles*, *Correction*, and *Wittgenstein's Nephew*, among others. It is typical for him to rage against the horrors of his own country, Austria. His writing is moving and horrifying, but also funny. His first-person narrators rave and fume, and the form of his novels is often one long paragraph. The writing is entrancing, spellbinding. His books were an important model for me when I was working on my own novel, *The End of the Story*, since what I was looking for was a sustained, emotional, controlled, single-breath, one-voice outburst—I included pauses (white spaces) but no chapter divisions, which would have implied control. I wanted to convey the sense, from the tone of the narration, that this was an autobiographical confession. (Other models were Elizabeth Hardwick's *Sleepless Nights* and Marguerite Duras's *The War* and *The Lover*.)

Here is the beginning of Bernhard's 1975 novel, *Correction*—a single sentence:

After a mild pulmonary infection, tended too little and too late, had suddenly turned into a severe pneumonia that took its toll on my entire body and laid me up for at least three months at nearby Wels, which has a hospital renowned in the field of so-called internal medicine, I accepted an invitation from Hoeller, a so-called taxidermist in the Aurach valley, not for the *end* of October, as the doctors urged, but for *early* in October, as I insisted, and then went on my own so-called responsibility straight to the Aurach valley and to Hoeller's house, without even a detour to visit my parents in Stocket, *straight* into the so-called

Hoeller garret, to begin sifting and perhaps even arranging the literary remains of my friend, who was also a friend of the taxidermist Hoeller, Roithamer, after Roithamer's suicide, I went to work sifting and sorting the papers he had willed to me, consisting of thousands of slips covered with Roithamer's handwriting plus a bulky manuscript entitled "About Altensam and everything connected with Altensam, with special attention to the Cone."

This opening sentence is more than ten lines long. (According to a note I made in the book, the first eleven pages have only sixteen sentences.) It is worth repeating, however, what I have previously said about Proust: that to be exact and economical does not necessarily mean to be brief. One can be verbose in a short poem, and one can be succinct in a long novel full of long sentences.

About the voice in that opening: it is immediately established as a voice filled with conviction. The sense of conviction is created by several things at once, stylistically: the almost pedantically correct construction of it, indicating high seriousness (and a degree of self-importance); the urgency of it, the sense we get that the narrator wants to tell us all about this; the level of detail about such things as the narrator's illness and Roithamer's manuscript; the narrator's strong opinions—his sarcasm in his references to such things as internal medicine and taxidermy; the use of italics stressing his opinion versus the doctors'; the naming of the people and places, as though the narrator and we the readers, too, recognize that these particular facts are important.

For me, Bernhard was already an admired and stud-

ied writer when I discovered that book of his in the airport. The book was *The Voice Imitator*, translated by
Kenneth J. Northcott. It contains 104 stories, each a
paragraph long. I had not even known that Bernhard
had written tiny stories.

6. Thomas Bernhard's short works and complex constructions

What is remarkable about these stories is not only their
tight structure, completeness, and negativity of attitude
but also the hypercomplex syntax of some of the sentences, as in the opening of *Correction*.

I have given students in writing classes the assignment to read, analyze, and then imitate stylistically one
of Bernhard's small stories. Younger writers these days
often have trouble constructing long, complex sentences. They often restrict themselves to short, simple
sentences, and when they try a longer, more complex
one, they run into trouble. I see this in otherwise good
writers—including good published writers. In this case,
the translator, Northcott, has reproduced the complexity with a skill that appears effortless.

In the following little story, about half its length is
contained in the first sentence; the second and third sentences are fairly short, though not simple; and the last is,
again, long and complex (I have numbered the sentences
for ease in finding them):

CONSISTENCY

[1] At the end of a philosophical discussion that
had tormented two professors from the University of Graz for decades and had brought not only

them but also their families to total ruin and which, as they are reported to have perceptively told a third colleague one day, like all philosophical discussions led to nothing and which, finally, in the nature of things, ruined and actually drove this colleague, who had also become embroiled in their discussion, insane, the two professors from Graz, after inviting their third colleague and adversary, out of habit, so to speak, into the house they had rented jointly for the sole purpose of their philosophical discussion, had blown the house up. [2] They had spent all the money they had left on the dynamite necessary for the purpose. [3] Since the families of all three professors were present in the house at the time of the explosion, they had also blown up their families. [4] The surviving relatives of one of the professors and adversaries, for whom the decades-long philosophical discussion—as they themselves had clearly demonstrated—had proved fatal, considered suing the state because they were of the opinion that the state's moral and intellectual bankruptcy had driven all three to their deaths, but they did not bring such an action after all, because they realized the futility of such an action.

Notice, again, how new material is introduced throughout even such a brief story, especially the idea of the state's responsibility introduced in the last sentence, which could not have been anticipated earlier.

Another tiny Bernhard story returns us for a moment to the territory of dreams. As with the first little story, the opening sentence is, in itself, about half the length of the story (again, I have numbered the sentences):

NEAR SULDEN

[1] Near Sulden, years ago, in a quiet inn to which I had withdrawn for several weeks so as to see as few people as possible and to have contact only with what was absolutely necessary, for which the area around Sulden is suited like no other—and it was above all for the sake of my diseased lung that I had gone to the remoteness of Sulden, which I knew from earlier days—a Herr Natter from Innsbruck, the only guest in the inn aside from myself, who stated that he had once been rector of the University of Innsbruck but had been dismissed from office because of a libelous attack and had actually been thrown into prison, though shortly thereafter his innocence had been established, told me each day what he had dreamed the previous night. [2] In one of the dreams he told me about, he had run around to hundreds of Tirolean authorities to get permission to have his father's grave opened, but this had been denied him, whereupon he had tried to open his father's grave himself and, after hours of the most exhausting digging, had finally succeeded. [3] He said he had wanted to see his father once more. [4] However, when he opened the coffin and actually removed the lid, it was not his father lying in the coffin but a dead pig. [5] As usual, Natter wanted to know, in this case, as well, what his dream meant.

Notice how the fourth sentence is carefully constructed to end with the unexpected element: the dead pig. Bernhard does not stop there, which would have left the story depending entirely on that surprise for its impact, but returns us to this character Natter's obsession with dream interpretation and his persistence, which are comical. The last sentence, though following naturally from earlier material, is still somewhat surprising.

7. A Bernhardian story

One of my own, quite recent, pieces was surely inspired by Bernhard, though it originated, like "Nancy Brown Will Be in Town" and "Hello Dear," both discussed earlier, in the material of an email. Once again, there are (at least) two sources for the inspiration: (1) my analytical readings of Bernhard's short pieces, all the closer since I was working on them with a class; and, more immediately, (2) the raw material—the email I encountered. The emotional impetus for the piece—since there is always, for me, strong feeling behind a piece of writing—was at least twofold: (1) amusement at what Bernhard does in his brief stories and at the content of the email; and (2) admiration for Bernhard's writing and a desire to do something similar, although I did not see the influence of Bernhard (obvious to me now) until after I had written it. My story, however, does not contain the elaborate Bernhardian constructions and is longer than his.

NEGATIVE EMOTIONS
A well-meaning teacher, inspired by a text he had been reading, once sent all the other teachers in

his school a message about negative emotions. The message consisted entirely of advice quoted from a Vietnamese Buddhist monk.

Emotion, said the monk, is like a storm: it stays for a while and then it goes. Upon perceiving the emotion (like a coming storm), one should put oneself in a stable position. One should sit or lie down. One should focus on one's abdomen. One should focus, specifically, on the area just below one's navel, and practice mindful breathing. If one can identify the emotion as an emotion, it may then be easier to handle.

The other teachers were puzzled. They did not understand why their colleague had sent them a message about negative emotions. They resented the message, and they resented their colleague. They thought he was accusing them of having negative emotions and needing advice about how to handle them. Some of them were, in fact, angry.

The teachers did not choose to regard their anger as a coming storm. They did not focus on their abdomens. They did not focus on the area just below their navels. Instead, they wrote back immediately, declaring that because they did not understand why he had sent it, his message had filled them with negative emotions. They told him that it would take a lot of practice for them to get over the negative emotions caused by his message. But, they went on, they did not intend to do this practice. Far from being troubled by their negative emotions, they said, they in fact liked having negative emotions, particularly about him and his message.

That is the piece as it stands, but it went through another change, and then a change back to its present form. After I had written it and saw the possibility that Bernhard had in part inspired it, I had the idea of making it even more Bernhardian by including overt violence in it. I added another paragraph, the following:

> Only one teacher was so angered by the message that for several days he was speechless. Then, instead of writing back, he went out in the middle of the night with a bag of excrement to the home of the teacher who had sent the message and wrote on his front porch, in excrement, "Negative Emotion."

I had doubts about that last paragraph. I sent the whole piece to a friend of mine to whom I send pieces occasionally. I told her I had a question about the piece that I would ask her after she read it. She wrote back that she liked it very much, but she didn't think the last paragraph belonged, somehow. Or rather, that was my interpretation of what I remembered of what she said. (This was some months ago.) Memory often falsifies, at least a little, and usually in the direction of the way you *want* to remember something. Her exact words, now that I've found them, were "I don't know why I don't like the last paragraph as much. If I don't know why, I'm not sure I should even say it. Somehow I like it ending with the seeming paradox of their liking having negative emotions (even though I know they were being sarcastic). But maybe I'm wrong."

She was confirming my own doubts, so I immediately got rid of that added paragraph.

8. The three-sentence daily diary entry

I recently had the idea of recording, every day, one brief experience in the form of three fairly short sentences. (I say "short" to preclude the sorts of sentences written by Bernhard in the very short stories above.) I haven't yet done more than two of these brief descriptions, and I am satisfied with only one of them, but I like the idea. Certainly it is an interesting way of imposing on yourself the daily diary entry—yes, I must make a daily entry, but it can be one that requires a careful choice of subject and then a careful choice of how to express the experience, and it can remain short.

Here is the first one I tried (since I did not write it down right away, as I so fervently recommend to others, I lost some of the wording, which I think was better):

> *The wind blew hard across the fields behind the old
> farmhouse.*
> *We were out for a walk, heading down toward the
> railway bridge.*
> *Below the road, a woman filling some bottles at an
> artesian well looked up and smiled.*

Very simple—Zen practice would say "nothing much." I first imagined this would be a little prose paragraph. Then, when I typed it out, I started each sentence on a separate line and found that that had a different effect, something of the effect of a haiku. In an earlier version, the first and third lines were longer than the middle one, the symmetry adding to the haiku effect, and that could be part of the prescribed form, if you liked. Of course, in the case of the haiku, the middle line is longer, not shorter.

9. Félix Fénéon

Maybe I was influenced, in conceiving of this form, by reading a few years ago the French man of letters, publisher, translator, and newspaper reporter Félix Fénéon (1861–1944). Fénéon did not publish a book of his own while he was alive. In response to a proposal to publish a collection of his own work, he remarked, "I aspire only to silence." He did, among his many other literary activities, write little fillers for the newspaper, very brief, usually sensational accounts of crimes or accidents, what we would call police blotter material and the French call *faits divers*, which literally means "various facts or deeds." Fénéon restricted these accounts to three lines of type (not necessarily three sentences), and worked carefully over making them, within the prescribed length and presentation of the facts, as vivid and expressive as possible, sometimes macabre, sometimes humorous or bizarre. After his death and then that of his mistress of fifty years, it was found that she had carefully preserved all his *faits divers* in an album. These were collected and published—there were 1,220 of them—and a few years ago a selection was translated into English by Luc Sante and published by New York Review Books under the title *Novels in Three Lines.*

Here are some of Fénéon's *faits divers*, or police blotter notices:

At five o'clock in the morning, M. P. Bouget was accosted by two men on Rue Fondary. One put out his right eye, the other his left. In Necker.

There was a gas explosion at the home of Larrieux, in Bordeaux. He was injured. His mother-in-law's hair caught on fire. The ceiling caved in.

In Le Havre, a sailor, Scouarnec, threw himself under a locomotive. His intestines were gathered up in a cloth.

Notary Limard killed himself on the landing stage in Lagny. So that he would not float away if he fell in, he had anchored himself with string.

Charles Delièvre, a consumptive potter of Choisy-le-Roi, lit two burners and died amid the flowers he had strewn on his bed.

The sinister prowler seen by the mechanic Gicquel near Herblay train station has been identified: Jules Ménard, snail collector.

Sante, in his introduction, compares Fénéon's three-line novels to Charles Reznikoff's *Testimony: The United States (1885–1915): Recitative*, a book-length poem that derived all its material from transcripts of criminal court cases. (Trial transcripts, by the way, along with oral histories, are productive resources for a writer studying how people, a wide variety, actually speak.) Reznikoff's research was massive: as he explained, he might go through a thousand pages of transcripts to find the material for a single poem. His accounts of, usually, disturbing incidents are, like Fénéon's, terse and abruptly concluded.

Both these works—Fénéon's three-line "novels"

and Reznikoff's *Testimony*—may have served as models, years after the fact, for a recent piece of mine called "Local Obits." This story consists of a number of very brief extracts from obituaries of local, more or less ordinary people—for example, Ethel, eighty-three, who loved to garden, and Richard, eighty-nine, who was a World War II vet and sang in the Polish glee club. Here, like Reznikoff (1894–1976), I am working with found material about strangers. Unlike Reznikoff, who composed poems of varying lengths with lines short and long from a considerable amount of material, I am confining the extract to, usually, just a few lines in newspaper obituary style. The entries are brief, like Fénéon's, but unlike Fénéon, I am selecting the material, not reporting it, and I am interested not in the sensational but in the oft-repeated ordinary.

I heard George Saunders say in an interview on the radio a few years ago that he believes the subconscious is not only very rich but also very well organized—which was a new idea for me. I had always known it was rich in accumulated material, but I had thought it was rather chaotic. If I apply what I think he meant to the way influence works for me, I'd say that the subconscious is storing things away, things like the Fénéon three-line "novels" and the Reznikoff *Testimony*, and that then, when I read the obituaries in my local paper and am touched by these lives and also by the way the obits are written, the influences of Fénéon and Reznikoff assert themselves, still without my knowing it, still subconsciously, and I write a piece in the form of "Local Obits." Maybe Saunders would say that the material was neatly shelved in my subconscious and filed under various headings, and that my efficient retrieval system zipped through and found them as models.

10. Sets of three lines and haiku: Padgett

Proceeding by association here, I'll go on from compositions in sets of three sentences or three lines to a little more about the haiku.

A writer friend of mine once said, whether seriously or not, that the only poem he had ever memorized was also one of the most useful, and that was the poet Ron Padgett's definition of the haiku, which is a haiku. It's called "Haiku":

First, five syllables.
Second, seven syllables.
Third, five syllables.

Neat, and memorable.

11. Bashō and his most famous haiku

For years, I've read, off and on, a slim little work by the seventeenth-century Japanese poet Matsuo Bashō—his *Narrow Road to the Interior* (as translated by Sam Hamill), which I first knew in a different version probably called *Narrow Road to the Deep North*. It has several captivating qualities: the beauty of the imagery, the spirit behind it, the moments of humor, the compactness, and particularly the form in which it is written. It is an account of a journey into Japan's remote northeastern region, or, metaphorically, into the poet's inner self. It is written mostly in prose but interrupted now and then by a haiku that describes or distills a physical or emotional moment at that point in the journey. There is thus a pleasing alternation—a moment of relief from the prose; then back to the prose. The form has a name in Japanese: *haiban*.

But I did not know until very recently about another haiku attributed to Bashō, one that is not in *Narrow Road to the Interior*. I discovered it through reading an article in *The New York Review of Books* by Ian Buruma, the Dutch writer and academic, about Japan:

> The great poet Matsuo Basho, traveling in the northeast of Japan in 1689, was so overcome by the beauty of the Island of Matsushima that he could only express his near speechlessness in what became one of his most famous haiku:

> > *Matsushima ah!*
> > *A-ah, Matsushima, ah!*
> > *Matsushima ah!*

I associate Bashō's near speechlessness with several things: Fénéon's remark that he aspired to silence; the fact that certain poets chose to stop writing poetry, either for many years, as in the case of Gerard Manley Hopkins and George Oppen, or forever, as in the case of Arthur Rimbaud (1854–1891), who gave it up around age twenty-one; and Proust's narrator in *Swann's Way*, when he was quite young, whose reaction to the assault of inspiration was the expressive but unrefined utterance: *"Zut, zut, zut, zut!"* (A complicated translation problem, by the way.)

I would also relate Bashō's Matsushima haiku to the paradox that when we are most powerfully moved, we are often least articulate—and this is something a fiction writer has to keep in mind when putting dialogue in the mouths of characters at emotional moments. Bashō's haiku may also remind us of the careful balance we need to maintain as writers. We may aspire to a certain degree of articulateness and eloquence in whatever our chosen form may be, but we must guard against crossing the line and indulging in an excessive eloquence or cleverness, one that distracts the reader from the work itself: we must be willing to stay modestly in the background and let the focus of attention be on the work itself.

12. Edwin Morgan and Louis Zukofsky

And following from the idea of silence, and brevity, I will end with what must be one of the shortest poems in print, having a three-word title and a one-word text. The poem is by a prominent Scottish poet, Edwin Morgan, who died in 2010 at the age of ninety.

Here is what James Campbell in *The Times Literary Supplement* had to say about him, quoting the poem:

> The event that might have pleased him most . . . was the publication of *Dreams and Other Nightmares: New and Uncollected Poems.* The book gives equal space to two faces of [Morgan] with which his readers will be familiar—the lunatic lexicographer and the anxious confessor—and contains the wittiest one-word poem ever written, "Homage to Zukofsky":

> *the*

This is actually a good illustration of the importance of a title in a short work, where it may do half the work, or even more: it prepares us for the text or body of the poem. Without the title, in this case, we would have only the word *the*. We would be left bewildered. As it is, the title here tells us that the poem is an homage to someone whose name we may or may not recognize. Campbell goes on to say: "It helps to know that Louis Zukofsky [1904–1978] is the author of the book-length poem '*A.*')" If we know this, and have even read some of "*A*" (an 826-page poem in twenty-four sections, written over about fifty years), only then can we appreciate the wit of Morgan's poem. (One section of "*A*," by the way, is only four words long.)

Morgan may also have had in mind a poem of Zukofsky's that he wrote at age twenty-two and that is regarded as his first major work. It is called "Poem Beginning 'The'" and is seen as a partly satirical response to his predecessors in the poetry world and in particular to T. S. Eliot's "The Waste Land." The poem much impressed Ezra Pound.

Edwin Morgan's "Homage to Zukofsky" certainly brings up once again a question that is regularly raised: How much does a reader have to know beforehand, in order to receive the full impact of a piece of writing, and is it all right for a reader not to receive that full impact? I had to pose myself that question, though I was not troubled by it, in the case of my short piece called "Samuel Johnson Is Indignant." The full body of the story is "that Scotland has so few trees." I think the story works even if you do not know who Samuel Johnson is, though it has more impact if you do.

In the case of Morgan's poem, perhaps a reader needs to know several things beforehand in order to get anything at all out of it. But I don't believe that this should stop Morgan from writing the poem exactly as it is, as he thinks best, and I don't believe that he needs to provide a footnote. Any piece of writing, after all, has only a particular, and limited, audience or readership. It is not necessary to try to appeal to everyone, or even to explain oneself.

2013

Fragmentary or Unfinished:
Barthes, Joubert, Hölderlin,
Mallarmé, Flaubert

A cooperative . . .

From Roland Barthes's introduction to *A Lover's Discourse*, in Richard Howard's translation: "What we have been able to say below about waiting, anxiety, memory is no more than a modest supplement offered to the reader to be made free with, to be added to, subtracted from, and passed on to others . . . (Ideally, the book would be a cooperative.)"

Of course, any book, and any piece of writing, is already part of a cooperative. It is, in itself as printed on the page, incomplete. It requires a reader to complete it. But the reader may also misunderstand it, distort it in favor of another idea, forget large parts of it, misremember it, create something different in misremembering it, etc. All these responses are perfectly legitimate parts of the cooperative act.

What is missing but is still present as empty space

In Peter Handke's novel *Across*, the narrator, an archaeologist who eventually concentrates his investigations on thresholds, is criticized early in his career because, as he is told, all he cares about is *finding* something. He goes on to say, in Ralph Manheim's translation, "It was in part this remark that impelled me to train myself at digs to look less for what was there than for what was missing, for what had vanished irretrievably—whether carried or merely rotted away—but was still present as a vacuum, as empty space or empty form."

The fragment

I would like to take the idea of the fragment as a form of writing and examine, explore, and digress from it, to consider ideas of wholeness, completion, incompletion, order, the writer's notebook, and certain writers who interest me in the ways their work relates to ideas of the fragmentary and the complete, like Joseph Joubert, writing 150 to 200 years ago, who resisted compiling collections of *Pensées* of the sort he was encouraged to produce by friends like François-René de Chateaubriand, and who planned and attempted various publishable "works" but left behind only notebooks of fragments or fragmentary entries, selections from which are now regarded as works; Friedrich Hölderlin, a poet whose late hymns and fragments were written in the early decades of the nineteenth century during a period when he lived in seclusion in a tower in Tübingen, apparently mad; Stéphane Mallarmé, fifty years or so after that, attempting poems during the time his eight-year-old son, Anatole, was dying and then dead; Barthes, who admits to a preference for the fragment, for writing in "brief bursts," as he calls them; and others.

Ruin as construction

Here are some thoughts by Eugène Delacroix, on the power of the unfinished:

> A building which is going up and where the details are not yet indicated gives one an impression that is different from what one gets from the same building when it has received its complement of ornamentation and finish. The same is true of a ruin, which is the more striking because of the lost parts. Its details are effaced or mutilated, just as in the building that is going up one does not yet see more than the rudiments and the vague indication of moldings and of the ornamented parts. The finished building encloses the imagination within a circle and forbids it to go beyond that. Perhaps the sketch of a work gives so much pleasure just because each one finishes it to his liking (*The Journal of Eugène Delacroix*, tr. Walter Pach, Grove Press [Evergreen Edition], New York, 1961).

Question: *Why* does this ruin appear all the more impressive?

Are the fragments I am considering, and other fragments, what remain (i.e., akin to the ruin) or what are still under construction? Or are they both at once—fragments left from what is still under construction?

(It may be added that Delacroix's writings themselves, of which we have a considerable quantity, remained fragmentary, scattered through letters and journals, although he made a start at writing a dictionary of the arts and of painting.)

Characterizing *fragment*

To characterize the fragmentary piece of writing is not easy: in the case of each writer who seems to me to write something like a fragment, the qualities would be a little different, so that there are more particular definitions than general definitions, though one can sometimes find at least a few common elements, pieces of a more general definition.

Hölderlin: The fragment can be the extreme form of what he was doing already in his late poetry, whose outstanding feature, says Richard Sieburth in his introduction to his translation of *Hymns and Fragments*, was defined by Theodor Adorno as "*parataxis*, that is, the juxtaposition, without explanatory connectives, of various syntactical and grammatical elements (as opposed to *hypotaxis*, the subordination or coordination of phrase or clause)."

(What I have written has come out, is presented, in what Barthes would think of as a horizontal structure—equal increments—rather than as a hierarchical structure, in which the parts are subordinated to an ultimate governing point or meaning. It is more *paratactic* than *hypotactic*.)

In the case of Barthes, a fragment is a "brief burst" or a "beginning." Speaking of himself in the third person, he comments, "Liking to find, to write *beginnings*, he tends to multiply this pleasure: that is why he writes fragments: so many fragments, so many beginnings, so many pleasures (but he doesn't like the ends: the risk of the rhetorical clausule is too great: the fear of not being able to resist the *last word*)" (*Roland Barthes by Roland Barthes*, tr. Richard Howard).

Joubert's fragments were, perhaps, in part, a way

of being perfectly clear: "Everything that is exact is short . . . because what is isolated can be seen better"; or "What is clear should not be drawn out too much. These useless explanations, these endless examinations are a kind of long whiteness and lead to boredom. It is the uniformity of a wall, a long piece of laundry" (*The Notebooks of Joseph Joubert*, tr. Paul Auster).

How Joubert describes thoughts in a book

"August 1 (*insomni nocte*). I would like thoughts to succeed one another in a book like stars in the sky, with order, with harmony, but effortlessly and at intervals, without touching, without mingling."

Notes

For Mallarmé, they are notes. He calls them, in a letter to Robert de Montesquiou written as Mallarmé's child was dying, "a few rapid notes," notes for an impossible work. "Hugo," he writes, "was happy to have been able to speak (about the death of his daughter); for me, it's impossible" (*A Tomb for Anatole*, tr. Paul Auster).

A more general definition—what I finally see that I mean when I think of the fragment, old or new—is a text that works with silence, ellipsis, abbreviation, suggesting that something is missing, but that has the effect of a complete experience.

How Barthes describes the fragment

"The fragment is like the musical idea of a song cycle . . . : each piece is self-sufficient, and yet it is never anything but the interstice of its neighbors: the work consists of no more than an inset, an *hors-texte*. . . . What is the meaning of a pure series of interruptions?" And further: "The fragment has its ideal: a high condensation, not of thought, or of vision, or of truth . . . but of music: 'development' would be countered by 'tone' . . . here it is *timbre* which should reign" (*Roland Barthes by Roland Barthes*).

How Joubert describes thoughts following one another

Joubert also looks to music for a simile: "Thoughts must follow one another and be connected to one another like sounds in music, through their relationships alone—harmony—and not like links in a chain" (*Notebooks*).

Maurice Blanchot, in his essay "Joubert and Space" (tr. Lydia Davis), which is included as an afterword in the North Point Press edition of Joubert's *Notebooks*, comments on Joubert's comparison of himself to an aeolian harp:

> The *Notebooks* accumulated images through which he tried to reconcile himself to his difficulties: "I confess that I am like an aeolian harp—which gives off some beautiful sounds but can play no songs." "I am an aeolian harp. No wind has passed through me." The aeolian harp: it is as though space itself has become instrument and music—an instrument with all the extent and continuity of open space, but music composed of sounds that are always discontinuous, disjointed, and unfettered. Elsewhere, he explains the gaps in his meditation

and the white spaces that interrupt his phrases by
the tension he must maintain in his strings so as
to resonate properly, by the slackening that results
from this harmony and by the long period of time
he needs to "recover his strength and tighten
himself again."

Fragment and whole

The word *fragment* implies the word *whole*. A fragment
would seem to be a part of a whole, a broken-off part
of a whole. Does it also imply, as with other broken-off
pieces, that enough of them would make a whole, or
remake some original whole, some ideal whole? *Fragment*, as in *ruin*, may also imply something left behind
from a past original whole. In the case of Hölderlin's
Fragments, they are the only parts showing of a mad-
man's poems, the rest of which are hidden somewhere in
his mind; or the only parts showing of a logical whole
whose logic is unavailable to us, fragments that seem
fragments only to us, while they seem to him to form a
whole—for there is only a thin line between what is so
new to us that it changes our way of thinking and what
is so new to us that we can't recognize it as a coherent
thought or piece of writing, can't see the connections
the author sees, or even sense that they are there. Or
fragments that seem to him to make a whole and to us,
eventually, also to make a whole, though from a different angle.

Or, as with Mallarmé's fragmentary poems for his
dead son, the fragment is something left from some pro-
jected whole, some future whole (i.e., fragments des-
tined one day to be pieced together with other elements

to make a whole); or the fragments of ideal poems shattered by grief; fragments comparable to the incoherent utterances of voiced grief; inarticulateness being in this case the most credible expression of grief: no more than a fragment could be uttered, so overwhelming was the unuttered whole. In the silences, the grief is alive.

What is missing?

We may call a piece of writing a fragment when something seems to be missing from it, when we feel it breaks off abruptly, or lacks some crucial element, does not develop where it might develop, or seems a part of something larger. But this depends on our expectations as readers.

We can contemplate a Mayan ruin in the jungle, and consider it a whole thing, though it is only a fragment of something that was once whole. In our experience, it is a whole, though a Mayan who lived at the time when the entire temple was there as originally built, and who used it, would see it now as broken. It is a whole for us because it is all we have experienced of it, and because it yields us a complete experience. While we recognize that it is a ruin, and broken, for us nothing is missing.

This is the case for the piece of writing that we recognize, historically or formally, as a fragment, but that is whole for us.

The poet William Bronk, writing in his 1974 set of prose pieces, *The New World*, about one area of the Mayan jungle, has a different way of describing how we see:

> We are looking at what we see, which no description gave us, which never existed. What we see is

new and if we mean to see it we must look at it as something new. What we see is not what is there, though surely something is there and we seem to see it.

Making a work

For the writer of a fragment intended as such, the fragment is complete and substantial, does not need more, and cannot make do with less. For some readers, also, this is true, but not for all readers. Therefore, in this case, as in others, it is the reader also making the work, seeing a work or not seeing a work, just as the writer—acting as reader, as receiver, of material—saw a work and wrote it so that, for her or him, it became a written work.

We can see (i.e., read) fragments written two hundred years ago as complete works, though their authors did not write them to be complete works.

We may read Joubert's, Hölderlin's, or Mallarmé's fragments as works, whereas they did not intend them as works. Barthes, of a more modern age, intended his fragments to form a work; he recognized in them a legitimate or useful or comfortable form.

How we see

Here is Barthes describing his attempt to copy a Persian composition of the seventeenth century: "I copy and na-ively connect detail to detail; whence unexpected 'con-clusions': the horseman's leg turns out to be perched right on top of the horse's breastplate, etc." (*Roland Barthes by Roland Barthes*). His copy of this picture is a faithful representation of the way he saw the picture, or at least one way he saw the picture (certainly of the process of his seeing and copying).

We do not see wholes, we see fragments. We are accustomed to, and maybe need, the illusion of living among, and perceiving, wholes. We may need to think we see the other side of the lamp as well as this side, or that this side is all that exists (i.e., that this side is the whole of it).

Any imposition of a particular order on the great random miscellany of possible subject matter contradicts or distorts another possible order. We could say that the more complete a piece of writing is—if in this case *complete* means more fully elaborated, more particular—the more limiting it is, the more it leaves out, and therefore the more partial it is. A densely filled, fully articulated novel by Henry James is also partial. Two works by Marguerite Duras, *The Lover* and *The War*, give the impression of being fragmentary because they are written in short sections that do not always, or immediately, seem to have obvious links; the sections add up to a large picture but one that seems incomplete because of the breaks or gaps between sections. Any complete picture is an illusion, however. A picture that seems less complete may seem less of an illusion, therefore paradoxically more realistic.

How Barthes arrives at his form

Barthes's approach (form) in the fragmentary works (e.g., *The Pleasure of the Text*, *A Lover's Discourse*, *Roland Barthes by Roland Barthes*): He is inspired by certain texts, and conversations with friends, and friends' accounts of other texts, and uses these as inspirations or goads in the evolution of his own thoughts—which is what many readers and thinkers do. What he then does that is not as common is to allow this written, published work to reflect this process: here, in physically separated "entries," he allows each inspiration to generate its own thought, in which the inspiration is absorbed and integrated into his reaction to it.

Of course, Barthes's reading is dictated by his interests—and I mean *reading* in two senses: what he chooses to read and how he chooses to read it, or interpret it (i.e., what he sees in it). His is a partial view, his own partial view.

Arrangements of fragments (order)

Barthes groups his fragments thematically into a book on love, or a book on himself. Within this book, created of thematically grouped fragments, he arranges the fragments in alphabetical order, or alphabetical order with departures, so as, he says of *A Lover's Discourse*, "to discourage the temptation of meaning."

In a diary or journal, probably in most writers' working notebooks, fragments are arranged not logically, not thematically—except from time to time, if a preoccupation continues or recurs over some days or weeks—but chronologically. As our minds also entertain a random, miscellaneous, repetitious series of thoughts that are linked not logically—most of the time, anyway—but associatively. Our journals, selections from our thoughts, are sometimes linked logically, sometimes associatively— if they are a close record of our thoughts, or if we are moved by reading one earlier entry to write an entry that follows from it—but their arrangement is above all chronological. Because our lives have a chronological arrangement. Our lives are in chronological order, if no other kind of order.

Our lives also contain possibilities for narratives: people do—writers and nonwriters alike—extract from the material of their lives single, meaningful narratives and present them as such, with, as Barthes says of love episodes, "a path which it is always possible to interpret according to a causality or finality—even, if need be, which can be moralized (*'I was out of my mind, I'm over it now' 'Love is a trap which must be avoided from now on'* etc.)."

(He also describes such a narrative in terms of a disease: "It develops, grows, causes suffering, and passes away.")

Imposing this coherent order on a series of events that was in reality mixed up with random, extraneous material, giving it a "meaning," is of course the "distortion" that Barthes talked about. One hears and sees what one is predisposed to hear and see, one interprets as one is biased to interpret; another will witness the same material and tell a different story. We see only one side.

The journal

Barthes says: "With the alibi of a pulverized discourse, a dissertation destroyed, one arrives at the regular practice of the fragment; then from the fragment one slips to the 'journal.' At which point, is not the point of all this to entitle oneself to write a 'journal'?" (*Roland Barthes by Roland Barthes*).

The journal or writer's notebook: a partial, externalized form of his or her mind. Just as, if we take notes on our reading, either in or out of our notebooks, so that we don't forget what we have read, then these notes become an externalized form of our memory.

My journal as my other mind, what I sometimes know, what I once knew. I consult my other mind and I see that although I do not know a certain thing at present, I once knew it; there it is in my other mind.

Barthes is self-centered

Barthes is self-centered, taking the word literally: he is centered on himself, centered in himself, and he is explicit in admitting this, using it, acting on it, assimilating it, and thereby achieving a paradoxical sort of distance from it and from himself. He himself becomes as much an object of interest to himself as other objects he examines. His mind in the act of apprehending fascinates him. In fact, if he occasionally refers to himself in the third person, as Joubert also does, perhaps it is precisely when he is most explicitly taking himself as an object of interest to himself.

What is unfinished

How different is it for Barthes to refer to himself in the third person and for Kafka, in his diary, to present himself as someone else, exaggerate and dramatize a situation he really finds himself in, and in this way create the beginning of a story? Many of these stories that he begins in his diaries don't go on, are unfinished. But how much more unfinished is an unfinished story in Kafka's diary than one of Barthes's "brief bursts"?

Doesn't it also have to do with our expectations? If

we did not expect the narrative, once begun, to continue, as we do not expect a nonnarrative statement in a journal to continue, then we would not even regard the story as unfinished. For Kafka it served a purpose, satisfied an impulse—nothing more had to be added.

The pleasure or pain of not finishing

In a short article I read recently on Sartre's political writings, the writer—whose name I can't remember—suggested that perhaps there were many works Sartre did not finish because he wrote for the pleasure of writing, not for the satisfaction of reaching conclusions. This seems to have something in common with what Barthes said about loving to begin. Kafka, on the other hand, appeared to be very distressed that he could not finish certain pieces of writing. Four years before he died, he wrote in his diary: "The misery of having perpetually to begin, the lack of the illusion that anything is more than, or even as much as, a beginning, the foolishness of those who do not know this" (October 16, 1921, *Diaries 1914–1923*, tr. Martin Greenberg). (Of course, this contradicts what I said above, that for Kafka nothing more need be added to a beginning of a story; in Kafka's mind, there was the expectation that the story should go on.)

Joubert is reproached, either by himself or by his friends, with not knowing how to finish. He answers in his notebook: "To finish! What a word. We finish nothing when we stop, when we say we have come to the end" (*Notebooks*). Reproached with having finished before any beginning, he says: "When the last word is always the one that offers itself first, the work becomes difficult."

What is allowed, formally, to be unfinished

I have always been more interested in *Bouvard and Pécuchet* than in *Madame Bovary*: to me, it was not only the preoccupation (subject) of *Bouvard and Pécuchet* that appealed (the autodidactic impulse carried to an absurd extreme) and not only the characters—the Laurel-and-Hardy or Beckettian couple, the androgynous or really sexless pair of males, males endowed with sentiment but no sexuality (this may be an inaccurate impression, left by a reading of the book decades ago), unaggressive, yet active, even passionate in their quests (i.e., pure minds? naked minds?)—but also the form of the book. It is horizontal rather than vertical (or paratactic rather than hypotactic): an endless series of episodes, endeavors, projects, a series that has only the feeblest of logical linking, a sequence that really has no logical conclusion because finality, causality, is not part of its nature and also because the book was in fact left unfinished by Flaubert. In this case, as in some others, can't we say that it may be appropriate to the very nature, the very enterprise, of the work to be unfinished? That this could be allowed formally?

The Frankfurt Edition

Sieburth, in his introduction to Hölderlin's *Hymns*, describes an edition that proposes a different way of reading fragments. This edition proposes to involve the reader in the text in a way that may stand as a paradigm for reading any fragment, as the reader is invited to take active part in its confusions, ellipses, and abbreviations.

"Whereas previous editions of Hölderlin had more or

less masked (the) authorial (and authoritarian) role of the editor," writes Sieburth,

> the so-called Frankfurt Edition currently in progress under the direction of D. E. Sattler challenges the sovereign procedures of traditional Hölderlin scholarship by inviting the reader to participate in the generation of the text. Sattler first gives a photographic reproduction of the manuscript, followed by a diplomatic copy that transcribes the spatial configuration of the original. This is in turn succeeded by a "phase analysis," which converts the spatial disposition of the page into a temporal sequence whose various stages of composition are indicated by different typefaces. Only at the end of this process is there finally printed a provisional version of the poem, or "reading text."
>
> What emerges from this new Frankfurt Edition, then, is not a closed canon of inert textual artifacts but rather a mapping of poems in process. . . . By presenting Hölderlin's texts as events rather than objects, as processes rather than products, it converts the reader from passive consumer into active participant in the genesis of the poem, while at the same time calling attention to the fundamentally historical character of both the reader's and writer's activity.

A possible performance of Mozart's *Requiem*

As Flaubert died before finishing *Bouvard and Pécuchet*, Mozart died before finishing his *Requiem*. What if this work were performed in a way similar to the approach of the Frankfurt Edition, so that the orchestra actually played it as it was left by Mozart in the manuscript, some parts fully realized, others suggested, a bar complete here and there, a theme alone in one instrument abruptly broken off. Would this be a performance with some of the same effect as Mallarmé's broken-off poems, his notes for poems? In other words, would we hear the grief in the silences? Would we be moved by the silences as well as, or as much as, by the notes and the words? Can't we say, coming back from a different direction to ask, really, the same thing, whether these fragments could not be regarded as a legitimate form?

When inarticulateness is not a defeat

Barthes justifies his own early choice of the fragment as form by saying that "incoherence is preferable to a distorting order" (*Roland Barthes by Roland Barthes*). In the case of Mallarmé, inarticulateness might seem preferable to articulateness when it comes to expressing a grief that is in fact unutterable. He writes, in *A Tomb for Anatole*:

> It is true
> that you have struck me
> and you would have carefully chosen
> your wound—
>   —etc.
>   —but
>   ——
>
>   and vengeance
> struggle between spirit and
>   death

One reviewer of the English translation, Sarah White, wrote that Mallarmé's was "a mind groping toward transcendence, then lapsing into grief and protest." He failed to transcend, he remained inside the grief, and the "notes," too, remain inside the grief. The notes become the most immediate expression, the closest mirroring, of the writer's emotion at the inspiring subject, the writer's stutter, and the reader, witnessing the writer's stutter, is witness not only to his grief but also to his process, to the workings of his mind, to his mind, closer to what we might think of as the origins of his writing.

Etc. and the invitation to the reader

Mallarmé did not take his "notes" to be finished works, publishable works, just as Joubert did not take the entries in his notebook to add up to a finished work. We, now, are the ones who read them as constituting a finished work. Sarah White, again, points out that "Mallarmé, despite his taste for sprung syntax, drastic ellipsis, and odd graphic arrangement, would never have released a poem containing the abbreviation 'etc.'"

Etc. is a sign of the process of thinking and writing. *Etc.* is a note within a note from the author to himself reminding him of the rest of a thought or an association so evident to him that he does not need to write it out. *Etc.* in a work released to a reader invites a witness, a closer witness to the process, the act of writing. *Etc.* invites or demands that the reader complete the thought, the association; *etc.* says that both writer and reader know how this continues. Mallarmé's *etc.* was not intended by him to be published but is published now and read by readers now not unused to finding *etc.* in a poem. The author did not intend these fragments as a work, but we, the readers, make them a work by reading them as a work, just as a writer may make a work by taking a text that was not meant to be a work and copying it, or parts of it, into his own work, which is a way of reading by writing or rewriting or rearranging, a form of reading that becomes so active that it turns into a kind of writing, in the hands of a writer.

Interruption

Doesn't the unfinished work tend to throw our attention onto the work as artifact, or the work as process, rather than the work as conveyer of meaning, of message? Doesn't this perhaps add to the pleasure or the interest of the text?

Any interruption, either of our expectations or of the smooth surface of the work itself—either by breaking it off, confusing it, leaving it actually unfinished— foregrounds the work as artifact, as object, rather than as invisible purveyor of meaning, emotion, atmosphere. Constant interruption, fragmentation, also keeps returning the reader not only to the real world but also to a consciousness of his or her own mind at work.

Two kinds of reading

When one's attention is drawn to the text as artifact or process, this may add to the pleasure or the interest of the text, but what happens to the act of reading?

I can identify roughly, at least, two different ways I read, depending on the text: I read *Anna Karenina* in somewhat the same way I read Stephen King's *Firestarter* in the sense that I lose sight of the text as artifact, the text becomes invisible, and I also lose sight of myself—my thinking mind, my discriminating mind. I lose my self as I lose myself in certain kinds of movies: the illusion is complete, the fiction has more reality than I do. I know people who do not like losing themselves this way and who never do—they remain critically awake (i.e., conscious of their thinking minds) during the movie; and some of them prefer not to read fiction.

The other way I read is the way I read when I read a work in which the text itself remains visible and present to me, an object of interest by its language and/or form; and in these cases I remain present to myself as well (i.e., conscious of my own thoughts).

Of these two ways of reading, years ago I read *Madame Bovary* the first way, *Bouvard and Pécuchet* the second way. Losing myself in the story of *Madame Bovary* was one kind of pleasure; involving myself actively with the form of *Bouvard and Pécuchet* was another kind of pleasure. I might go a step further and say that when I read *Madame Bovary*, Flaubert's mind seemed—was?—further away from me; when I read *Bouvard and Pécuchet*, my mind encountered Flaubert's mind; Flaubert himself was more present in *Bouvard and Pécuchet* than he was in *Madame Bovary*. Returning to the movie comparison, I could also imagine that it is easier to make a movie from a written work in which the text disappears—for me, *Madame Bovary*—than from one in which the text is foregrounded as object of interest.

The generosity of the fragment

Here, again, is Blanchot on Joubert: "What he was seeking—this source of writing, this space in which to write, this light to circumscribe in space— . . . made him unfit for all ordinary literary work" (*Notebooks*)—or, as Joubert said of himself, "unsuited to continuous discourse." Blanchot, continuing, proposes that Joubert preferred "the center to the sphere, sacrificing results to the discovery of their conditions, and writing not in order to add one book to another but to take command of the point from which it seemed to him all books issued."

Whether intended as works or not, these fragments can be characterized as less mediated than other forms of finished works (i.e., closer, really or apparently, to the origin of their writing, apparently more ragged, cruder, less refined, more revealing of the process of the writing, closer to being the raw data of the writer's thought).

The less mediated a work is, the more personal, in a sense, and the more private, the more closely involved the reader feels in the process of the work and the more she or he participates or feels participation in the creation of the work, whence its generosity, and its modesty.

Form as response to doubt

Doubt, uneasiness, dissatisfaction with writing or with existing forms may result in the formal integration of these doubts by the creation of new forms, forms that in one way or another exceed or surprise our expectations. Whereas repeating old forms, traditional forms, implies a lack of desire or compulsion, or a refusal, to entertain doubt or feel dissatisfaction with them.

To work deliberately in the form of the fragment can be seen as stopping or appearing to stop a work closer, in the process, to what Blanchot would call the origin of writing, the center rather than the sphere. It may be seen as a formal integration, an integration into the form itself, of a question about the process of writing.

It can be seen as a response to the philosophical problem of seeing the written thing replace the subject of the writing. If we catch only a little of our subject, or only badly, clumsily, incoherently, perhaps we have not destroyed it. We have written about it, written it, and allowed it to live on at the same time, allowed it to live on in our ellipses, in our silences.

1986

Thirty Recommendations
for Good Writing Habits

The following are just my personal pieces of advice. They won't be the same as someone else's, and they may not fit your life or practice, but maybe you'll pick up something useful.

1. Take notes regularly. This will sharpen both your powers of observation and your expressive ability. A productive feedback loop is established: through the habit of taking notes, you will inevitably come to observe more; observing more, you will have more to note down. Here are some examples from my own notebooks and also from the Austrian fiction writer Peter Handke's notebook selection titled *The Weight of the World*. Other notebooks that might serve as useful models are Kafka's and the painter Delacroix's.

Observe your own activity.

From my notebook:

a. "I keep hoping for a new and interesting email, and for hours now it has been the same subject line: 'Used Kubota tractor for sale.'"

b. "I kept smelling a smell of cat pee but could not find where it was coming from, until I found the cat pee—on the tip of my very own nose."

From Peter Handke's notebook:

c. "Someone [a stranger] drops something and I pull my hand out of my pocket, but that's all I do."

Observe your own feelings (but not at tiresome length).

From Peter Handke's notebook:

a. "At the sight of a woman with enormously protuberant eyes, my irritation vanished."

From my notebook:

b. The feeling of love, it seems, in my response to Peter Bichsel's stories—they are *loving* stories. They awaken in me a feeling (love) that I am then quicker to feel in response to other things.

Observe the behavior of others, both animal and human.

From my notebook:

a. Little kitty crouches down and flattens her ears (in the entryway, in front of the glass door) so that she won't be seen by the dead leaves whirling around outside.

b. Grandpa is over there under the tree working on his retractable umbrella.

c. That very handsome dark-haired and dark-eyed young man walks up and down the aisle of the train so many times to show us how nice he looks in his cream-colored summer suit and white shirt. He will continue to walk up and down until he is sure we have all seen him.

(In this case, the observation has already turned into something a little more, even as I write it, because I am adding something to it that I imagine, or can pretend I imagine, about the man.)

Observe the weather, and be specific.

From my notebook:

a. High wind yesterday blew women's long hair, women's long skirts, crowns of trees, at dinner outdoors napkins off laps, lettuce off plates, flakes of pastry off plates onto sidewalk.

Apropos of weather and precision, here is the 1970 *Merriam-Webster's Collegiate Dictionary*'s chart of the Beaufort scale—a scale in which the force of the wind is indicated by numbers from 0 to 12. This source is "just" a dictionary, but the images are vivid because of their specificity and the good clear writing in the dictionary, and because the increasing strength of the wind on the scale becomes, despite the dry, factual account, dramatic.

Beaufort Number	Name	Wind Speed, MPH	Description
0	calm	< 1	calm: smoke rises vertically
1	light air	1–3	direction of wind shown by smoke but not by wind vanes
2	light breeze	4–7	wind felt on face; leaves rustle; wind vane moves
3	gentle breeze	8–12	leaves and small twigs in constant motion; wind extends light flag
4	moderate breeze	13–18	wind raises dust and loose paper; small branches move
5	fresh breeze	19–24	small trees with leaves begin to sway; crested wavelets form on inland waters
6	strong breeze	25–31	large branches move; overhead wires whistle; umbrellas difficult to control
7	moderate gale *or* near gale	32–38	whole trees sway; walking against wind is difficult
8	fresh gale *or* gale	39–46	twigs break off trees; moving cars veer
9	strong gale	47–54	slight structural damage occurs; shingles may blow away
10	whole gale *or* storm	55–63	trees uprooted; considerable structural damage occurs
11	storm *or* violent storm	64–72	widespread damage occurs
12	hurricane	≥73	widespread damage occurs

I have to say, as an aside, that I'm sure I learned something about writing clear and exact prose from the very precise definitions in this same dictionary, which I acquired at age twenty-five and consulted constantly.

Observe other types of behavior, including that of municipalities.

From my notebook, while traveling:

a. To commemorate the Saint-Cyprien victims of the flood of 1875, the city erected . . . a fountain.

(I revised this, in the notebook: I changed the order a little to avoid a succession of prepositional phrases. My sentence originally read: "To commemorate the victims in Saint-Cyprien of the flood of 1875, the city erected . . . a fountain." That version may, after all, be perfectly all right, or even better.)

Note facts.

As a writer, whether you are writing fiction, nonfiction, or poetry, you must be responsible for accurate factual information about how a thing works, if you're writing about it. You will have to be well informed about such things as the weather, biology, botany, human nature, history, technology; such matters as color spectrums and the behavior of light waves, etc., etc. This means that, over time, you will learn a good deal. Here's an example of a piece of knowledge acquired while traveling:

Question: can you figure out three reasons why trees were planted along this canal in a French city?

My answer, noted in my notebook:

a. trees planted along canal for three reasons: shade for boatmen, help slow evaporation of water, hold earth in banks. Often planted at exactly equal intervals.

Note technical/historical facts.

Here are some notes I took in the Cluny Museum in Paris, about construction methods in ancient Rome:

a. "Courses of limestone (rows) intersected by leveling courses (bands) of horizontal bricks forming a construction named *opus vittatum mixtum* [banded mixed work], a reference to the layering techniques and to the mixing of different materials."
b. "The floor . . . is made of Roman concrete, *opus caementicium*, a mix of stones and lime mortar . . . probably covered in stone slabs or mosaics."

Important: Take notes at the time, because you will forget much, if not everything, later—you will inevitably either forget the moment entirely or forget a part of it, so it won't be as complete or interesting when you do note it down.

a. Here is Samuel Johnson on the subject of travel writing: "He who has not made the experiment, or who is not accustomed to require vigorous accuracy from himself, will scarcely believe how much a few hours take from certainty of knowledge."

On the subject of taking notes, I want to add one last thing, and that is about public transportation: I do a lot of writing and note-taking on trips: in airports, on airplanes, on trains. I recommend taking public transportation whenever possible. There are many good reasons to do this (one's carbon footprint—on the ground, in any case—one's safety, productive use of time, support of public transportation, etc.), but for a writer, here are two in particular: (1) you will write a good deal more waiting for a bus or sitting on a train than you will driving a car, or as a passenger in a car; and (2) you will be thrown in with strangers—people not of your choosing. Although I pass strangers when I'm walking on a city street, it is only while traveling on public transportation that I sit thigh-to-thigh with them on a subway, share the armrest with them between our airplane seats for hours on end, stare at the back of their heads waiting in line, and overhear sometimes extended conversations. It takes me out of my own limited, chosen world. Sometimes I have good, enlightening conversations with them.

2. Always work (note, write) from your own interest, never from what you think you should be noting or writing. Trust your own interest. I have a strong interest, at the moment, in Roman building techniques, thus my notation above, taken down in the Cluny Museum. My interest may pass. But for the moment I follow it and enjoy it, not knowing where it will go.

Let your interest, and particularly what you want to write about, be tested by time, not by other people—either real other people or imagined other people.

This is why writing workshops can be a little dangerous, it should be said; even the teachers or leaders of such workshops can be a little dangerous; this is why most of your learning should be on your own. Other people are often very sure that their opinions and their judgments are correct.

3. Be mostly self-taught.

There is a great deal to be learned from programs, courses, and teachers. But I suggest working equally hard, throughout your life, at learning new things on your own, from whatever sources seem most useful to you. I have found that pursuing my own interests in various directions and to various sources of information can take me on fantastic adventures: I have stayed up till the early hours of the morning poring over old phone books; or following genealogical lines back hundreds of years; or reading a book about what lies under a certain French city; or comparing early maps of Manhattan as I search for a particular farmhouse. These adventures become as gripping as a good novel.

4. Revise notes constantly—try to develop the ability to read them as though you had never seen them before, to see how well they communicate. Constant revision, whether or not you're going to "do" anything with what you've written, also teaches you to write better in the first place, when you first write something down.

I have already given some examples of revision, since it is an inveterate habit of mine when I reread anything I've written. I will give more examples as I go along and explain more about the importance of this later.

5. If you take notes regularly, sitting in an airport, for example, you can "grow" a story right then and there. Revising it, you can give it a good shape and pace. Here are some notes I took sitting in an airport lounge at a table near a Starbucks. They later turned into a finished story. They begin with some dialogue I hear that strikes me:

a. "Caramel syrup or caramel drizzle?"
   "Sorry?"
   "Caramel syrup or caramel drizzle?" (I look up; it is a tall slim woman with a ponytail buying the drink. She's an airline employee in the Starbucks line.)
   Long pause for deliberation.
   "I'll take the drizzle."
   (I see her now from behind, over there, her blond ponytail and sticking-out ears, drinking her caramel drizzle. As she deliberated, I was deciding that drizzle was a smaller amount of caramel than "syrup," even though "syrup" must be involved in the "drizzle.")
   Later, she walks away with another airline employee, the empty cup in her hand, the caramel drizzle inside her.
   And then she turns out to be the attendant on our flight—her name is Shannon—so her caramel drizzle will also be going to Chicago with us.

In between my observations of the flight attendant, there were other notes, first a comment about something I had experienced trying to learn Dutch, and then another "people" observation, as follows:

> b. Stout, cheerful, rather dandyish man dressed in preppy clothes—tweed jacket, bow tie, loafers, etc.—starts off down the airport corridor in pursuit of a boy of six or seven in camouflage clothes who is galloping away. Stout man calls cheerfully back to woman at table, who is evidently boy's mother: "James and I are going potty!"

Then I go back to observing the stewardess.

6. Taking notes as you sit outside at a café table, you can also begin to develop a poem. This is the same wind as noted before, at the same café table. I did not write it to be a poem, but later I think it almost reads as one:

> a. In the wind, the grass is bowing and the Queen Anne's lace is nodding.
> Now, as though blown by the wind, come the runners in the footrace.

Here is how the revision worked: Originally I did not have "In the wind" at the beginning. I was sitting there in the wind, I knew it was windy, I knew why the grass and the Queen Anne's lace were bowing and nodding. But when I read it over with fresh eyes, I could see that I needed to say the wind was blowing; otherwise the reader might hesitate or take time figuring out why the grass and flowers were moving. You want the impact of what you write to be *unobstructed*; you don't want confusion or hesitation in the reader's mind.

I say "the reader" for convenience, by the way. The fact is that when I revise in my notebook, I'm revising for the sake of the piece itself, to make it work. I'm not thinking about any reader. I may never do any more with it than leave it in the notebook.

7. Another advantage of revising constantly, regardless of whether you're ever going to do anything more with what you've written, is that you practice, constantly, reading with fresh eyes, reading as the person coming fresh to this, never having seen it before. This is a very important skill to develop, and one that probably develops only with time and practice (although some people recommend various tricks, such as printing different drafts of your work in different fonts).

Another way to see your work freshly is to leave it alone and come back to it after time has passed. I will quite often begin a piece of writing, even hastily, getting a few lines or sentences down, with a title, and then leave it and work on other things, and sometimes I leave it for so long—weeks or months—that when I see the title again I wonder what it is, and even when I read it I don't recognize it, having completely forgotten it existed.

8. Sentences or ideas reported from reality *out of context* can be wonderful. But then, when and if you use them in a piece of finished writing, beware of how much context you give them.

Context can mean explanation, exposition. And too

much of it can take away all the interest the material originally had. Here are some more notes, effective alone,
without context, less effective with context:

More notebook entries:

a. "When Maris was in his sixties, he often seemed
   tired of life." (from Wikipedia article about the
   Dutch painter Willem Maris)
b. "Another of Tennyson's brothers, Edward
   Tennyson, was institutionalized at a private
   asylum, where he was deemed dead." (from
   Wikipedia article on Tennyson)
c. "Alas I'm in Denver." (email)
d. "I can always get someone to open a window
   in Paris." (email from schoolmate about learning French)
e. "The children at The Children's Center are interested in building a castle." (email)

In this last example, part of the vividness of the entry is the language: the repetition of *children* and then
the word *interested*, which somehow seems an odd choice
for characterizing the children here. And then the picture conjured up by children building a (real) castle. This
would not have been as striking if the situation as a whole
had been more fully explained and the language had
been slightly changed, thus: "The children at the day-care
center want to build a castle out of blocks."

f. "I need a plumber." (email)

9. Go to primary sources and go to the great works
to learn technique. This was the advice of Matsuo

Bashō, the seventeenth-century Japanese master of the haiku.

Read the best writers. Maybe it would help to set a goal of one classic per year at least. Classics have stood the test of time, as we say. Keep trying them; if you don't like them at first, come back to them. I tried Joyce's *Ulysses* three times before I read it all the way through. (It helped that I was living in Ireland at the time, where I saw Joycean and Beckettian characters all around me.) I haven't yet read *Don Quixote*, but I think I'll actually enjoy it. There is a lot more to say about learning from the best writers, and I'll say a little more in a moment.

10. How should you read? What should the diet of your reading be? Read the best writers from all different periods; keep your reading of contemporaries in proportion—you do not want a steady diet of contemporary literature. You already belong to your time.

You should be reading a lot—reading different kinds of books but also reading in different ways: sometimes fast, and sometimes slowly. Sometimes just absorbing what you are reading, losing yourself; at other times analyzing as you read, developing your awareness of how a writer achieves an effect; sometimes stopping to analyze closely just one sentence or one paragraph.

Digression on analysis

Examples of analysis:

a. I used to do this with the Dr. Donahue health column in the daily paper where I lived. Why did I have the impression that Dr. Donahue, in his column, was so caring, so sympathetic? I would read the column sentence by sentence from the beginning to find out. Much of it was neutral, clearly presented medical information that might have turned cooler or warmer at any moment. But then came the note of caring; it involved the use of the second person—"you"—and then the advice: "You will want to make sure you leave the compress on for five minutes." Along with the advice there might come a note of self-deprecation: "It sounds ridiculous to ask an exhausted person to exercise." Despite being the expert, he never sounded superior.

b. Much more recently I was analyzing the humor of the British novelist Barbara Pym, a writer I enjoy: I would start at the beginning of a chapter and proceed, again, one sentence at a time. She was not funny, not yet, she was rather neutral, and then—aha, there it was, the first funny moment. And then I would ask, How does she do it?

Incongruity is at the heart of humor, so often. In the following example, it's the contrast between the gravity of the first statement, which raises our expectations of serious news, and the anticlimax or change of register in the second statement. I can't find the passage, so I'll have to approximate it.

Two people are sitting together and talking at a church reception. One is a man very involved in the internal affairs of the church. The other is a woman, the narrator, a visitor to the town attending the reception out of courtesy.

He said: "I have had serious news."

"Oh," I asked, alarmed. "What is it?"

He leaned toward me and lowered his voice: "There is a fungus growing on the walls of the choir vestry."

You may not find that funny; maybe one has to have been following the story from the beginning and also to have become completely attuned to Pym's quiet and constant humor. And one's sense of humor is an individual thing, in any case.

I'm analyzing just how Barbara Pym achieves her funny moments, not because I want to learn to be funny, but just because it interests me. But I also know that close analysis is *in itself* instructive. Please remember that. Analyzing, in itself, will sharpen your perceptions and sharpen your skills as a writer.

Analyzing will help you solve problems: if you have trouble with endings, read and analyze endings; if you have trouble with lush descriptions, see how descriptions function for different writers. For any problem you have, there will be an answer in the close analysis of one or more good writers.

Read closely, and learn to analyze texts.

11. Other books to have on hand:

Books of writing exercises, if you find them useful. One I like is Brian Kiteley's *The 3 A.M. Epiphany*. He has not only exercises to do but also little stories of his own experience to go with them.

When you aren't inspired to work on whatever it is you should be working on, do an exercise, or a series of them. Make up your own exercises. Do them even if you feel dull and unimaginative. Something may come of it, and it is better than doing nothing.

12. Important practical tip: After a session of writing, leave some clear time in which you can note down what your brain will continue to offer you. In other words, do not go directly from writing to lunch with friends or to a class. Do *not* go straight to your emails or your phone. Leave at least fifteen minutes completely open. Do the dishes or take a walk or a shower—do something physical in which you can remain open to your random thoughts. Your brain will offer you a few more good ideas during this time. Don't lose them by silencing them with other activities.

13. If you want to be original, don't labor to be original. Rather, work on yourself, your mind, and then say what you think. This was Stendhal's advice. Actually, he said: "If you want to be witty, work on your character and say what you think on every occasion." Where did I find this quote? In my *New Basics Cookbook*.

But I prefer my adaptation of his advice: If you want to be original, cultivate yourself, enrich your mind, develop your empathy, your understanding of other human beings, and then, when you come to write, say what you think and feel, what you are moved to say.

Which may bring us to five (or six) cardinal rules.

The five cardinal rules (or six)

(1) Work on your character. (2) Work on your handling of language so that you know what you're doing and can do it well and be in control. (3) Know your language—its

words and phrases and idioms—deeply through every kind of study of it. (4) Say what you want to say without inhibition, in the way you want to say it, regardless of what other people might think (but with sensitivity to the feelings of others). (5) Work hard (write a lot), and be patient.

I'll say it again, slightly differently: (1) Work closely on your technique. (2) Separately, develop your mind and character. (3) When you write, write freely, as you want to, following your own interests. (4) Work hard; be painstaking in your revision. (5) Be patient; let time go by if you have to. (6) Disregard what other people may think (but not what they may feel).

We will revisit some of these cardinal rules in separate sections.

Example of a writer following her own bent

a. In a recent book of poems, *Works and Days*, which is a sort of springtime diary, with brief entries in prose and poetry from April into June, Bernadette Mayer includes in many of the poems non-words that are sets of mixed-up letters, inspired by Jumble, the word puzzle:

bufial ilbafu fsiul
walfed dewfal flawed

This is a funny, quirky thing to do—but those Jumble words are not there because Mayer said to herself, Now, how can I be original, how can I do something different, unusual, and eye-catching? They are there because it amused and interested her to put them in—the impulse grew organically out of her own interests and preoccupations.

This is what I mean about character and work: your nature, your character, your whole being will produce the kind of writing you do. (That is why we hate clichés so much: they don't reflect your own, very individual person; they are borrowed ideas, in outworn language.)

That those Jumble words were included in the diary because of Mayer's own interests is one important point about those poems; the other is that she did not then censor her impulse—she did not say to herself, That's silly, I'd better not do that. She trusted her own instincts—if doing this interested her, it was interesting, and those Jumble words belonged in the poems.

And you may not even be able to articulate why you want something in a piece of writing—that is when you have to trust your instincts.

14. Apropos of censoring. Let us look at privacy versus publishing. Your notebook, or whatever you first write on or in, should be private, and there you should not censor at all, unless something offends even you too much to write it down. Then, when you come to the point of making your writing public, there are bad reasons to censor and good reasons to censor. A couple of good reasons to censor: You don't want to hurt or offend other people, especially those close to you, although sometimes a writer will decide he has to publish something even if it does hurt or offend. I say "he" in this case because I am thinking of Karl Ove Knausgaard, the Norwegian novelist, who wrote a "novel" in six fat volumes that was obviously a thinly veiled memoir and that did offend or outrage some of his family members.

A second good reason to censor is—in my opinion, anyway—that we don't need to increase the burden of obscenity and violence, including hate speech, which we already have enough of in the world.

A bad reason to censor is, as I have probably said or implied already, the fear of what some unspecified, or specified, group of fashionable people, or one's ambitious friends, or a conventional-minded reading public will think. Related to that, another bad reason to censor is fear of not selling your work—that's a terrible reason.

By "censoring," I don't mean just deleting offensive or hurtful material; I mean also deleting or omitting things you think someone else may think are odd or silly, like Jumble words.

15. Back to the idea of patience, for a moment: Be patient; don't rush your work or try to finish before you're ready. Be prepared to sit on it for days, weeks, months, years if necessary—keep revisiting it. Work on something else in the meantime. Return periodically to a piece that is giving you trouble. Someday you may understand what the trouble is.

16. Work on your expertise with the technical aspects of writing English. Know what you're doing, and what other writers are doing—specifically.

Read books about language, and about style: most highly recommended of all is Virginia Tufte's *Artful Sentences: Syntax as Style*. This should be nearby in your room, whether you ever manage to read all the way through it or not. Dip into it regularly and read a little.

You should have a good history of the English language; and of course you need a thesaurus and reference books on grammar, usage, rhetoric, etc. Anything and everything that makes you pay more attention to language per se, in itself, not just as a workaday "vehicle" for your ideas and your plot. And I say books, rather than online resources, for a reason: although online resources are handy, many of them are to some extent inaccurate, hastily assembled, and/or poorly written; they may be none of those things, but you simply can't be sure. So in addition to online resources, use books, even, or especially, older editions. You could almost say that the farther back in time you go to find them, the better they will be, or at least the more carefully edited. And a lot of what is in them won't be out of date.

If you can't think of a good exercise and you're stuck, try writing a "thesaurus" story, in which you use all possible near synonyms of a word.

English has two predominant, parallel sets of vocabularies, Germanic and Latinate. English is incredibly rich. Here is an eloquent list of near synonyms for *abusive*, for example (almost all of them Latinate).

a. "calumniating, castigating, censorious, contumelious, defamatory, derisive, disparaging, insolent, insulting, invective, libelous, maligning, obloquious, offensive, opprobrious, reproachful, reviling, rude, sarcastic, scathing, scolding, scurrilous, sharp-tongued, slanderous, traducing, upbraiding, vilifying, vituperative."

Which are the Anglo-Saxon or Germanic words? *Rude*, *scathing*, *scolding*, *sharp-tongued*, and maybe *slandering*. I'm not sure of *slandering*. You should know your language well enough so that you have a pretty good idea whether a word is Latinate or Germanic.

Some will surprise you, but you should be right most of the time.

I prefer to say "near synonym," by the way, because I don't like to use the word *synonym* anymore. Part of the beauty of the language is that every word is actually a little different or very different—in its meaning, its history, and its associations.

Apropos of the two sets of vocabularies: Be aware of the history of the English language—know at least roughly how it evolved before the Norman Conquest, and how it continued to evolve afterward. Why is the Norman Conquest so important? In 1066, the Norman French conquered England and imposed upon the conquered peoples the language of Norman French, which was a Latinate language, a language descended from the particular form of Latin (what we call Vulgar Latin) spoken in France by the invading and occupying Romans. The Norman French imposed their language on the existing language, which was Old English, a West Germanic language.

17. Learn as much as you can, as often as possible, about the origins of the words you're using. You will use them more accurately, and it is also interesting.

Did you know that *gregarious* and *egregious* both have the word for "flock" or "herd" at their origins? (If you are gregarious, you like to mingle with the flock; if a thing is egregious, it stands out from the herd.)

Sporadic and *diaspora* both have at their origins the idea of sowing seed. (And mushrooms reproduce from spores.)

In the history of the abstract word *ostracize* are pottery shards.

In the word *precarious* is prayer.

In the words *rodent* and *erode*, there is the idea of gnawing.

The buried metaphor in *caprice* and *capricious* is the behavior of a typical goat.

At the origin of *sabotage* lies the French word for a wooden shoe, *sabot.*

Words that appear, or are, abstract almost always have at their origins something concrete: herd, seed, pottery shard, a rodent gnawing, a goat. Know what that concrete thing is. Your use of the abstract word will then be more accurate.

Your use of the word should be in harmony with its origins, not in conflict. For instance, if you describe a man's clothes as being "dilapidated," this choice will be in conflict with the metaphorical origin of the word, which contains *lapis*, or "stone." (A wall may be dilapidated, or a building, but not a pair of trousers.)

18. Pay attention to the sounds of the language.

Some people hear, in their head, everything they read. Others do not. Some writers like to read aloud what they have written, to hear how it sounds. Others can hear what they've written without reading it out loud—though they may hear something more once they do read it out loud.

What you write should be pleasing to hear—unless, of course, you want it to be displeasing, or awkward. In either case, you want to take fully into account how your word, phrase, or sentence sounds.

The sounds of the more abstract, more Latinate vocabulary in English, by the way, are quite different from the sounds of the Anglo-Saxon, or Germanic, vocabulary, which teems with words that are short, abrupt, sometimes percussive (think of the difference, for instance, between *impecunious* and *broke*). We may return to the sounds of your language, but meanwhile—let's relate the sounds of your language to your diet of reading.

19. Be sure to read poetry, regularly, whether you are a poet or a writer of prose. I hope, of course, that if you're a poet, you are already reading a lot of poetry. You will not develop, as a writer, if you don't read. You won't write as well, if you're a prose writer, if you don't read poetry.

The poet William Bronk's definition of a poem (I can't remember where I read it) included the words *condensation* and *serious concerns*. Of course, not all poems involve "serious concerns." That was what he thought of as the most important characteristics of a poem. His poems were dense and compact and certainly expressed serious concerns.

It is important for you to absorb, regularly, a poem's concentrated attention to language, and its economy. I spoke earlier about the strangers you may come to know when sharing your armrest with them on an airplane flight. One young man I met that way who was, maybe, a lawyer—I can't remember—and a great reader admitted sadly that he was afraid of poetry. He was afraid he wouldn't understand it and did not like being in that position.

If you're afraid of poetry, or think you dislike it, as a friend of mine dislikes water, then find a way to begin reading it, maybe by starting with the most prosy poems.

In fact, that is an idea for an anthology of poems—to start the book with the easiest, most prose-like poems and progress to the most obscure and difficult.

I have another friend who said, last time I saw her, "I don't like poetry." We began to debate this. I was indignant. I said, "But poetry is not just one thing. There are many different kinds of poems and poets. Somewhere there must be a poet or at least a single poem that you like." Then she remembered that—it was true—her book club had read Anne Carson's *Autobiography of Red* and she had liked it. I liked that book, too. It is a long narrative poem in sections, some of which, in their language and settings, reminded me of James Agee's novel *A Death in the Family*, which I think is one of the superb American classics.

We don't see each other often enough so that we could really get into a discussion of her initial statement—"I don't like poetry." But later I realized that I have probably been caught saying, or thinking, "I don't like jazz." And that would be just as blind, general, and inaccurate. It has made me stop saying I don't like jazz and realize that, yes, actually, I like some jazz, like Miles Davis and Sidney Bechet. Probably even quite a few others. John Coltrane.

20. Be curious—be curious about as much as possible. Think, generally, about how curious you are, or are not, as a person. If you are not very curious, think about why not. And try to cultivate curiosity. If you are curious, you will learn things, and the more curious you are, the more you will learn. And curiosity may lead you deeper and deeper into all sorts of subjects.

My latest example of curiosity and the pursuit of answers is the three lines of bricks in the Roman towers in the French town of Bourges. (I should really say *courses* of bricks; *course* is the correct word for a layer of bricks; James Joyce, especially, was very particular about using the correct term for a thing—he seemed to delight in it.) For a full week, in Bourges, where I first noticed this pattern, I wondered about those bricks. I was sure they were not just decorative—there must have been something in the construction of the towers that called for them. Then, at the Cluny Museum in Paris, I found a mention of them, though maybe not yet the complete answer.

But there are many more things to be curious about: at the Culinary Institute of America, how do they teach the students the right way to uncork a bottle of wine? When you blow on an ant, trying to move it, and it doesn't move, why is it so good at bracing itself? Does it have strong little muscles in its little legs? Why, exactly, does power corrupt?

And don't underestimate the value of spending time wondering about something, like those three courses of bricks, while *not* immediately finding the answer by looking it up on the internet, as you stand there in the street in front of the towers. *Wondering* means that you try to answer the question yourself, first; you are more alert to picking up clues, trying to figure it out; and that means also that you will come up with various possible answers that may open yet other avenues of interest, so that the whole subject has time to expand and develop in your mind *before* you find the answer. About those bricks, I had time to wonder: Do they somehow stabilize the structure? Does it have to do with absorption of moisture? What do I know, anyway, about the relative porousness or permeability of bricks versus stone?

After I copied out, here, the journal entry I made in the Cluny Museum, I found another I had copied out from a book in French that I had bought on the trip and was reading. It provided more of an answer, embedded in a sentence (here translated into English) about something else: "a row of three superimposed bricks which served as *agrafes* for Roman builders." But what were *agrafes*? This is crucial, naturally, but I have only now looked it up: it means staples, fasteners, or hooks. I'm closer to understanding, but I still don't quite get it.

21. Speaking of not looking things up right away: Free yourself of your device, for at least certain hours of the day—or at the very least one hour. Learn to be alone, all alone, without people and without a device that is turned on. Learn to experience the purity of that kind of concentration. Develop focus, learn to focus intently on one thing, uninterrupted, for a long time.

Which reminds me of a class discussion that took place in a fiction workshop, once, about the most significant historical events of the twentieth century. I had given the perhaps misguided assignment of asking the students to create a timeline of important events in the twentieth century. I do habitually give impulsive assignments that don't always turn out well. I had in mind that we should all be able to locate ourselves generally in the twentieth century, or any century, for that matter, in relation to a few important dates. I still think that's important. If you read in the biography of a writer that his best work was done after World War II, you need to know the dates of World War II. Important events of the first half of the twentieth century might be, at the very least, World War I, the Great Depression, and World War II.

Here is a possible sequence, for the United States anyway: the Gilded Age; World War I; the Roaring Twenties; the Great Depression; World War II; the Korean War; the Vietnam War. And, closing the century, the development of the personal computer and the creation of the internet.

In the class, we had a good and protracted discussion exclusively about American history, with some of the history buffs going into amazingly sophisticated detail about a number of events whose importance I was hardly aware of, like the mechanization of the cotton industry. One student remarked later that part of her fascination with what was occurring in class was that the discussion relied entirely on what information was contained in our brains—no one consulted a device.

(Another impulsive assignment of mine was for the students to attempt, outside class, during the week, to come up with a list of all the words they could think of that began with *wr*. I forget where that assignment came from, probably from trying, myself, to think of those words and realizing how relatively few of them there were. The rule was that of course you could not look them up in a dictionary or online—you had to try to remember them yourself, but you could ask another person. This assignment had a rather interesting outcome, when we realized what all these words, or most of them—not the Cornish-derived *wrasse*, referring to a type of fish—had in common.)

22. I want to skip back to the idea of not having too much context, *context* meaning explanation, or exposition.

Saying less rather than more, which sometimes means cutting some of what you have, can be very effective: for one thing, it speeds up the pace of the writing a little; for another, the more explanation you cut, the more active the reader's mind has to be, making connections. The more active the reader's mind, the happier the reader is, usually. That's why we like jokes, or one reason why—because the joke happens in our minds; we the listeners are the ones who make the connection.

23. Cutting can be effective: it quickens the pace and involves more happening in a shorter space. But this does not mean that everything has to be short. You can write three thousand pages (as Proust did in *In Search of Lost Time*) and still be economical. In this case, economical simply means not saying more than you need to.

24. Keep in touch with the physical world. There is a lot of emphasis on sex and violence—two forms of physicality—in our culture. That is partly a result of lazy, unimaginative writing—writers for popular entertainment fall back on sensationalism to attract an audience. But maybe it is also a crude kind of substitute for the physicality that has in general been lost from our daily life. Imagine how physical life used to be. There was much more contact with animals, for instance, such as horses, cows, and chickens; the trades and crafts were individual and physical and very present on the street (the blacksmith, the shoemaker); and smells were more prevalent—horse manure, mildew, people's sweat and unwashed clothes, tobacco, woodsmoke, the dust of the roads, flowering plants, etc.

Here is a description of dust by the Bengali English writer Nirad C. Chaudhuri, whose autobiography, by the way—speaking of long books—is in two thick volumes, the first alone, called *The Autobiography of an Unknown Indian*, numbering 506 large pages. He is a patient writer of great skill. He writes at greater length than you would expect about the dusty road and going barefoot when he was a child. The passage is lovely, and economical. His thoroughness writing about the road reminds me of the thoroughness and beauty of James Agee in *Let Us Now Praise Famous Men*.

Here is just a part of the Chaudhuri passage:

> We held this soft deep dust in great affection. It offered not simply the childish delight of being able to make dust castles, but something more profound. . . . The best part of the pleasure of walking was to feel one's bare feet sinking in the dust, just as the keenest edge of the joy of kicking, that activity so natural in children and so essential for them, was in raising dust as high as the head. . . . Our road . . . was so sensitive that we could always tell which way people had gone by looking at the footprints. . . . At midday, after the great litigious crowd had gone towards the courts, the toes all pointed westward, and in the early morning eastward. In addition, in every section of the road coinciding with each house-front, there were one or more bigger depressions, showing where the pariah dog or dogs belonging or voluntarily attaching themselves to that particular house had slept the night before.

In your prose or poetry, consider how present or absent the physical world is, meaning the world as perceived through the senses. We are physically in the world, we perceive it through our bodies. Use the five senses in your writing if you want the physical world to be more a part of it: consider sight, hearing, smell, taste, and touch. Here are some more examples from a writer particularly good with description, especially smells, which are often neglected in descriptions. The examples are all from V. S. Naipaul's *A House for Mr. Biswas*:

> The blanket was hairy and prickly; it seemed to be the source of the raw, fresh smell he had been smelling all day.

> For eight months, in a bare, spacious, unpainted wooden house smelling of blue soap and incense, its floors white and smooth from constant scrubbing . . .

> . . . trying to hide the smell of drink and tobacco on his breath.

> The musty smell of old thatch was mingled with the smell of Mrs. Tulsi's medicaments: bay rum, soft candles, Canadian Healing Oil, ammonia.

Cormac McCarthy is another writer in whose work the physical world is very present, as it is in Thomas Hardy. In the work of others, such as Anthony Trollope, though he writes in engrossing detail and with great subtlety about the machinations involved in love and politics and finance, it is hardly present at all. As you read, it is a good idea to observe this particular trait; pay attention to how the physical world is treated by the author.

25. Dialogue. As I have said, there are good and excellent writers who do not make their worlds very
physical. There is no rule. Again, each writer's writing
should reflect the whole of that person, should grow
organically out of that person's being, character, and
history.

So Grace Paley was, it seems, more interested in talk,
in opinions and beliefs—political convictions, life stories,
characters, friendships. Lush description is simply not her
thing. You could take a paragraph of a Grace Paley story
and see where or when the physical world, the senses,
come in. But here, let's look at dialogue, which is so important in her work.

Dialogue is an integral part of the interpersonal
interactions central to her stories. A good example of
her use of speech is the opening of her very short story
"Wants." Another is the monologue of Aunt Rosie, the
narrator of "Goodbye and Good Luck," which opens
as follows:

> I was popular in certain circles, says Aunt Rose.
> I wasn't no thinner then, only more stationary
> in the flesh. In time to come, Lillie, don't be
> surprised—change is a fact of God. From this no
> one is excused. Only a person like your mama
> stands on one foot, she don't notice how big her
> behind is getting and sings in the canary's ear for
> thirty years. Who's listening? Papa's in the shop.
> You and Seymour, thinking about yourself. So
> she waits in a spotless kitchen for a kind word and
> thinks—poor Rosie . . .
>
> Poor Rosie! If there was more life in my little
> sister, she would know my heart is a regular col-

lege of feelings and there is such information between my corset and me that her whole married
life is a kindergarten.

Another writer worth looking at to see how much
he relies on dialogue alone is the Irish novelist Roddy
Doyle. He is very funny. His subject is family life.

26. More about dialogue. Listen to people talking and
copy down the choicer bits of what you hear. Copy
phrases, sentences. In this way, you will learn how people
really speak. We don't usually speak very coherently or
neatly. We are often very brief in our exchanges. We often communicate in sentence fragments—that is, when
we're not being overly long, stumbly, and messy, as we
grope to express what we mean. Your dialogue should
reflect how we speak, though it will often be notched up
a degree or two in order to be more intense, more colorful, and more dramatic. But above all, dialogue should
not consist entirely of neat, complete sentences.

A little story developed in my notebook out of a single line of dialogue overheard at the next table in a Soho
restaurant. The story consists of a (very long) title and
two lines:

> MATURE WOMAN TOWARD THE END
> OF A DISCUSSION OF RAINCOATS OVER LUNCH
> WITH ANOTHER MATURE WOMAN
> She says, in a reasonable tone,
> "It doesn't *have* to be a Burberry!"

Here, again, what interests me is probably a couple of
things: first, what a single line of speech reveals about a

person's culture, background, class, and character; and second, the language itself, in this case the word *Burberry*. It is, really, a funny word, in itself, but it also carries a freight of meaning for some people.

Language always catches my attention—as in the notebook entries recording "caramel drizzle" and "going potty."

I relish the way people talk. And it is not just the combination of words, the sound of the language, the perhaps unexpected vocabulary, but also, of course, what it reveals about the people who are speaking.

Here is more dialogue recorded in the notebook:

a. Youngish couple in airport shop, with baby, staring at a shelf:
Husband: "Let's go somewhere else—these are all packaged."
Wife: "But that's what we're *looking* for!"

In fact, a favorite recent hobby of mine is listening to people who are having these short conversations so as to arrive at a decision together—this is especially good to listen for when you are traveling, because that is when couples are often making decisions together, acting as a single unit. And they are a little tense or preoccupied, so they are not likely to notice you listening in on their conversations.

b. Older married couple standing outside the restrooms in the airport:
Woman: "I'll wait here."
Man: "You're not going to go?"

Woman: "Well, maybe I should."
Man: "It might be a good idea."

A long wait in a doctor's or dentist's waiting room is another opportunity for eavesdropping and taking notes.

c. A rather gloomy elderly man sits next to his wife in the eye doctor's waiting room. He is looking around the room. He says to her, after a silence, looking not at her but at a door next to the receptionist's desk:

"They're going to come through that door there."

What I liked here was, first, the language—"that door there"—and the drama it suggested, and, second, the way the old man supplied to his wife a small and quite unnecessary item of information, as though thinking aloud.

Here is some Denis Johnson dialogue. It fulfills no less than six requirements of dialogue for this kind of fiction: (1) it sounds natural, (2) but it is more vivid and more interesting; (3) it reveals character or is in character; (4) it reveals the relationship or is true to the relationship; (5) it reveals or enhances the characters' situation; and (6) it enhances or advances the story.

This passage is a small part of a great deal of dialogue in Johnson's story "Steady Hands at Seattle General"— really, the whole story is dialogue, after the introductory couple of paragraphs that set the scene and one later, very brief paragraph of description. One patient (the first speaker) is shaving his roommate in a rehab or detox:

> "Someday people are going to read about you in a story or a poem. Will you describe yourself for those people?"
> "Oh, I don't know. I'm a fat piece of shit, I guess."
> "No. I'm serious."
> "You're not going to write about me."
> "Hey. I'm a writer."
> "Well then, just tell them I'm overweight."
> "He's overweight."
> "I been shot twice."
> "Twice?"
> "Once by each wife, for a total of three bullets, making four holes, three ins and one out."
> "And you're still alive."
> "Are you going to change any of this for your poem?"
> "No. It's going in word for word."

The story ends (roommate speaking first):

> "Well, I'm older than you are. You can take a couple more rides on this wheel and still get out with all your arms and legs stuck on right. Not me."
> "Hey. You're doing fine."
> "Talk into here."
> "Talk into your bullet hole?"
> "Talk into my bullet hole. Tell me I'm fine."

27. A few last pieces of advice, the first about complex characters:

As you are observing people, observe the traits of complex people in particular. We are all mixtures of qualities: be aware of this, look for it, analyze your own complexity and that of the people you are close to or know well; reproduce this degree of complexity in your more important characters. What does *complex* mean? You might start with the idea of contradictory, and then see what other qualities go to make up a complex character.

28. Learn at least one foreign language in your life, either on your own (it can be enjoyable) or in a class; read regularly in that foreign language; it will give you perspective on English and teach you more about English; *and* it will develop your mind and character—to go back to that.

Here is the same advice from Sparrow, in his entertaining small-format book called *How to Survive the Coming Collapse of Civilization and other helpful hints!*:

> 18. STUDY A FOREIGN LANGUAGE
> It doesn't matter which language you study. What's important is confronting words like *szökik*.*
> *Hungarian for "jump."

29. Translate at least one piece of writing, no matter how short, in your life—you owe it to your fellow Anglophone readers, who may be monolingual, and you owe it to the literatures of other cultures. The English language is so dominant in the world today that when a writer is translated into English, he or she immediately reaches a larger audience, potentially worldwide, an audience that may include a translator who will in turn translate the work further, into yet another language.

And unlike what you may have assumed, or been taught, the most important skill you can have as a translator is not expertise in the foreign language, but the ability to write well in your own language.

30. Finally, maintain humility with regard to language and writing.

2013

VISUAL ARTISTS:
ALAN COTE

Energy in Color:
Alan Cote's Recent Paintings

Alan Cote is an abstract painter who lives and paints in an old brick school building, vintage 1930. His studio is the former gym and auditorium, where the community used to gather in the evenings, coming in by the building's side entrance, for talent shows and the like. The stage is at the far end of the large space, up a few steps, and now serves as his office. The deep and spacious main part of the room, where the little orchestra played and the audience sat, can accommodate comfortably his tall, double-sided drawing table, his three sturdy carts of paint cans, his rolling scaffolding, the stacked canvases leaning against a side wall, and the one large wall on which he paints. The arched windows on two sides are lofty and ample, filling the space with floods of northeastern and northwestern light. Cats wander in and out, sit on one or the other of the two large speakers and watch what he is doing, or settle to sleep on a chair before a low table piled with books, or stretch out along the tops of the leaning canvases.

After fifteen years of the life of a New York City painter (Greenwich Street in Tribeca, when that part of town was the fruit, vegetable, and dairy market district and rents were $200/month; when dealers sought painters instead of vice versa), Cote moved north a couple of hundred miles to live and work in a vast old tugboat shop that looked out on the Rondout Creek, a tributary of the Hudson. In the early spring he could hear the ice booming; waterfowl nested in the rotten, half-submerged barges against the far bank. Now he has moved again, farther north and deeper into the country, at the edge of a rural village. Here he has increasingly concentrated his focus on what can be done within a few consistent constraints. He finds there is great freedom within constraints—even, perhaps, more freedom than with no constraints at all.

Cote's paintings have always been large, occasionally, in the past, filling an entire wall of a sizable gallery. He sometimes does a small or very small painting, but this is a rare departure. A number, at various times, of the earlier paintings were shaped canvases, but most of his paintings, over the years, have been single rectan-

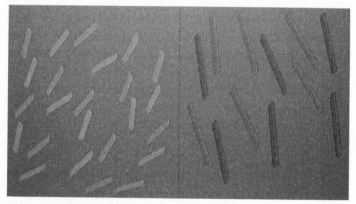

Figure 1 (2013, 72 × 130 in.)

gles or squares. Now, for the past two decades or so, he has been working with two-panel paintings. This was a form in which he worked briefly some decades ago, and, oddly—as the painter has little control over the eventual fate of his work—some of those panels were sold separately, consigned to exist the rest of their lives on their own. One hangs, without its partner, in a college library. Its matching panel is in a museum collection; another he has reacquired, and it leans against other paintings in his storage barn, while its partner is in a private collection somewhere out West.

This, then, is one consistent feature of Cote's recent paintings. Each of the two panels is painted with a colored ground, the colors of the two grounds being sometimes radically different; sometimes exactly the same, as in the orange/orange painting, Figure 1, as reproduced here; and sometimes close in color and/or tone—*tone* meaning lightness or darkness of the color—as in, for instance, Figure 2, the darker yellow/lighter yellow painting in which the two yellows converse and interact, the activity heightened because the tones are so close.

Why two panels rather than a single rectangle? What is the different effect of two panels on the viewer? Whereas the single canvas tends to act somewhat as a window, the viewer looking directly at and into the canvas, with the two-panel painting, the relationship is radically altered: there is interaction between the two panels, with viewer either as onlooker—some of the tension shifting from the relationship between viewer and painting to the relationship between the two panels—or as participant in a triangular relationship: panel to panel to viewer. Another consistent feature has been the

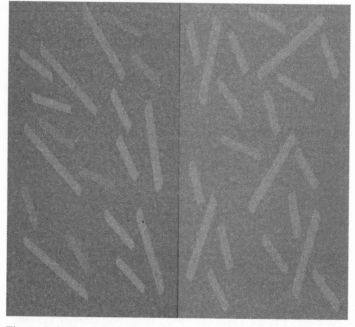

Figure 2 (2014, 84×92 in.)

repeating shapes painted on the grounds, which could be called bars, but which Cote calls by a more neutral, and nonreferential, name—elements. Cote sees the element as something between a line and a shape, and having some of the characteristics of both. For a time, the elements were thinner, and precisely taped before being painted, whereas now the human hand is allowed a more visible presence. They are drawn directly on the ground in colored pencil, using a shaped cardboard guide. They are then painted freehand. The result is precise, geometrical, and neat, but not mechanically precise, not ruler-straight; rather, there is the slightest imprecision in the straight line, which subtly evokes the presence and motion, and the vulnerability, of the fallible human hand: they are not intended to be perfect.

The ends of each element used to be sharper, and are now more curved; with a curving rather than sharp end, not only does the eye move more slowly as it traverses the painting, but the motion of the hand is also more apparent, and thus the hand itself is more obviously present.

The elements were for some years, in the 1980s and early 1990s, horizontal and vertical. Now, and going back more than fifteen years, they are diagonal. The horizontal line can be a challenge because it often suggests landscape. Cote chose to free himself of that reference and work with the diagonal. The diagonal is inherently more unpredictable. It is alive, dynamic rather than static: there is more motion in it. "The painting has to have visual energy that is apparent. That visual energy is the *necessity* of a painting," he says.

Sometimes that motion is explosive, even dramatic, as in Figure 3, with grounds of different shades within a single panel, longer elements, and more insistent motion in one direction (if we see them moving left to right); sometimes it is quieter, more meditative, the elements floating up the canvas and toward the space above, beyond the limits of the painting; or across the canvas; or drifting down, as in Figure 4, with its shorter, relatively thicker elements, gentler colors, and random-seeming (not random in actuality, of course) placement on the ground. (Naturally, but also disconcertingly, one viewer will see motion up, and another down, in the same elements.) These diagonals, painted as they are, could be seen as a geometric gestures.

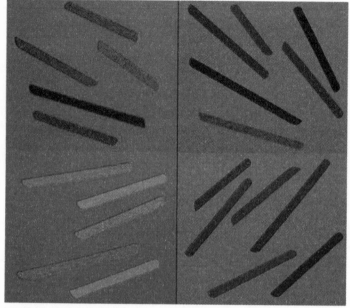

Figure 3 (2009, 84×96 in.)

The angles of their placement are sometimes steeper and sometimes flatter (i.e., more toward the vertical or more toward the horizontal): the elements in the white/blue-ground painting, Figure 5, are the most horizontal that Cote has done in many years. Most often, though not always, the elements are contained within the edges of the canvas, not touching the edges or moving off them either at the outer edges or at the center. Most often, each element is separate from the others, moving independently, though it is subtly associated with a finite number of others by the sharing of tone or color.

The elements are usually arranged in equal numbers

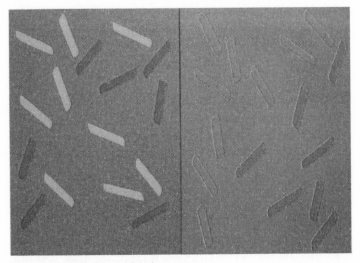

Figure 4 (2013, 70 × 100 in.)

on the two panels, but not always. In Figure 1, with its orange/orange grounds, for instance, a different balance is achieved: the elements on the right panel are twice as long as elements on the left panel, but half in number. In Figure 2, darker yellow/lighter yellow, they are asymmetrical in number but achieve balance through the fact that the smaller number of elements have greater optical radiance.

Thus, what changes from one painting to the next, besides the overall dimension of the painting and the colors of the grounds, are the numbers and sizes of the elements, their placement on the canvas, their orientation, and, of course, their colors and tones.

Another constant is Cote's manner of applying the paint that will form the ground: in many layers, but thin, even, and flat, rather than textured. Cote prepares the canvas by applying three coats of gesso before applying three or four coats of ground. What might seem a mechanical activity serves a purpose, which is to give him a deeply assimilated sense of the size, and the dimensions, of each panel. Cote's intention is that the paint should not call attention to itself, as it would in a more thickly applied, textured surface. His aim is to avoid that distraction—toward texture, toward the paint, toward the gesture, toward the history of applying the paint— from his primary concern, which is attention to color and tone. Cote's primary interest is in color, along with placement; and the activity of the drawn in relation to the activity of the color. He is interested in the energy in color, and in realizing that energy, the life that is in color. What is its life? Its life is the emotion it conveys, since it is not serving to depict something. Although his paintings are not figurative, not about phenomena, do not depict things in the world, they are nevertheless about human relations and emotions, via the life and energy in color itself.

What occurs in the process of developing the painting is this: in his preliminary drawings, which are done on a small scale and without color, and then through his color studies, which go through many changes before resolving in decisions about the placement and color of the elements, Cote finds an initial, working "solution" to the "problem" posed beforehand by the painting; he evolves an idea of what the painting will be; and he decides on the colors, tones, and placement of the elements in the painting—how to relate what is behind (that is, the ground) to what is in front (that is, the elements). He finds certain directions he wants the painting to take. This is done intuitively; he gravitates toward certain relations of color and tone.

Then, as he actually engages in painting it, the painting once again opens itself to question; the painting changes, becomes active in determining its own evolution, refuses certain solutions, suggests others, evolves in unexpected directions. It grows from his observation of it, not from something outside of it. Cote thus works his way from the known into the unknown, and the painting, as a result, is new to him, a new presence. Even as he works with a set of choices similar to those of previous paintings, the painting must be, he says, a painting he has never done before. At the same time, he is working from disorder, in the process of the exploration, to order, in the finished outcome. "Logic should allow for illogic within it," he says.

What does not change, within the process of creating the painting, is the color of each ground, once determined, and the size and positioning of the elements on the ground. What does change, over days and weeks, is the color and/or the tone of the elements. By organizing the placement of the elements beforehand, he allows for freedom in his use of color and tone. In some paintings, as in Figure 3, the differences among the colors or tones of the elements are obvious; in others (for instance, Figure 5, red, white, and blue), the elements on the two panels contain the same colors, yet because the grounds are different, the colors of the elements also appear to be different. Or, in one panel of a given painting, though not in the other—as in the right-hand panel of Figure 4— the difference in tones of the elements may be almost imperceptible at first (especially in reproduction, but even in the presence of the painting itself) and then gradually become more and more conspicuous the longer one continues to look, until it seems as obvious, in the end, as it was hard to perceive in the beginning. (But, Cote points out, you don't have to know the colors are the same; you just have to experience what effect this has on you.)

As the painting evolves, then, the color and/or tone of the elements changes; and in fact, in consequence, the ground itself, though its color and tone are not touched again once they have been applied, also changes in response to the changes in colors and tones of the elements applied on it. In some sense, all the preparation of the drawn elements and the colors of the grounds is done in preparation for then altering color and tone within the elements, to create the relationship between the elements and the grounds, and also, more surprisingly, between the two grounds. For each ground itself is active in the painting, its activity determined by the elements on the surface. Conversely, Cote may establish symmetry in the different aspects of the painting, through sequences and sets of numbers, and then has the option of unbalancing it through the colors he puts on the elements. The painting, in the end, because of the particular use of color and tone, may feel *un*balanced, working against the symmetry supplied by the drawn elements.

Most complex, then, is this question of balance, the relation of symmetry and asymmetry in the paintings, the interplay of different kinds of balance between the numbers of elements, their sizes, and their colors. The two-panel structure itself implies, as a premise, a concern with balance, and the symmetry or asymmetry of the elements continues and complicates the preoccupation with balance.

To look at balance or symmetry in a little more detail, we may follow what is happening within a single painting. In the white/blue-ground painting with red-orange elements, Figure 5, Cote worked from a series of decisions—about the horizontality of the diagonals, about the ground color choices of dark blue and pure white, about the length of the elements. These particular diagonals appear almost horizontal. The lengths of the elements are the same on both panels: there are two sets of four each, with what seems like an "off" middle between the sets. There are three "spines": one implied vertical in the middle of each panel and one physical vertical where the two panels meet. Each set of four elements within each panel is of four different colors, but those colors repeat within each panel, though reversed in order: 4321 and 1234. The elements are asymmetrical in position, but symmetrical in number and color. They are deep in tone because the blue ground is deep in tone: the tones of the red-oranges need to be deep in order to be in the right relation to the deep blue, for us to sense that they have an attachment to the blue. (On a scale of 1 to 10, in depth, the elements would be a 7 or 8.) The interaction of the elements and the grounds is contrapuntal: the blue *comes to* the red-oranges; the blue *gives* to the red-oranges and the red-oranges *give* to the blue at the same time as they set up an opposition to it. The white ground separates from the elements, pushes them out toward us, whereas the blue ground magnetizes the red-orange elements, so that they relate chromatically to it. They therefore relate both chromatically and contrapuntally.

Because of the arrangement of the drawn elements, those on the blue ground appear to rise from the implied vertical between the two sets of four, whereas those on the white side appear to descend from the implied

Figure 5 (2014, 40×92 in.)

vertical. The ends of the elements on the left are tapered one way, the ends of the elements on the right are tapered the other way.

Cote works with contrasts and oppositions: the balance of planned versus intuitive or spontaneous; of disorder evolving into order, of measured versus rough, of ground and elements; of simplicity (of parts) versus complexity (of the whole).

The formal constraints are privately imposed; the results are then public.

So it is within these repeated constraints that Cote explores what can be done—and perhaps the possibilities are infinite—with depth versus surface, with activity, dynamism, symmetry, asymmetry, balance, motion versus stasis, motion into and out from the canvas, motion up and down the canvas, convexity versus concavity of the painting, motion of the elements versus the ground, prominence of the elements versus the ground, using simple factors to create a complex work, and more.

Viewers find the paintings electric. Some find that a painting appears convex, the middle coming out toward them: they walk up to the painting to make sure. Some viewers see the elements moving up, while others see them moving down, moving quickly or slowly. A painting of his has no particular *narrative meaning* or *message*, says Cote. You don't read it; you work on it visually. You have to look at it over time. You have to want it.

It is like music, he says: We accept sound; are we willing to accept color—the way things look? That is harder. We are used to accepting music—it has always been abstract.

2014

WRITERS (2)

"Emmy Moore's Journal"
by Jane Bowles

Many of Jane Bowles's typical superb narrative characteristics are evident in just the first two pages of this
small story: the clear and forceful narrating voice; the odd
female protagonist; the humor arising from this eccentric protagonist's worldview; her obviously tenuous hold
on "reality"; the inevitable distinct and funny secondary
characters (here, the "society salesman" whom the narrator has "accosted" in the Blue Bonnet Room); the
pathos of the main character's valor, disorientation, and
ultimate defeat.

A closer look, tracing the progress of the story over
just these two pages, sentence by sentence, shows the
following shifts: The story opens without prologue or
preamble, with a clear and plain declaration in simple,
forceful language, by a strong first-person voice: "On certain days I forget why I'm here." Already, we experience
this narrator as emphatic but not quite in this life or not
quite competent. In the second sentence, we sense a certain insecurity: "Today once again I wrote my husband
all my reasons for coming." The fact of her introducing
him as "my husband," instead of by his name, suggests
that she wishes to stress his role in relation to her rather

than his unique individual identity in a larger public world. In the third sentence, her reliance on him ("He encouraged me to come") as well as her insecurity ("each time I was in doubt") is further stressed. She hesitates, he urges. In these first three sentences, we haven't yet seen any sign of the humor that is almost omnipresent in Bowles's writing. In the fourth sentence, it appears: first, along with a reiteration of her husband's authority, there is the oddity of the faux-clinical phrase "state of vagueness": "He said that the worst danger for me was a state of vagueness." Then comes the name of the hotel, so prosaic, so deliberately flat or unromantic (for a hotel): "so I wrote telling him why I had come to the Hotel Henry." (Compare her naming of Camp Cataract, in her short story of the same name.) Still in the same sentence, there is then a third moment of humor: "—my eighth letter on this subject."

But with that statement, something else has crept in. The narrator is declaring that she is writing to her husband for no less than the eighth time about why she has come to the Hotel Henry. Since this is unarguably many more times than would seem necessary to anyone else, it suggests that the narrator is someone obsessed, or highly anxious, perhaps neurotic, perhaps even seriously disturbed. The fourth sentence is not yet over, though, and now the tone changes: "but with each new letter I strengthen my position." With this change in tone comes another moment of humor, arising from the disproportion between the language used by the narrator, which might be that of diplomacy or international relations, and the subject: why she has come to the Hotel Henry. The new tone is one of sudden self-confidence.

Now the long paragraph continues in the same confident tone, which evolves, even, to sound a note of defiance: "Let there be no mistake. My journal is intended for publication." And develops, further, into the heroic, now colored by delusions of grandeur: "I want to publish for glory, but also in order to aid other women"—the choice of the lofty *aid* over the more common *help* enhancing, with a single word, the suggestion that the protagonist has unrealistically high ambitions. (Compare, in "Camp Cataract," this wonderful bit of dialogue: "'Not a night fit for man or beast,' [Harriet] shouted across to Sadie, using a voice that she thought sounded hearty and yet fashionable at the same time.")

The paragraph then relaxes a bit, rambling on with some disjointed information about her husband, his knowledge of mushrooms, herself, her physical attributes, her Anglo stock ("Born in Boston"), and some incoherent generalizations about "the women of my country." Eventually the narrator trails off altogether, lapsing into uncertain, repetitive speculations about Turkish women and their veils.

Typically, given the skewed hierarchies of Bowles's characters, the event with the best possibilities for some drama is tossed away within a parenthesis at the end of the second page: "(written yesterday, the morrow of my drunken evening in the Blue Bonnet Room when I accosted the society salesman)." The subject of drink will reappear in a deadpan, touchingly simple statement later in the story: "When I'm not drunk I like to have a cup of cocoa before going to sleep. My husband likes it too." As for the unfamiliar term *society salesman*, it will be defined through the unfolding of the story—although the incident will not be fully narrated—and the man himself, an exceptionally wealthy department-store clerk, will soon be described with Bowles's typical vivid precision and ear for the percussive possibilities of English as "a man with a lean red face and reddish hair selling materials by the bolt."

Jane Bowles's half-unworldly, off-kilter heroines are of course versions of aspects of herself, in her troubled course through an often flamboyant or exotic bohemian life to her end in a clinic in Spain, where, weakened by alcoholism and a previous stroke, she died in May 1973, at the age of fifty-six, soon after, in fact, writing "Emmy Moore's Journal." It may be too easy to say with hindsight, but the bleak return to the bottle at the end of the story—really, the story's bleakness throughout—seems to announce Bowles's imminent capitulation in her decades-long struggle with the challenges of her life, which included many episodes of manic-depressive psychosis, and of her writing, which was hard won from severe and recurring writer's block. Back in 1967, John Ashbery called her "one of the finest modern writers of fiction in any language." Although she is still considered one of the best by many contemporary writers and readers, she remains stubbornly underrecognized.

2012

Osama Alomar's Very Short Tales
in *Fullblood Arabian*

Osama Alomar, a young Syrian writer who has been living here in the United States for the past five years, belongs at once to several different important literary traditions. Most immediately evident are two: that of the writer in exile, either voluntary or involuntary, from his own country and culture; and that of the writer of very short stories.

The plight of a writer who has an established reputation in his own country, and none at all here in his adopted country, is a plight shared, of course, with immigrants of other professions, including, for instance, the Puerto Rican lawyer who leaves a thriving practice on the island to manage a small grocery store in Cambridge, Massachusetts; or the Jewish scholar or physician who flees Nazi Germany to work in a textile factory in New York. It involves the profoundly disturbing change in his identity in this new world, and often in his own eyes. His identity in his new community is, in a sense, an involuntary disguise; and he faces the challenge of holding his two identities in balance, adjusting himself to the new, keeping alive the old. Alomar left a culture in which his prizewinning fiction and poetry had been published in four collections to date, appeared regularly in literary journals, was shared out loud with appreciative others in convivial living-room gatherings. By contrast, his writing is known here to only a few. How fortunate, then, that with the publication of *Fullblood Arabian* he will begin to find an audience in the United States and in the larger Anglophone culture.

The other tradition to which Alomar most obviously belongs—in this case by choice—is that of the very short story. But this tradition is complicated, for within the genre, we have different traditions and different types. While Alomar is working within his own particular cultural heritage, he is of course also sharing in a wider international legacy of the very short story or prose poem, the more contemporary part of which spans more than a century at least: from the prose poems of Baudelaire in the mid-nineteenth century to those of Francis Ponge and other French poets of the twentieth; the lyrical and nostalgic real-life stories of the early twentieth-century Viennese Peter Altenberg and the quirky numbered "handbook" instructions of the Bohemian/Czech Dadaist and pacifist Walter Serner; the Austrian Thomas Bernhard's grim and syntactically complex paragraph-long stories in *The Voice Imitator*; the self-denigrating, anticlimactic, quarrelsome tales of the Soviet Daniil Kharms; the lyrical autobiographical sequence of the Spanish Luis Cernuda; and the pointed philosophical narratives of the contemporary Dutch writer A. L. Snijders (whose own chosen term, *zkv* or *zeer korte verhaal*—very short story—means exactly the same thing as Alomar's *al-qisa al-qasira jiddan*); to mention only a few.

And then there are the literary traditions in which the

very short story shares, and Alomar's work with it, including moral tales, fairy tales, works of magical realism, coming-of-age novels, and so forth ad infinitum. I read, for instance, Alomar's "Conversation of the Breezes" and I hear, suddenly, an echo of the voice of the swallow in Oscar Wilde's very moving late nineteenth-century tale "The Happy Prince." I read his "Sea Journey," in which a weary office worker dreams of delirious adventures in the waves and wakes to find he is late for work, and I am reminded not only of Kafka but also of the great early twentieth-century Dutch writer Nescio, both of whom so vividly evoke the man of imagination stuck within the rigid entrenched bureaucracy of the madly irksome office routine. Again I think of Nescio's classic, *Amsterdam Stories*, with its interrelated stories of three pals growing up together, and also of a long early section of the multivolume *My Struggle*, by the contemporary Norwegian Karl Ove Knausgaard, when I read Alomar's "Dividing Line," one of the rare longer stories in the book and a succinct and crystalline tale of adolescent exuberance, heedlessness, rebellion, and epiphany. And—to return to the short form—Alomar's insidious and powerful tale "The Hammer and the Nail," deploying personification with such utter ease and inevitability, reminds me of the terrifying absurdist domestic fables of the contemporary American poet Russell Edson, while the eccentricity and anguish underlying the occasional simple friendly tale remind me of the weird and powerful twentieth-century Brazilian Clarice Lispector, one of whose main forms was also the short story.

Although my frame of reference may be international, it is not particularly Syrian, which is of course my own loss. I have turned to Alomar's translator, C. J. Collins, to learn what, in Alomar's Syrian or Arabic heritage, have been the sources of his inspiration, particularly in the short form, and he has given me some interesting insights into the history of the form in the Middle East, both recent and older. There was an explosion of this form of writing in Syria in the 1990s; it became popular in magazines and newspapers as an expression of frustration at Syria's bureaucracy, corruption, and lack of freedom of expression, since the short-short form allowed for more ambiguity than did the novel, for instance, and thus made it easier to write social and political critiques without drawing unwanted attention. In an economically depressed time, too, there was a demand for the densest, briefest, most compressed of stories; a longer literary work was in fact a luxury—time to write was scarce, and authors were expected to pay up front for publication of their books and to take responsibility for distributing them to bookstores. A book was expensive to buy, at a time when Syrians had little disposable income, whereas newspapers, besides being more accessible and affordable for readers, paid authors relatively well, and reliably. So access to literary works in those years tended to come through what was published in newspapers or shared informally, often orally; short-short stories were shared and circulated as freely and easily as we in this culture would share a joke.

One of the best-known contemporary practitioners of the Arabic-language short story is the Syrian Zakaria Tamer, now in his eighties—many of his story collections have been translated into English and are available here. Going back another fifty years, there is the Lebanese literary and political rebel Kahlil Gibran, with his formally innovative spiritual stories or prose poems, hugely popular in the American counterculture of the sixties and an important influence on Alomar (Gibran himself being profoundly influenced by the earlier cosmopolitan Syrian prose poet Francis Marrash, who died in 1873). But the very short form has its roots in various Arabic literary traditions that go back to the Middle Ages and before, one important example being the mammoth story compilation *One Thousand and One Nights* (whose multicultural origins lie in the tenth century or arguably even earlier) and fable traditions like the *Kalila wa Dimna*, a third-century Indian set of interrelated animal fables imported into Arabic in the eighth century.

The personification of animal characters in the *Kalila wa Dimna*, for instance, finds its direct descendent in the naturalness and conviction with which Alomar personifies many of his protagonists, whether they be natural elements—the ocean, a lake, fire and water, breezes, clouds—or everyday objects such as a wistful and ambitious drop of oil, that cruel hammer and that gullible nail, a proud bag of garbage—or, yet again, abstractions such as freedom and time, allowing us to move easily into the alternate reality created in so many of these stories, whose forms range from moral fable to political fable to political allegory, to myth, to realistic moral tale, even to undisguised political statement, as in the title story, with its crushing final sentence.

The range of forms within this collection of stories is matched by the versatility with which Alomar shifts tone, subject matter, and even structure from one story to the next. While some of the tales are explicitly angry or bitter, others are ironically detached, and still others make their point with a piece of sly wit, one of these being "The Pride of the Garbage," in which a bag loaded with trash, in its vainglory, is satisfied only if it is placed on the very top of the heap of bags bound for the dump. Formally, some stories proceed straight to the final shock or stunning image, as in "The Drop," with its beautiful closing opposition of earth and sky. In others, the focus shifts smoothly, subtly, and naturally throughout the story, so that, to our surprise, the subject turns out to be something quite other than what we expected.

One of these might be "Expired Eyes," in which the firm grounding of the plot in a realistic situation (a man enters his apartment after a day at work) allows us to accept its fantastical, perhaps futuristic ending (the man goes to his doctor to acquire a set of new eyes): here, realism is skillfully deployed, along with a reverberating emotional truth, in the service of fantasy. In Alomar's stories, however, fantasy never devolves into mere whimsy. His magical imaginative creations are, every one, inspired by his deeply felt philosophical, moral, and political convictions, giving these tales a heartfelt urgency.

"Tongue Tie," one of the simplest, neatest, and hardest-hitting, in its humorous restraint, ably illustrates this and can be quoted in full, being also one of the briefest:

> Before leaving for work I tied my tongue into a great tie. My colleagues congratulated me on my elegance. They praised me to our boss, who expressed admiration and ordered all employees to follow my example!

2013

Haunting the Flea Market:
Roger Lewinter's
The Attraction of Things

28. If we choose to take Lewinter's story for the truth—
and it is no doubt close to the truth, since Lewinter con-
siders it a piece of autobiography—we could say this: if
his mother had had her way, he would not now be living
alone in Geneva writing, translating, and allowing himself to be weirdly, mystically involved with such things
as Kashmir shawls, plants, and men-strangers glimpsed
in the flea market or invited up from the street, but
would be an academic, an academic married to a woman
named Michèle.

31. What is his world? It is: his literary work, his intellectual preoccupations, his mother and father, his friendships, his flea market searches, his eccentric and erratic
love life.

22. The flea market as commerce in used things, or usually used things—things available only by chance, and,
often, seldom; things presided over by the dealers in
these rare, often much-desired commodities—who chose
them, endorsed them, now display them, and put a value
on them; things often imbued with the intimacy of

having belonged to others; things covered by a patina of the touches of others.

27. Some of the names in the book are: Margaretha Honegger, Musset, Binswanger, Kazuo Ohno, Alfred Hitchcock, Anthony Perkins, Moriaud, Sandra

6. He is like Maurice Blanchot in that he resists summary. The way to read his work being to experience it word by word and phrase by phrase, to live it and live inside it as it goes forward. Not to try to reduce it to a précis.

5. Some of these long sentences require more than one reading: read them all the way through and then all the way through again; or read each phrase more than once and go on to the next.

29. More names: André Bonnard, Spontini, Sophocles, Rosa Ponselle, Neury, Callas

30. The end of one paragraph spins off into a realm abstract, sometimes mysterious, sometimes only half understood, on first reading. Example (in Careau's exact translation): "with a patience that I didn't understand was intended for me, orienting me then in the space from which, through her gaze, radiated the highest pitch of divine madness." After which, in the beginning of the next paragraph, we are returned calmly to a more quotidian reality, and grounded: "On Friday, May 27, at noon, while, at my father's, I attended to the meal . . ."

7. A new paragraph is indeed experienced as a fresh start—following a deep breath—rather than as a continuation. Or, as a continuation, but from a fresh angle.

4. Wilhelm Fränger, Bosch, Musil, Georg Groddeck, Martin Grotjahn, Geneviève Serreau

34. His asides. How strange is this punctuation!: the dash followed by the comma, something we don't do in English. It often indicates that we have come to the end of an aside before a pause, or before the second of a pair of commas. There are many asides. They imply a hierarchy of thoughts. Not a hierarchy in importance, necessarily, but a hierarchy of order, how information is presented within a particular sentence. The asides are contained within pairs of dashes, and also within pairs of commas.

21. Godefroy, Gérard, Schütz

20A. Another eccentricity of punctuation: a colon followed within the same sentence by another colon. He presents us with this idea, and then, still within this idea, presents us with another. A colon, or more than one, or a semicolon, or more than one, may also be contained within a pair of dashes, the dashes being widely separated, to hold all that information. And perhaps it is not so much about asides and more about containment. The punctuation of containment within a sentence. Like the containment of the flea market objects, within the rooms of his apartment.

3. He is perhaps, with his own elaborate constructions, agreeing with Proust's idea that one thought, however long or complex, however qualified or digressive, should be contained within a single sentence.

19. Marcella Sembrich, Rainer Maria Rilke, St. John of the Cross

9. Convincing are the repeated "whens" and "whiles." Implying an earnest effort to locate events in time; the evident effort implying the narrator's seriousness: he is endeavoring to be accurate, and we should trust him.

26. He seems to be establishing some essential information—as though "for the record."

8. There is also an illusion of dependability regarding his specific dates, frequently offered: "It was in February 1980 that I first heard of La Argentina"; "In July, one Saturday at the flea market"; "since the previous September." The firmness with which dates and days of the week are supplied seems to tell us that this report is true, that this report is trustworthy. But of course we should be a little wary in trusting it.

23. La Argentina, Roger Kempf, Madame de La Fayette, Denis Diderot, Marivaud, Suzanne Cordelier

24. The proprietors of the booths or stalls at the flea market are also named, in a matter-of-fact way, as though they and their presence are inevitable: Julmy, Leuba, Novel, Pauline Cohenoff. They are often named only with single names, without description—as though for persons of such solidity and importance, description is superfluous. The proprietors of the stalls become oracles, or minor gods or goddesses, like Aeolus, Aether, Aristaeus, Artemis, Asclepius. They grant favors—precious items, precious goods—in return for a tribute, which is money. As well as, no doubt, the tribute of respect.

38. There is the touch of the dealers on these objects, and the touch of others before them on the objects that

Lewinter's protagonist (who is evidently Lewinter himself) will in turn touch, and then there is the touch of strangers on the body of the protagonist, strangers who have also been brought home from public places, brought in off the street, and who have also been touched by others, possibly many others.

35. Anne-Lise, Ria Ginster, Joseph Roth (whose novel *The Radetzky March* is found at the flea market)

36. As though the flea market were the only possible source of goods, as in the case of the Roth novel, acquired for his father for one franc. If you can't find it there, by chance, then you will have to read something else.

32. Alexandre Brongniart, Houdon

36A. As though this were during a time of war, or this were a black market. *You* want a pound of ball bearings; *I* want Roth's *Radetzky March*.

33. Stall proprietors Lometto, Fontanet, Madame Inès, Csillagi

37. Sabine, at the Ange du Bizarre, Audéoud

2016

Red Mittens: Anselm Hollo's Translation from the Cheremiss

[UNTITLED]

FROM THE CHEREMISS

TRANSLATION BY ANSELM HOLLO

i shouldn't have started these red wool mittens.
they're done now,
but my life is over.

I rarely cry over a poem. Maybe it is easier for me to cry over something that is not so good, something in which the sentiment is very obvious, very frontal, completely lacking in subtlety and finesse. The bluntness of the sentiment may be relaxing, and maybe it is easier to cry when you're relaxed, or when your brain is not asked to be very perceptive. When I read a really good poem that moves me, I am at the same time slightly distracted by how good it is, and by considerations of the ways in which it is good. I am so interested in how it works that my thinking brain is as engaged with it as my heart is. Of course, sometimes my brain is engaged first and then, afterward, my heart, and part of my emotion comes simply from how good the poem is. But I would not cry over that—it would make me happy. Even a sad or very serious poem that was very good might make me deeply happy, or deeply happy at the same time that I am moved, almost to tears.

I want to talk about this very brief poem, a translation by Anselm Hollo—who died not many years ago (2013)—because it has both moved and mystified me for the past thirty years or so that I have kept it nearby, sometimes in front of me on a bulletin board and sometimes in my memory, though in that case somewhat inaccurately reproduced, even though it is so brief. In the physical form in which I have it, it is printed on a postcard published in 1980 that has suffered from the passage of the decades, two corners chipped away, one edge slightly torn, the front still whitish but fly-specked, the back not yellowed but browned, almost burnt, with age.

Anselm Hollo was born in 1934 in Finland, and after living in Germany, Austria, and England, he finally settled in the United States in the late 1960s. He had a long career of writing eccentric, rebellious poems ("give up your ampersands & lowercase 'i's / they still won't like you / the bosses of official verse culture") and translating (from no fewer than five languages). I do not believe I ever met him in person, but I corresponded with him briefly. I have just reread the one letter I can find from him, and I can tell from it that I wrote him twice about this poem, forgetting, the second time, that I had written him before. The first letter he did not answer, the second he did. He told me then: "The little poem is a translation from traditional Cheremiss/Mari folk sayings, and I still like it too."

Several things about the poem mystify me. One is that within such a very short span (sixteen words) it inclusively conveys so many contradictory emotions: pathos and humor, absurdity and seriousness, apparently frank and

earnest statement, and obviously fictive storytelling. Part
of the fiction is the narrator him- or herself: who is this
"i"? Surely not the poet. Another part is the knitting
of the red wool mittens—surely the poet did not knit
them, and surely no one knit them, not even the fictional
"i." They are a fiction. (I may of course be wrong on
all these counts. But then that would be another way in
which we have been misled by the poet, teased into believing he is telling a tall tale.)

Then there is the fake monumentality of the project,
as conveyed to us: it has taken a lifetime to knit these
mittens; they were the project of a lifetime; there was an
intention to knit them and it was carried out—though
at what cost! That is the absurdity. The project was monumental, and absurd. But, importantly, the voice of this
fictional narrator is not absurd. The voice is plain, earnest, direct, scared, alone at the end. There is nothing
fictional about a life being over. Hollo's own life is in fact
over, though long after he translated the poem.

That the life is over is one part of what I find moving,
in particular that it is over with just one thing, the poem
implies, accomplished—those red wool mittens. One
thing, it would seem, that consumed so much attention,
that consumed so much of other things, perhaps—time,
skill, devotion—that the life itself went by almost un-
noticed. The one thing was accomplished, but the life is
over. And the one thing was hardly monumental, really,
in the end.

What mystifies me is also something I find profoundly
satisfying. The question is: How can a three-line poem
that is on the surface quite simple and direct—three plain,
everyday statements—continue in some way to surprise
me, each time I read it, not by its content, which I don't
forget, but by something else? I think I may have one pos-

sible answer to what that is: it may be the change of register within the poem. The opening statement is one that any of us has probably made over and over, in irritation or regret, about one thing or another—that we never should have started whatever it was. The second statement, too, is a familiar one, one we might make about the first, whatever the project was. We are tired, annoyed, impatient with ourselves—it's done now, but we regret it. But the third statement is out of all proportion to what has gone before—huge, devastating, vastly greater and of a significance entirely different from that of the first two statements. The disproportion or incongruity is the source of the humor of the last line, but also of its pathos. It is comically disproportionate, but agonizingly true, as though, really, the poet is saying: I never should have started this life, because I have lived it but now it is over.

The poem may also continue to surprise me because it always slightly eludes me; try as I may, I can never quite assimilate it. I find this quality in the poem exemplary, because it is doing the rare thing that a good piece of writing strives to do and sometimes manages: it never dies, it never becomes stale and familiar, it perpetually renews itself; it is born and lives over and over; it begins, continues, and ends, without losing its freshness and surprise; it continues to have an impact. Smart and capacious though we readers are, the poem avoids being learned by us—it defies assimilation.

That is a lot to say about such a brief poem, but it seems to ask for it.

2015

In Search of Difficult Edward Dahlberg

Between *Two Years Before the Mast* (by Richard Henry Dana, Jr., published in 1840, written while he was still an undergraduate at Harvard, after interrupting his studies for health reasons to spend, in fact, something over two years intermittently before the mast as a common seaman sailing from Boston to California and back) and Robert Creeley's *The Collected Prose* (containing a piece called "Three Fate Tales" that includes a description of a mouse and its shadow moving across the snow under a full moon into the storyteller's shadow and thence onto the storyteller's arm as a cat and its shadow wait), on the shelf there are three books together: *Bottom Dogs* (City Lights Books, 1930, 1961); *The Edward Dahlberg Reader* (New Directions, 1967); and *The Leafless American* (McPherson and Co., 1986). Another I thought I had, once I am reminded of it, is missing—where is it?—*Because I Was Flesh.* Is it on another shelf in the house, somewhere upstairs? No—another apartment, another life? I see the spine clear as day—somewhere.

I am looking because of a conversation last night over dinner in a restaurant sitting at a long table across from Ursule Molinaro (whose entire novel *Positions with*

White Roses is narrated by a woman who is sitting on the long side of the dinner table with her parents—this is the "normal daughter," the "visiting daughter") and her publisher Bruce McPherson, and next to Matthew Stadler. Also present, but presently out of earshot at the far end of the long table full of people, is Lynne Tillman (*Cast in Doubt, Madame Realism, The Broad Picture*), who had invited Molinaro out from the city.

I ask Ursule what she thinks of Dahlberg. But that is after she has asked me, and the company in general, about Jane Bowles, whom she does not like, preferring Paul Bowles, as though one must choose between them. She likes Buzzati, Giorgio Manganelli, and one of our present company, Stadler, as well as Jaimy Gordon, also published by McPherson and Co.

Also on the list: Frederick Ted Castle, his startling and compendious suitcase of a book, *Anticipation*. Castle himself was a bit rough-edged when met coming up the stairs in a bar and addressed with admiring words by a fan descending the stairs some years ago, but *Anticipation* is inviting to read in the way of a journal or letter—open, personal, giving the impression of easiness and flexibility and good humor in the writing—and is, in addition, vast, wide-ranging, informative, opinionated, humorously self-conscious, formally adventurous, exact, and written with crystal clarity. In fact, it answers very well to a description of storytelling that Creeley gives in the introduction to his *Collected Prose*, a description I discover when poking around in the book in search of the tale I remember, the one that included the mouse in moonlight: "that intimate, familiar, localizing, detailing, speculative, emotional, unending talking." As often happens, perhaps especially in the case of a book I admire,

I did not finish reading *Anticipation*. I progressed 150 pages or so into it, about twelve years ago. Enough to know, though, as in the case of Dahlberg, that it interested me very much, and should even be set on the shelf of "possible models"—in other words, I thought of trying something like it someday.

But aren't there some shared qualities in Jane Bowles and Molinaro? For instance, the dry humor (Molinaro: "A man with many wives and little money, or perhaps it was: a little wife and much money"—I am quoting perhaps inaccurately from memory). And the characters who appear so ladylike—as for instance Molinaro's Mrs. Feathergill—but conceal sometimes criminal or potentially criminal depths. The pitiless eye for behaviors, foibles, the clear style, and the device of repeated epithets, as for instance Molinaro's "the Hispanic-looking boy."

Now the two across the table become enthusiastic about Paul Bowles. I have a large place in my heart for Jane Bowles, but agree with them that Paul Bowles's *The Sheltering Sky* is admirable as a piece of writing, if horrifying, of course, as a tale. I continue to think of the McPherson list, and come to Dahlberg. I bring up his name, and the general opinion at the table goes against him.

I know Dahlberg interests me, though, again, I have read only a little, a long time ago, a few passages from one book or two. That was enough at the time, enough to learn something from, and to know to keep that book, and keep it handy. I always intended to read more of it, the rest of it, and more of his other books, just as I always intended, and still intend, to read the rest of other books, the whole of many other books, on my shelves, later—as though, when I retire. But retire from what?

What about Dahlberg? Why do I not hear his name often? Was he surly, too, brusque in social exchanges, like the interesting stylist Ted Castle? Is that why certain writers so emphatically do not like him? Will one be forgotten, no matter how fine a writer, if one is sufficiently unpleasant or offensive in company or in friendships? Did he suffer too much, and announce his suffering? Robert Creeley, I will later discover, called him "the necessary Job of our collective American letters." Does McPherson publish only nice or at least civil women and cranky, crabby men? No, also on the list is David Matlin (*How the Night Is Divided*), perfectly civil, whom I encounter by chance some days later, in time to ask his view of Dahlberg. We are sitting at a picnic table by an old hotel. Matlin's tempered response is that Dahlberg was an important influence on certain American poets, including perhaps Charles Olson. He mentions also how superb he finds *Do These Bones Live*, a series of essays on the social and spiritual isolation of American writers, first published in 1941.

I know little about Dahlberg, really, beyond, perhaps, that his handling of language, his vocabulary, entrance me, his directness, his frankness—this is enough for me to want to keep him on the shelf, even if I have seldom picked up the books. Over that dinner, which is already receding into the past, someone had remarked, in defense of Dahlberg perhaps, that he was an underappreciated writer. Here, again, I thought, this recurring question comes up, of underappreciation and, in fact, overappreciation of writers, also of other artists. (I have been thinking, lately, of the general underappreciation

of Haydn and overappreciation of Mozart that seem
beyond correction by now—though I, too, change my
mind about that upon hearing some particular movement or melody.) Paul Bowles being also underappreciated, as is Jane Bowles. The American public may resent
expatriate Americans and withhold appreciation from
them. But then, though Dahlberg did sometimes live
abroad, expatriatism is surely irrelevant in his case. The
defender of Dahlberg had pointed out that his work
might be underappreciated because the material is so
harsh, so difficult or unpalatable, painful. Although . . .
what about Céline? he had added.

I search around in what I have, to explore this further. Here is *Bottom Dogs*, with an introduction by D. H.
Lawrence. Dahlberg's dedication reads: "For my Friend
Jonathan Williams." So he had, at the time, at least one
friend. Dahlberg comments, in his preface, written in
Spain in 1961, for a later edition: "When I finished *Bottom Dogs* in Brussels and returned to America, I was
quite ill in the hospital at Peterborough, New Hamp-
shire. . . . I was slow in recovering. The real malady was
Bottom Dogs."

Lawrence's introduction begins: "When we think of
America, and of her huge success, we never realize how
many failures have gone, and still go to build up that success. It is not till you live in America, and go a little
under the surface, that you begin to see how terrible and
brutal is the mass of failure that nourishes the roots of
the gigantic tree of dollars." (By "failure" I think Lawrence must mean poverty and the labor of the poor at
the very bottom of the social ladder.) Skimming further, I see the word *America* or *American* repeated
many times: "savage America . . . American pioneers . . .

American position today . . . position of the Red Indian . . . American soil . . . deep psychic change . . .
The American senses other people by their sweat and their
kitchens . . . their repulsive effluvia . . . American 'plumb-
ing,' American sanitation, and American kitchens . . .
American nausea . . . American townships . . . repulsion from the physical neighbour . . . *Manhattan Trans-
fer . . . Point Counter Point . . .* They stink! My God, they
stink! . . . Theodore Dreiser and Sherwood Anderson."
Still nothing about Dahlberg himself. What will Lawrence say? Ah: something about Dahlberg's main character, Lorry, and then the conclusion: "The style seems
to me excellent, fitting the matter. It is sheer bottom-dog
style, the bottom-dog mind expressing itself direct, almost as if it barked. That directness, that unsentimen-
tal and non-dramatized thoroughness of setting down
the under-dog mind surpasses anything I know. I don't
want to read any more books like this. But I am glad to
have read this one, just to know what is the last word in
repulsive consciousness, consciousness in a state of repulsion. It helps one to understand the world, and saves
one the necessity of having to follow out the phenom-
enon of physical repulsion any further, for the time
being." Bandol, 1929. He has also said: "The book is
perfectly sane: yet two more strides and it is criminal in-
sanity." That was enough for Lawrence, who was, however, Dahlberg's friend. Repulsion: I think of Céline
again. A literature expressing physical repulsion.

To place Dahlberg, in one sense: he was an American realist or naturalist preceding the line that stretches
from James T. Farrell to Jack Kerouac.

Inside the book, there is a biographical note, probably written by Dahlberg himself, describing his grim

beginnings, then his wide experience of the more difficult working world, but also his sound education:
"Dahlberg was born in 1900 in a charity maternity
hospital in Boston and at the age of five committed to
a Catholic orphanage. Before reaching his twelfth year
he was an inmate of a Jewish orphan asylum, where he
remained until he was seventeen." Occupations, after
that: Western Union messenger boy, trucker, driver
of a laundry wagon, cattle drover, dishwasher, potato
peeler, busboy, longshoreman, clerk. Education: the
University of California and Columbia University—
later, however, in *Because I Was Flesh*, he referred to
what he encountered in these institutions as "canon-
ized illiteracy" and remarked that "anybody who had
read twelve good books knew more than a doctor of
philosophy."

A standard reference book enhances the early picture,
describing him as "the illegitimate son of an itinerant
woman-barber"—who is depicted still more particularly
and colorfully, elsewhere, as "the Junoesque owner of the
Star Lady Barbershop of Kansas City."

In Dahlberg's own words (Lorry is Dahlberg as a
child):

> She moved from town to town, selling hair
> switches, giving osteopathic treatments, going on
> again when she felt the place had been played out.
> In this way she hoped to save a little money and
> establish herself in some thriving city. She had
> taken Lorry with her wherever she went.

Paul Carroll, who edited and introduced *The Dahlberg Reader*, describes Lawrence's introduction to *Bot-*

tom Dogs as "shrill, chilly." (I would add, following more or less Carroll's rhyme scheme, that it also seems *unwilling*.) In his own introduction he announces: "Three major themes distinguish Mr. Dahlberg's writings: his dialogue with the body; his criticism of other writers; and his condemnation of the modern world."

Carroll goes on to say: "Certainly there is no prose like Dahlberg's prose in all of American literature. At its best, the Dahlberg style is monumental and astonishing," evolving from "hard-bitten, bony, slangy" to "supple, bizarre, a weapon of rage and authority," and peaking after decades with "cadence and dignity . . . and . . . rich, queer erudition." Dahlberg was also described—by Sir Herbert Read, an English poet and champion of the importance of the arts to education and industry—as "a lord of the language, the heir of Sir Thomas Browne, Burton, and the Milton of the great polemical pamphlets." Yet he spent most of his years in poverty, lacking "respectable" recognition.

He despised contemporary America, rigorously hated it and condemned it, hated all that was mechanized and sophisticated that separated people from the natural world. "As for myself," he said in a letter to Sherwood Anderson, "I'm a medievalist, a horse and buggy American, a barbarian, anything, that can bring me back to the communal song of labor, sky, star, field, love."

His circle, at various times, included Anderson, Ford Madox Ford (whom he described, before he knew him well, as a "Falstaffian bag of heaving clothes"), Josephine Herbst, Karl Shapiro, Isabella Gardner, Jonathan Williams, Allen Tate, E. E. Cummings, William Carlos Williams—the last two of whom Ford grouped with Dahlberg as three "neglected" authors. He was also supported by Williams, by Archibald MacLeish, and by Robert Duncan.

The *Reader* includes literary essays, personal letters, portions of the novel *The Sorrows of Priapus*, and chapters from the autobiographical *Because I Was Flesh*. Jonathan Williams took the cover photograph of Dahlberg, and Alfred Kazin contributed a quote to the back cover that calls this "one of the few important American books published in our day." I skim through.

Here is Dahlberg coming down hard on Melville.

> *Moby-Dick*, a verbose, tractarian fable on whaling, is a book of monotonous and unrelenting gloom. . . . *Moby-Dick* is gigantology, a tract about a gibbous whale and fifteen or more lawless seamen. . . . In a book of half a millennium of pages, the adjectives alone are heavy enough to sink the Theban Towers . . . 'moody,' 'mad,' 'demonic,' 'mystic,' 'brooding,' 'crazy,' 'lunatic,' 'insane,' and 'malicious.' . . . Melville was as luckless with his metaphors. . . . His solecisms and hyperboles are mock fury. . . . This huffing treatise is glutted. . . . Melville's jadish vocabulary is swollen into the Three Furies.

Who else did he vilify? Here is a partial list, from Carroll's introduction—"What he said [at a party given for him by Isabella Gardner] about Hemingway, Faulkner, Eliot, Edmund Wilson, Pound, and, I believe, the New Critics was univocal, brilliant, sour, erudite, and unanswerable." One of the reference works adds to that list: Fitzgerald. Among the few whom he praised were Thoreau, Sherwood Anderson, and Dreiser.

Did he tend to like, in the prose of others, the sort

of thing he did himself? For one, he employed a stout, pungent Anglo-Saxon vocabulary, including unfamiliar words, with beautiful sound: "A low, squab mist hovers over the bay which damps the job-lot stucco houses" (*Because I Was Flesh*). I look up *squab* to understand this curious way he is using it. I don't immediately find any adjective, but I do find these nouns, which together give him the soft sensuousness of his metaphor: fledgling pigeon about four weeks old; short fat person; couch; cushion for chair or couch.

Another feature of his style is his manner of combining this punchy Anglo-Saxon vocabulary with literary and classical allusions in vivid descriptions: "The playgrounds in back resembled Milton's sooty flag of Acheron. They extended to the brow of the stiff, cindered gully that bent sheer downwards toward a boggy Tophet overrun with humpback bushes and skinny, sour berries." I enjoy the way "boggy Tophet" rolls off the (squab) tongue and make a halfhearted attempt to find Milton's sooty flag of Acheron.

As I sample his prose, here and there, another quality I find is the moment of irony and the glint of humor in the careful, self-conscious word choice that remind me again of Jane Bowles: "The sight of the poultry seemed to make him listless."

The preface to *The Leafless American* by Robert Creeley (written in 1986, in Waldoboro, Maine) refers us back to the subject of America again, and "the immense loneliness of this country's people," particularly the isolation of American writers:

It may be that there is truly no hope for any one of us until we remember, literally, this scarified and dislocated place we presume humanly to come from, whether the body of ground we claim as home or the physical body itself, which we have also all but lost. Dahlberg has made this determined gesture of renewal and recognition again and again in his work, and if he is, as some feel, the necessary Job of our collective American letters, he is also a resourceful friend to any who would attempt their own instruction and survival in the bedlam of contemporary life. . . . Because we have neither a history simply available to us nor the resource of a community underlying our acts, no matter their individual supposition or nature, we work in singular isolation as writers in this country. Unlike our European counterparts who work in modes and with words long established by a communal practice and habit, we have had to invent a syntax and address appropriate to the nature of our situation. . . . Therefore the extraordinary rhetorical resources of Dahlberg's writing are intensively American in nature.

Americans are the subject of the first essay in *The Leafless American*. The other short pieces concern the decline of souls in America ("May no one assume that these granitic negations comfort me"—I relish the word *granitic*); Kansas City ("a smutty and religious town . . . Homer detested Ithaca, and let me admit, I hate Kansas City"); Spain; Rome and America ("The difference between the Roman and the American empire is that we are now adopting the licentious habits of a Poppaea, or a Commodus, or a Domitian, without having first acquired stable customs, deities, or a civilization"); an unfavorable review; literature's place of low esteem in American culture at the time of writing (I can find no dates of first publications of these pieces—but certainly just now the place of literature is not one of high esteem here); Stephen Crane; Sherwood Anderson ("We are now in the long, cold night of literature, and most of the poems are composed in the Barren Grounds"; "Barren Grounds": I suspect the reference is to *The Pilgrim's Progress*, and I look through the book—another I will someday read—but I cannot find the phrase); Oscar Wilde (to whom Dahlberg is more or less unsympathetic, which disappoints); Nietzsche (sympathetic); cats and dogs, in what appears to be a parable set in biblical times; "The Garment of Ra" in a poem of many pages; the problem of governing, or not governing, one's desire.

At the book's end, there is a portrait of Dahlberg consisting of diary entries reporting encounters with him, by the American poet and artist Gerald Burns: "[1.8.73] . . . His outerworks were hard to breach, but I got through them twice without harm"; "[12.29.73] . . . He said a wonderful thing about people who don't like Ruskin." Burns reports that Dahlberg's favorite Pascal quote is: No man fears himself enough. His second favorite: Men are always surprised by their characters. "I had heard he was down on blacks," says Burns, and goes on to give some evidence of this. A bigot? Céline again, and Knut Hamsun. And that other old question again: Are we willing to admire the artistic work of a racist, a misogynist, or an anti-Semite? Are we willing even to read it? How bad does the bigotry have to be before one has to stop reading? How good does the writing have to be for one to consent to read it?

A few months ago I took part in, and then later read the results of, a survey organized and written up by the French literature professor and literary critic Alice Kaplan,

on the question of Céline and his standing among writers
now. Of the sixty-five writers who responded to the survey, thirteen said that Céline's political views had no effect
on their reading of him. At the other end of the spec-
trum, some (number not specified) refused to read him at
all. Among these was, in fact, Paul Bowles, who said, "I
have avoided him for five decades." (Other writers mentioned in the article who have been spurned for political
reasons—their work not read because of ideologically un-
acceptable positions in their texts or their lives—were Paul
Eluard, Pound, Heidegger, and Paul de Man.) One writer
who did read Céline, and was excited by the style, and the
urgency, of Céline's writing, felt that the effects of the politics were part of the complexity of the work. He said the
politics "deepen[ed] an appreciation of the dystopian and
repulsive character of this work." In the article, Edward
Dahlberg is mentioned in passing, being defined—along
with the early James T. Farrell, Dos Passos, and William
Saroyan—as a "proletarian lyric writer."

As I explore the question of Dahlberg, I find I am
doing my own limited, informal survey in casual conversations, when I encounter other writers. Two poets
more or less my age (born in the mid to late 1940s) did
read Dahlberg, but many years ago, in college, and have
only remote memories of his work, no particular impression. One essayist and translator my age was very excited
about Dahlberg in college, but would not read him now,
reacting now against what he sees as the "eighteenth-
century" style. (I don't agree about that character-
ization.) He also says that whereas he used to think
Dahlberg was a sweet man who turned into a monster
only when he wrote, he later came to believe that Dahlberg was in fact always a monster.

One fiction writer about five years younger knows the name but has never read him, has no impression of him, associates him with the thirties but confesses she may be mixing him up with another writer who writes about cats (possibly in verse form). Another fiction writer ten years younger has or may have (he is away from home and cannot check) a book of Dahlberg's on his shelf, not read, acquired ten years ago on the recommendation of another writer he admires, perhaps James Purdy but perhaps another, this book being one of the two to three hundred books not yet read that he keeps because they promise to be of value to him eventually. His strong impression, though he has not read Dahlberg, is of a vigorous playfulness in forms both short and long. Another writer still younger has no sense of Dahlberg at all, associates nothing with the name, though he knows the name. He asks when Dahlberg died. In the early eighties, I say incorrectly—the actual date is 1977. The younger writer suggests that age may be a factor in his own case—the younger the writer I ask, the less well acquainted he or she is with Dahlberg. (And it is true that those City Lights and New Directions books on my shelf appeared before and during the years when I and those two poets were in college.)

There may be something in that, or there may not, but in fact when I question one last writer, who is also the oldest, born in the first decade of the century, just a few years after Dahlberg, she becomes animated. Dahlberg? Oh yes—he was delighted to meet her husband, a literary critic. She and her husband met him in the mid-1940s on Cape Cod. He offered some sort of practical help to them, where they were staying in Wellfleet, which resulted in a misunderstanding concerning a bag of dirty laundry left in front of Dahlberg's door. "He was highly insulted!" she says. "I wish I still had his letter!" She goes on to say more generally: "Crazy fellow, crazy guy!" About his work, however, she is, like the others, vague. "Offbeat," she says, "not mainstream, anyway."

Cape Cod comes into the following, which I don't think is at all eighteenth-century. It is quite plainspoken and contemporary sounding, with just a touch of formality here and there ("I arose"), with a Hemingwayesque string of *and*s, and brandishing one ornate, pleasingly hyperbolic metaphor:

> One evening I saw her staggering about in the room, jostling against the sink and the steamer trunk. She turned to me, throwing out her hands; the tears hung upon her sagging face, and I saw there all the rivers of sorrow which are of as many colors as there are precious stones in paradise. She said to me, "I am going to die, Edward. Let me sign over to you what I still have left."
>
> I stood there, incapable of moving. Had it come, the void, the awful and irrevocable chasm between us? What should I do? Instead of taking this shrunken heap of suffering into my arms, I only shook my head. I had already stolen too much from her; I had not the strength either to lift up my guilt or to say more.
>
> Every night after that when she lay on the cot, she continued to grease her face and arms and neck with her lotions, and before going to sleep, I came to her and knelt on the floor beside her cot and kissed her, and then I arose and went to my own bed.

With the money she had given me I purchased an old house on Cape Cod and a secondhand car, and one night my wife and I sat in the car outside the flat saying goodbye to my mother. Then I watched this shamble of loneliness, less than five feet of it, covered with a begrimed and nibbled coat, walk away from me. (*Because I Was Flesh*)

I take a random look at some of the critical works I have kept on the shelf, more from a sense of duty, or caution, than eagerness to read. In Harry Levin's *The Power of Blackness*, there is no mention of Dahlberg. (But Richard Henry Dana, Jr., comes up three times. According to Levin, Melville associated himself with Dana, as he associated Ishmael with Queequeg, through the metaphor of Siamese twins. Melville praised Dana's contribution as a sincere and sympathetic witness to the sailor's way of life—"a voice from the forecastle." Melville admitted to Dana that it was hard to get poetry out of blubber. In this and another book, one about Melville, Dana's "flogging scene" is described as being more forceful, more moving, than Melville's. I also learn that Melville once asked—lamenting, in a spirit not unlike Dahlberg's, that the mystery of unexplored America had vanished—"Are the green fields gone?")

Dahlberg is not mentioned by contemporary theorists like Terry Eagleton, in the books I have. In a memoir by Alfred Kazin, I am in the right decades, but there is nothing about Dahlberg. (I learn, though, somewhat to my surprise, that the critic Edmund Wilson—one of those reviled by Dahlberg—saw nothing in Kafka, as he saw nothing in Dickinson or Frost.)

In the correspondence of James Laughlin and William

Carlos Williams there is a little more: that Dahlberg was
a member of the "Friends of William Carlos Williams,"
formed by Ford Madox Ford in 1939; that Williams
thought well enough of Dahlberg's *The Flea of Sodom*,
published by New Directions in 1950, to write something about it for the press, saying to Laughlin: "its a
unique & valuable book even tho' overpacked with wild
metaphor" (Creeley, though, I learn later, found it at the
time "dismal . . . unreadable, [a] sick, sick book"); and
that New Directions also published Dahlberg's *The Sorrows of Priapus* in 1957 with drawings by Ben Shahn.
I also learn that both Dahlberg and Shahn appear in
Book 5 of Williams's *Paterson*. Dahlberg's appearance
takes the form of a longish letter by him apparently
written from Spain. ("Plato took three journeys to Di-
onysius, the Tyrant of Syracuse, and once was almost
killed and on another occasion was nearly sold into slavery because he imagined that he influenced a devil to
model his tyranny upon The Republic," he tells "Bill,"
before talking about his morning shopping excursions
with his wife to the *panaderia* and *lecheria*.) At one
stage, before the final revision of Book 5, there was,
instead of the letter from Dahlberg, a letter from Cid
Corman. Other letters included in Book 5 are from Josephine Herbst, Allen Ginsberg ("I mean to say Paterson
is not a task like Milton going down to hell, it's a flower
to the mind too"), and Ezra Pound. I learn also, since
I continue to read backward and forward in the letters, that New Directions published Paul Bowles's *The
Sheltering Sky* in 1949 and that the book sold twenty-
five thousand copies, and that such successes (as, also,
the sales of Tennessee Williams and Thomas Merton)
made it possible for Laughlin to publish, as he says (in

1950), "kids like Hawkes." Born close to the same year as Dahlberg (1900) were Ben Shahn, Bennett Cerf (founder of Random House), Josephine Herbst, William Faulkner, F. Scott Fitzgerald.

He was of his time in America, he had the support and admiration of other writers contemporary to him, he was published by good and forward-looking presses, his writing was and sometimes still is acknowledged by other good writers to be very good, he was an important influence on certain younger writers; his subject matter was not only luscious, rhapsodic, touching, but also often sad, sordid, discouraging, something that some readers preferred to avoid; and his own nature was not only generous and passionate but also curmudgeonly.

I suppose I have been trying to answer the question of why, though Dahlberg seems to be considered worth writing about as an American author (his name appears often enough on certain lists), he is so rarely mentioned now, his work so unknown to American writers writing today. Is an answer taking shape having to do with his cantankerous, thorny personality (his "sensitive, touchy and bitter temperament regarded even by friends as somewhere between difficult and impossible," according to Tom Clark's *Charles Olson: The Allegory of a Poet's Life*); his isolation ("Blessed and burdened with one of the great voices in American literature he has long likened himself to Ishmael and Job and lived an eremitic life of writing, caring only to please himself"—Paul Carroll's introduction to the *Reader*); his offensive degree of bigotry or narrowness ("he dwelt in agreement with Homer and Euripides, neither of whom 'regarded woman as a moral animal'"—Clark's *Olson*); his glorification of rusticity and American roots and landscape, not particularly in

fashion nowadays, though his dismay over environmen-
tal degradation is very much of our times ("Perhaps no
American writer since Thoreau has been so enamoured
of our natural history, our woodlands, meadows, rivers,
and their creatures. These are the gardens we left for
lucre's apple"—Carroll in the *Reader*); his strong identification in subject matter and to some degree in style
with a proletarian literature very identified with its time
and thus, perhaps, feeling dated to us—how often do we
even use the word *proletarian*?; stylistically, his heavy
use of literary and classical allusion, also not fashionable
now?

> There are five trash towns in greater New York,
> five garbage heaps of Tofeth. A foul, thick wafer
> of iron and cement covers primeval America, be-
> neath which cry the ghosts of the crane, the mal-
> lard, the gray and white brants, the elk and the
> fallow deer. A broken obelisk at Crocodopolis has
> stood in one position for thousands of years, but
> the United States is a transient Golgotha. (*Because
> I Was Flesh*)

It occurs to me, before I settle in to read one of
Dahlberg's own books, to follow up on what Matlin said
about Charles Olson. I read around in the biography I
have by Tom Clark and discover that indeed Dahlberg
was a father figure to Olson in the beginning of their
relationship, in the mid-1930s, a Bloom to his Stephen
Dedalus, that Dahlberg influenced him in his education,
his reading, and his style. Interestingly, I discover as I
browse how Melville was involved in their relationship at
every turn—Dahlberg encouraging and helping Olson in

the beginnings of the Melville project that resulted eventually in *Call Me Ishmael*; the severing of their relationship being ostensibly caused by jealousies over certain of what Olson felt were his own ideas about Melville that appeared in Dahlberg's essay on Melville; their partial or temporary reconciliation coming about over the publication of Olson's book.

As I read about Olson, glimpses of Dahlberg's personal and professional life keep appearing, most often dark ones, filled with unhappiness: divorce; child-custody suits; a thankless job teaching freshman composition at a Brooklyn college; and "latterly," in Clark's words, Dahlberg having "descended to the meanest of free-lance wastelands."

I am eventually led to Olson's essay "Projective Verse" and Dahlberg's appearance in it: "Now (3) the *process* of the thing, how the principle can be made so to shape the energies that the form is accomplished. And I think it can be boiled down to one statement (first pounded into my head by Edward Dahlberg): ONE PERCEPTION MUST IMMEDIATELY AND DIRECTLY LEAD TO A FURTHER PERCEPTION."

Before I desist from my exploration of Dahlberg, under pressure of time, I am left with a thought about his possible importance being, for one thing at least, his influence on Olson's development as a writer and particularly on *Call Me Ishmael*: for Olson, *Do These Bones Live*, along with William Carlos Williams's *In the American Grain* and Lawrence's *Studies in Classic American Literature*, served as models of, as Clark says, "a loosely constellated associative structure from which an unstated central thesis might be allowed to emerge as a strong cumulative pattern or sense."

Having situated Dahlberg sufficiently for my purposes, for the time being anyway, I will go on to read at least *Bottom Dogs*, meanwhile looking for a copy of *Because I Was Flesh*. It will be interesting, as I will now be on the lookout, to see which, if any, Dahlberg titles turn up in secondhand bookstores. One friend has told me that Dahlberg's own library was sold, after his death, to a secondhand bookstore now in turn defunct, and that my friend bought, there, Dahlberg's own copy of Ford Madox Ford's *Selected Letters*, in which Dahlberg had underlined, he says, every "perfect Dahlberg sentence."

Then again, I haven't yet read its neighbor on the bookshelf, Dana's *Two Years Before the Mast*, either—a title that turns up regularly in library sales—and I like the prospect of a good adventure book, especially one with such an immediate opening: "The fourteenth of August was the day fixed upon for the sailing of the brig *Pilgrim* on her voyage from Boston round Cape Horn to the western coast of North America. As she was to get under weigh early in the afternoon, I made my appearance on board at twelve o'clock, in full sea-rig, and with my chest, containing an outfit for a two or three years' voyage." Especially an adventure book that includes some language I will not necessarily understand.

1997

Gustave Flaubert's *Madame Bovary*

"Yesterday evening, I started my novel. Now I begin to see stylistic difficulties that horrify me. To be simple is no small matter." This is what Flaubert wrote to his friend, lover, and fellow writer Louise Colet on the evening of September 20, 1851, and the novel he was referring to was *Madame Bovary*. He was then just under thirty years old.

Picture a large man, handsome though fleshy and prematurely balding, with clear green eyes and a voice that could be loud and gruff (he was known to "bellow," both while trying out his sentences and while having dinner with his friends), bent over his desk, working with a goose-quill pen (he abhorred a metal nib) by lamplight. He writes very slowly and painfully, drafting—and revising—much more material than he will keep in the end. His concentration is deep, intense, and enduring; he stays with his work for many hours at a time. His mother will sometimes leave the house all afternoon to do an errand in town and find him, on her return, in exactly the same position as when she left.

Generally, he starts writing in the early afternoon and continues until the early hours of the morning, breaking only for dinner. His study is a spacious room on the second floor that looks out past a tulip tree over a towpath to the river. Although he has put in a long day of meticulous work, he often, then, at one or two in the morning, perhaps as a form of release, writes a long letter to Colet. It is thanks to his letters to her, which continued until their breakup two and a half years later, that we can follow so closely his progress on the novel.

Because he discards a good deal of material, and prunes back severely the material he keeps, he produces very few finished pages—he variously reports one page per week; one every four days; thirteen pages in three months; thirty pages in three months; ninety pages in a year. (This in contrast with the ease of his first version of *The Temptation of Saint Anthony*, drafted earlier—five hundred pages in eighteen months, he said.) Yet he makes steady progress. His closest friend, the poet Louis Bouilhet, comes almost without fail every Sunday, and during those visits Flaubert reads aloud to him what he has done that week. Bouilhet responds, often severely: he likes it very much; or Flaubert should cut further; or there are too many metaphors.

Flaubert spent about four and a half years writing the novel, staying closeted with his work for months at a time, only periodically taking the train to Paris for some days of city life and sociability with friends, though he did not always stop writing when he was there.

He finished the novel sometime in March 1856; it was then accepted for publication by his longtime friend Maxime Du Camp, one of the editors of *La Revue de Paris*, and was published serially in that journal in six installments from October 1 to December 15. Henry James describes coming upon it in this form "when a very young person in Paris" and picking it up "from the parental table." "The cover . . . was yellow, if I mistake not." He recalls "taking it in with so surprised an interest," as he read it "standing there before the fire, my back against the low beplushed and begarnished French chimney piece."

Although certain scenes had been cut from this version as a precaution—which perhaps had the opposite effect, of arousing suspicions—the government brought charges against it for being a danger to morality and religion. The trial took place on January 29, 1857—but lasted only one day; Flaubert and the magazine were acquitted a week later. When the book appeared as a single volume that April, it bore a second dedication, to Marie-Antoine-Jules Sénard, the forceful and eloquent Rouen lawyer who had defended him.

The very approach that made the novel vulnerable to prosecution by the Second Empire government was what made it so radical for fiction of its day—it depicted the lives of its characters objectively, without idealizing or romanticizing, and without intent to instruct or draw a moral lesson. The novel, soon to be labeled "realist" by his contemporaries—though Flaubert resisted the label, as he resisted belonging to any literary "school"—is now viewed as the first masterpiece of realist fiction. Yet what made it so radical at the time is paradoxically hard for us to see, when we read it, for the very reason that, in fact, *Madame Bovary* permanently changed the way novels were written thereafter, and so its approach by now seems completely familiar to us.

Flaubert was born December 12, 1821, in his family's apartment in a wing of the hospital of which his father was chief surgeon, in the port city of Rouen. He showed an interest in writing from a very early age and published his first work at sixteen, but was persuaded by his father to attend law school. Suffering his first epileptic attack at age twenty-three, he was forced (though without reluctance) to give up his law studies and from then on devoted himself almost exclusively to writing. By that time he had already begun the first version of his novel *A Sentimental Education*.

The family had acquired a large, comfortable house overlooking the Seine in the hamlet of Croisset, a few miles from Rouen, and it was here that he settled. After the death of both his father and his sister in 1846, the household was to consist, for many years, of Flaubert, his mother, and his little niece Caroline, whom he helped to raise, as well as the servants that looked after them. Aside from some traveling, some vacations by the seaside at Trouville, and some intervals of living in Paris, he spent most of the rest of his life at Croisset.

Drawn to the exotic, he wrote a draft of another novel, *The Temptation of Saint Anthony*, but suspended work on it in 1849 when Bouilhet and Du Camp so disliked it, after a marathon four-day reading, that they suggested he throw it in the fire. He did not abandon either of his early novels, however: he was to finish *A Sentimental Education* in 1869 and *The Temptation of Saint Anthony* in 1872.

He had, therefore, already written a great deal, though to the literary world he was unknown, before he began what was to be his first published novel.

To counter Flaubert's tendency to wax lyrical and effusive in response to exotic materials, Bouilhet suggested that he take as the subject for his next novel something quite mundane. The story of Madame Bovary is based, in fact, on two local dramas: the adultery and subsequent suicide of one Delphine Delamare, the wife of a local public health officer, and the disastrous spending habits and ultimate financial ruin of Louise Pradier, the wife of a sculptor Flaubert knew personally. A third influence on the novel was the regional fiction of Balzac, whom Flaubert greatly admired. The book would be about not only a woman whose character fatally determined the course of her life but also the place in which she lived and its confining effect on her. After first considering Flanders as a setting, Flaubert settled on his native Normandy, which he knew so well.

The main action of the novel unfolds squarely within the July Monarchy of Louis Philippe (1830–1848), an interval of relative calm in French history and, for Flaubert, the years that had embraced his adolescence and early adulthood. Unlike *A Sentimental Education*, the novel contains relatively little hint of political unrest: here the drama is domestic and local, and the larger outside world hardly intrudes.

It was during the reign of Louis Philippe, known as the *roi bourgeois*, or "Citizen King," because of his bourgeois manner and dress, that the middle class was most explicitly defining itself as distinct from the working class and the nobility. And one of Flaubert's motivating forces in his approach to the material of the novel was his scorn for the bourgeoisie, though he readily included himself in its ranks. What he despised, really, was a certain type of bourgeois attitude—later codified in his *Dictionary of Received Ideas*. It included traits such as greed, a love of material things, raw ambition, shallow culture, intellectual and spiritual superficiality, and above all a mindless parroting of sentiments and beliefs.

He delighted in attacking this kind of behavior wherever he witnessed it: his letters are full of jabs and gibes, whether against a pompous cousin visiting Croisset for the day or a fellow writer in Paris proud of having been invited to dine with a government minister.

The novel is full of markers of the culture of his time that we in our time may not recognize as such: La Chaumière dance hall in Paris; Pompadour clocks and statuettes; the poet Béranger; the novelist Sir Walter Scott; fireworks; tourist attractions in Italy; and a plethora of importations from across the Channel, including horse racing and a tendency to drop English words and expressions into casual conversation. Flaubert is holding up a mirror to the middle- or lower-middle-class world of his day, with all its cherished fads and fashions. French readers who belonged to that world would recognize themselves (or an acquaintance or a family member), and either blush or laugh complicitly: they, or their parents, might play whist in the evening (as did the king himself), or display a similar piece of coral on the mantelpiece or the same print on the parlor wall; perhaps it was their aunt who, like Emma, coveted a tilbury—that fashionable English carriage—or a mouth-rinsing bowl on the dinner table; or perhaps a self-important uncle who, like the pharmacist Homais, hoped to be awarded the cross of the Legion of Honor.

It is not as clear to us, reading the novel in the twenty-first century, that the choices made by Flaubert's characters are not necessarily thoughtful and individual choices, but rather symptoms of a blind adherence to conventional—and often questionable—taste. But what Flaubert called stupidity was not limited to the bourgeoisie. Or rather, if he had a lifelong habit of watching for stupidity and relishing examples of it, he found it in "all of humanity"; all of humanity was bourgeois. He could not shave his face, for instance, without laughing at the stupidity of it.

In a letter written to Colet as he was drafting the scene in which Emma and Léon meet for the first time, he explains that what interests him is the grotesqueness of a supposedly lofty conversation between two sensitive, poetic individuals that is in fact wholly made up of cli-chéd ideas. He realizes early on that he has set himself a formidable task: to take this grotesqueness as his subject, to write a novel about shallow, unsympathetic people in a dreary setting, some of whom make bad choices and come to a horrific end. There will be no romanticizing the subject—in fact, the whole project is opposed to the romantic. The heroine, infatuated with romanticism, comes to grief because of it—because of her craving for impossible dreams, her refusal to accept the ordinariness of her own life and its limited possibilities for happiness.

Nor is there any moralizing on the part of the author—one reason the novel was so vulnerable to attack by the government. The story contains no sermon to point out its moral; it has no "good" moral exemplar to offer in contrast to the "bad" woman that Emma is. The author does not condemn her behavior, but, rather, may even have some sympathy for her, nor does he pass judgment on any of the other characters. The story is un-compromising: the heroine commits adultery and then suicide; her good husband dies, too; her innocent child is fated to have a hard life; the evil moneylender who has been the instrument of Emma's downfall prospers; the conniving, hypocritical, and disloyal "friend," Homais, is rewarded with a coveted medal.

Flaubert chose to create characters who are less than admirable, and to treat them with ironic objectivity—he remarks in another letter, as he works on the scene between Emma and Léon, "This will be the first time, I think, that one will see a book that makes fun of its young leading lady and its young leading man." Yet he goes on to say that "irony takes nothing away from pathos." Which is echoed by Nabokov, writing about the novel: "The ironic and the pathetic are beautifully intertwined."

Flaubert wants his readers to be moved by the characters. He states explicitly, for instance, in the case of Charles's grief: "I hope to cause tears to flow with the tears of this one man." Again, in another letter: "In my third part, which will be full of comical things, I want people to cry."

And although there is hardly a sympathetic character among them—some readers may feel that possible exceptions to this are Emma's father; or the pharmacist's assistant, Justin; or Charles himself—we do feel at least glimmers of sympathy or liking, at moments. It may be true that every one of Homais's statements is a completely conventional "received idea," yet it is hard not to enjoy his cunning, his enterprise, and his intellectual explorations, or even to agree with him sometimes. One cannot help feeling some respect for Emma's bravery at the end, her moment of true affection for Charles, her interest in what is happening to her. "She was observing herself curiously, to see if she was in pain. But no! Nothing yet. . . . 'Ah! It's a small thing, really—death!' she thought; 'I'll fall asleep, and everything will be over!'" We are indeed moved, though perhaps not to the extent Flaubert may have hoped—the prevailing irony may distance us too much from the story, even as it may enhance its dramatic horror.

Nor is he himself unaffected by them. "I am in their skin," he says—though he later qualifies that skin as "antipathetic." We know that he sometimes found himself weeping as he wrote, and that he so identified with Emma during her last days that he was physically ill.

Flaubert's aim was to write the novel "objectively," leaving the author out of it. Although he had many vehement opinions (Zola describes how he could not tolerate being contradicted in an argument), and although *Madame Bovary* is filled with political and social details that reflect these views, Flaubert's technique is to present the material without comment (though the occasional comment does slip in). Simply to report the facts, to give a painstaking description—of a ridiculous object, for instance—should be comment enough. Flaubert remarks in another letter to Colet, of the scene in which Emma goes to the curé for help: "The episode is to have at most six or seven pages without a single reflection or explanation coming from the author (all in direct dialogue)."

Everything was to be conveyed, then, not through authorial comment, but through acute psychological portraiture—including direct dialogue, which, for Flaubert, functioned more to portray character than to move the plot forward—as well as through the details of the scenes. Detailed description would bring the reader into the presence of the material. To be effective, the details had to be carefully chosen, closely observed, precisely described, and striking, as in the depiction of Emma's bridal bouquet, after she has thrown it into the fire, being consumed by flames: "The little cardboard berries burst open, the binding wire twisted, the braid melted; and the shriveled paper petals, hovering along the fireback like black butterflies, at last flew away up the chimney."

If the novel is to move or interest a reader, Flaubert will have to transform what he sees as a sordid world, wholly through the power of his style, into a work of formal and stylistic beauty—all the while writing it in a manner against his own natural inclinations. He says outright many times that he is afraid he won't pull it off: everything must depend on the style.

Flaubert worked from successive plans, following them and subsequently revising them. He wrote numerous drafts of every passage, often rewriting and perfecting it before cutting it out altogether—at one point he estimated that to achieve 120 finished pages he had written 500. In rewriting, he would watch out for poor assonances and weak repetitions of sounds and of words (especially *qui* and *que*, which he occasionally underlined and apologized for even in his letters)—Zola remarks, "Often a single letter exasperated him."

In keeping with his plain, almost clinical approach to the material, he schooled himself to be very sparing with his metaphors. Often enough, an earlier version, one that he cut out of the finished manuscript, was more lyrical than the one he let stand. Proust, for one, writing more than sixty years after the publication of the novel, regretted the absence of metaphor, since he believed, as he said, that "only metaphor can give a sort of eternity to style." But he admitted that there was more to style than metaphor alone.

Proust goes on to say that in all of Flaubert there is not a single beautiful metaphor. Yet here is another lovely comparison to a butterfly: in the famous consummation scene in Part III of the novel, after she has given herself to Léon for the first time in the closed carriage that careens through Rouen, Emma tears up the note of rejection she had written him, now useless, and "a bare hand passed under the little blinds of yellow canvas and threw out some torn scraps of paper, which scattered in the wind and alighted, at a distance, like white butterflies, on a field of red clover all in bloom."

If objective description was his literary method, that objectivity was always imbued with irony. To see and judge a thing with a cool eye was to judge it with the irony that had been a part of his nature since he was a child. This irony pervades the book, coloring each detail, each situation, each event, each character, the fate of each character, and the overarching story.

It is present in his choice of names: that of the old rattletrap coach, called "Swallow"; "Bovary" itself, along with several other character names that play on the French for *ox*; that of the evil moneylender, Lheureux ("the happy one").

It is present in the words and phrases in the novel to which he gives special emphasis—in the manuscript, he would have underlined them, of course, as he does similar language in his correspondence; in print, they are italicized. They appear throughout the novel, starting on the first page with *new boy*. With this emphasis, he was drawing attention to language that was commonly, and unthinkingly, used to express shared ideas that were also unquestioned. Some, such as *new boy*, are relatively innocuous; others may reveal a malevolent prejudice, such as the comment made by Madame Tuvache, the mayor's wife, to her maid (reported as indirect speech), when she learns that Emma has taken a walk alone with Léon: *"Madame Bovary was compromising herself."*

Flaubert's irony is present in the eloquent juxtapositions he creates between the "poetic" and the brutally commonplace, with an effect that is sometimes humorous, sometimes shocking, but that always draws us up short, breaks the "mood," whether of romance or grief, that another author might have chosen to sustain. An exquisite passage—often a description of nature—will be undercut, as though, here, Flaubert is also undercutting his own lyrical impulse, by what immediately follows it, a banal, mundane comparison or action. There are numerous examples.

Emma, for instance, is lying on the ground in the woods, still tremulous from her first lovemaking with Rodolphe, in tune with the natural landscape around her, which is fully and sensuously described; but the passage concludes with the flat statement that Rodolphe, a cigar between his teeth, is mending a bridle. Much later in the story, in a boat with Léon, Emma feels a chill at the thought of Rodolphe with other women; the boatman, who has unknowingly upset her, spits into his palm and takes up his oars. Crushingly, pathetically, after Emma's death, as she is being laid out, one of the women working over her admires her beauty in rather glib terms—how alive she looks!; immediately after, as she lifts Emma's head to set the wreath on her, black liquid runs out of the dead woman's mouth. Flaubert the obdurate antiromantic could not be more clearly in evidence than at this moment.

As in the above examples, it is the incisive specificity of the poetic details and then the abruptness with which Flaubert "cuts" to the equally specific but disturbing or brutal details that jolts us so.

Some of these ironic juxtapositions produce not horror, or pathos, but humor.

For instance, during the scene at the agricultural fair, the poetic and romantic exchanges between Rodolphe and Emma, who are observing from a window above, in the town hall, are punctuated (without authorial comment) by the sober announcements of awards for agricultural advancements in such areas as "manure" and "use of oilseed cakes."

There is humor, also, in the juxtaposition of disproportionate elements, as, for instance, in the case of the writings of Homais, who is a journalist as well as an apothecary: sometimes it is the grandiosity of his style that is out of keeping with the banality of his subject (for instance, cider); or, as he reports the festivities, it is the glorious colors in which he paints them in his article that have little relation to what we know of them in all their paltriness and insufficiency.

Then again, the disproportion may lie not in Homais's writing, but in his manner—between his pomposity, in a moment of embarrassment with the grieving Charles, and the obviousness of his statement: "Homais thought it suitable to talk a little horticulture; plants needed humidity."

Yet complicating our reactions to these moments is, in one instance, during the awards ceremony at the agricultural fair, some modicum of respect for the concerns of the proponents of advances in agriculture, and, in another, as Homais waters Charles's plants after his tactless question about the funeral, some sympathetic understanding of the pharmacist in his moment of embarrassment. Our emotional responses to the incidents of the novel are never entirely unmixed, which is of course one of the sources of its power.

Because Homais is something of a writer, and a character obviously much enjoyed by Flaubert (who refers to him affectionately in his letters as "my pharmacist" and occasionally likes to use an expression Homais might have used), it is hard not to think that he must represent a comment on the role or the practice of the writer, or one aspect of it. In fact, late in the novel, Flaubert the great reviser insinuates a moment of self-parody that would be comical if it weren't subsumed by the drama of Emma's fatal illness. As Emma nears her end, Homais must send word by messenger to the two doctors who might be able to save her. He goes home and bends to his task, but although speed is of the essence, he is so agitated (and so particular about his prose style) that he requires no less than fifteen drafts to find the right wording.

Twice, at least, we are allowed to experience an event and then to read Homais's written version of it. Homais's material (like Flaubert's) is mundane and subject to lapses into mediocrity—the fireworks at the conclusion of the agricultural fair are damp and they fizzle, a complete failure. But he transforms this material, inflates it, gives it importance and success, by a grandiloquent style that Flaubert, tongue in cheek, describes in a letter as "philosophic, poetic, and progressive"—and by his outright lies. A piece of writing, Flaubert seems to be demonstrating, may always be false: the writer has the power to transform reality as he wishes. Words, particularly in print, have the perfidious power to misrepresent and betray. And eloquence is especially dangerous: the better one can write, the more persuasively one can lie.

Although Homais is the only "professional" writer in the book, other styles of writing appear in the course of it: Emma's father's letters; the speeches of the officials;

Rodolphe's farewell note to Emma; Charles's instructions for the coffining. Flaubert, entering fully, always, into his characters' points of view, shifts gears convincingly as he moves in and out of these other styles, no less alien to him, perhaps, than the style of narration of the novel as a whole. His own natural style, after all, he says in one letter, is that of *Saint Anthony*: what he wishes he could be writing are "grand turns of phrase, broad, full periods rolling along like rivers, a multiplicity of metaphors, great bursts of style."

What he is trying to achieve in this book, instead, is a style that is clear and direct, economical and precise, and at the same time rhythmic, sonorous, musical, and "as smooth as marble" on the surface; with varied sentence structures and with imperceptible transitions from scene to scene and from psychological analysis to action.

Though he did not write poetry himself, in a letter to Colet (a poet) Flaubert complains: "What a bitch of a thing prose is! It's never finished; there's always something to redo. Yet I think one can give it the consistency of verse. A good sentence in prose should be like a good line in poetry, *unchangeable*, as rhythmic, as sonorous."

Yet Proust, in the course of his vehement response, in 1920, to a negative article about Flaubert, commented admiringly on what he called Flaubert's "grammatical singularities," which, he said, expressed "a new vision"; our way of seeing external reality was radically changed by Flaubert's "entirely new and personal use" of the past definite, the past indefinite, the present participle, certain pronouns, and certain prepositions. He went on to talk about other singularities: Flaubert's unprecedented manner of using the imperfect tense and indirect discourse, his unconventional handling of the word *and*—omitting it where one would expect it and inserting it where one would normally not look for it—his emphatically "flat" use of verbs, and his deliberately heavy placement of adverbs. But it was Flaubert's innovative use of the imperfect tense that most impressed Proust: "This [use of the] imperfect, so new in literature," said Proust, "completely changes the aspect of things and people."

The imperfect, or *imparfait*, tense in French is the form of the past tense that expresses an ongoing or prevailing condition, or a repeated action. It is most usually conveyed in English by *would* or *used to*. Expressing a continuing state or action, and thereby signaling the continuity of time itself, it perfectly creates the effect Flaubert was seeking—what Nabokov, in his lecture on the novel, describes as "the sense of repetition, of dreariness in Emma's life." Thus, early in her marriage, Charles's (tiresomely predictable) habits are described using a string of verbs in the imperfect: "He would return home late. . . . Then he would ask for something to eat. . . . He would take off his frock coat. . . . He would tell her one by one all the people he had met . . . he would eat the remains of the beef hash with onions . . . then go off to bed, sleep on his back, and snore."

While the imperfect, as agent of "background" description and habitual activity, was traditionally, before Flaubert, subordinated to the simple past tense, used to narrate finite action, with Flaubert, the habitual and the ongoing are foregrounded, and the division between description and action is blurred, as is the division between past and present, creating a sustained immediacy in the story. Even the speeches of the characters are often reported indirectly in the imperfect (as, for instance, in the mayor's wife's comment quoted above: *"Madame Bovary was compromising herself"*), allowing Flaubert to slip seamlessly into a character's point of view without abandoning the detachment of the third-person narration. The narration remains dynamic despite the fact that a large proportion of the book, in Flaubert's view at least, is exposition or preparation for action.

In a letter to Colet of January 15, 1853—sixteen months into the writing of the book—Flaubert worries about proportions: "I have now lined up five chapters of my second part in which nothing happens." This was an exaggeration, of course, but he felt there was going to be a great quantity of exposition, or prologue, and then very little unfolding action, before the conclusion. This, too, had not been done before—telling a story with so little action. He believed that those proportions were true to life: "A blow lasts a minute but is anticipated for months—our passions are like volcanoes: always rumbling but only intermittently erupting." Yet he worried that the demands of aesthetics required something different.

If Proust calls *A Sentimental Education* "a long report" in which the characters do not really take part in the action, Flaubert calls *Madame Bovary* a "biography," one that takes the form of an extended analysis of one woman's psychology. But he believed that it could, even so, have the pace of action: "It also seems to me not impossible to give psychological analysis the rapidity, clarity, passion of a purely dramatic narration. This has never been tried and would be beautiful." It would seem, in fact, that this was just the sort of action that really interested Flaubert: the subtle shifts of feeling created in a reader by description and by psychological analysis. "I maintain that images are action," he says. "It is harder to sustain a book's interest by this means, but if one fails it is the fault of style."

Another striking characteristic of his psychological portraiture is the evenhandedness with which he gives validity to multiple points of view at the same time, without promoting one over another, and thus reproduces, remarkably and unusually, the multiple conflicting self-interests that occur in real life all the time.

Abruptly, without comment, he "cuts" from one character's preoccupation to another's. Just when we are wholly absorbed in Léon's impatient vigil in the cathedral, for instance, we are recalled to the very lively emotions of the tiresome verger, whom Léon is slighting, and the reality of his "fury"—after all, a large part of his identity is involved in showing people the cathedral's points of interest. Or we remain captivated, imaginatively, by Emma's lingering bliss after her "honeymoon" with Léon until we are deflected by Homais's equally real anger at Justin during the jam-making scene. And then there is Homais's comical but heartless preoccupation, as Emma is dying, with producing a good lunch for the visiting doctor; or the blind man's arrival at Yonville in search of the promised cure for his terrible deformity just as Emma breathes her last; or the innkeeper's distraction, as she worries about the competition from a rival inn, while Charles is trying to unburden his grief to her.

At such moments, Flaubert is constantly reminding us that even as we are caught up in one drama, another, of real importance to someone else, is taking place right next to us—as in life. But through his abrupt changes of point of view he is also manipulating us, as readers: just when we are most absorbed in one character's drama—as when we are losing ourselves in a lyrical description—he interrupts and undercuts it.

Many of Flaubert's transitions are indeed imperceptible, while others are abrupt; at still other points in the novel the narration suddenly makes a rapid advance, covering months or years in a paragraph or two. But there is a tight unity to the novel as a whole, rising not only from its extreme economy—in which every element serves more than one function—but also from its recurring words, phrases, images, and actions. A small sampling would include butterflies (actual and metaphorical, as in the passages quoted above); constructions in layers (Charles's schoolboy cap, the wedding cake, Emma's nesting coffins); Emma's fitfully recurring attraction to religious faith; Homais's quoted writings; Charles "suffocating" with emotion twice near the end of the book and the theme of suffocation in general; the same phrase—*bloquer les interstices*—used first literally, to describe "filling the gaps" between Emma's body and the sides of the coffin; and then figuratively during the awkward last conversation between Rodolphe and Charles.

Particularly prevalent are recurring images involving water, the sea, and boats. These include the "skiffs by moonlight" in Emma's convent reading; the gondola in her daydream of a future life with Rodolphe; the actual "skiff by moonlight" in which she and Léon go to the island each evening of their three-day "honeymoon"; and the gondola-shaped bed in the hotel room where they meet thereafter every week.

Most striking, however, is the repeated image of a sealed vessel (carriage, casket, coffin) tossed about in the waves of a troubled sea. Its first notable appearance is in the opening speech of the agricultural fair, as a pompous official pays homage to the king, "who guides the Chariot of State amid the unceasing perils of a stormy sea." Later, as Emma gives herself to Léon during the prolonged ride through the city, the king is replaced by the driver of the hackney cab, steering (rather carelessly) "a carriage with drawn blinds that kept appearing and reappearing, sealed tighter than a tomb and tossed about like a ship at sea." Here, Flaubert has taken the speechifier's mixed metaphor and added the simile (another layer) of the sealed tomb. Finally, he repeats the comparison at the end of the novel, as Emma's nesting coffins, hammered and soldered, are borne to the cemetery: "The bier moved forward in little jolts, like a boat pitching with every wave."

Such is the tight construction of the novel, and the utter conviction of the detailed descriptions and psychological portraits throughout, that we compliantly ignore, most of the time, any passing questions we may have either about inconsistencies in the plot or about implausibility in plot elements, the most conspicuous being that Charles never suspects any of Emma's betrayals, never notices the sound of the sand striking the shutters as he and she sit reading, never receives an anonymous letter from a busybody. (And how does he, deeply in debt by the end of the novel by reason of Emma's extravagances, pay for her three coffins?) If space and time as handled in the novel are both "elastic," as has been said by some critics, so is plausibility. And yet this is not a distraction as we read—it is barely noticeable. The requirements of psychology take precedence over plausibility and consistency in time and space, and the psychology is entirely persuasive.

2010

VISUAL ARTISTS:
EARLY TOURIST
PHOTOGRAPHS

Dutch Scenes: A Portfolio of Early Twentieth-Century Tourist Photographs

Opposite: Boys with cart on beach. The Dutch boys—variously in sweater, smocks, shirt with bib, and clogs—are nestled around or perched on the shafts of a sturdy cart equipped with baskets that must have something to do with fishing for shrimp, eel, oysters, or fish, or with gathering seaweed. In the background, holidaymakers, either foreign or Dutch, stand at the shoreline in more cosmopolitan dress, and a horse is partly visible, there either to pull a "bathing machine" or, more likely, to assist with some aspect of the fishing industry.

Just as there is no single type of lace bonnet in Brittany, but rather many variants, there is no single Dutch national costume, despite what we might think from looking at the illustrations on cookie tins or the outfits on little Dutch dolls. Beginning as early as the sixteenth and seventeenth centuries, each region—sometimes each island or even village—in the Netherlands developed its own characteristic way of dressing: a small, close-fitting white cap here, a large-winged black cap there; a striped apron here, black stockings on Sunday there; a several-stranded coral necklace in many areas but not all. In the nineteenth century, as Holland evolved from a number of provinces under one central government into a more unified single entity, the traditional costumes, in response to this threatened loss of identity, became even more individual and more locally particular.

One influence on the development of distinctive dress seems to have been the relative isolation of the different communities. Many communities in the coastal parts of the Netherlands were originally established on islands only later joined to the mainland through the ever-ongoing land reclamation that has been so integral to the creation of the Netherlands. The combination of this isolation and the requirements of climate and work— farming and fishing for the men, household care and market vending for the women—led to the development of such costume elements as stout, waterproof, roomy woolen pants for the men, warm skirts with multiple petticoats for the women, always a cap of some sort to keep the head warm, wooden clogs. Different religious groups within the same region would be characterized by their own distinctive dress, just as, in the United States, the Amish and Hutterian communities continue to dress

Marketplace at Middelburg, Zeeland. In the foreground, *visleur-sters*, or fish peddlers, from the village of Arnemuiden; in the middle ground, shoppers; in the background, market stalls in front of the well-known *stadhuis*, or town hall.

in their characteristic fashions. The enforced leisure in winter and stormy weather may well have encouraged the development of the elaborate ornamentation characteristic of some costumes: the embroidery on a bodice or the quantity of lace in the voluminous "fall" of a head covering. One more element in the costume was the display of wealth: silver coins on the men's jackets or pants, jewelry on the women's caps.

For instance, Volendam, to the northeast of Amsterdam, and the nearby peninsula, Marken, once an island, are close geographically, but their predominant religions and traditional costumes are different. The peaked white cap with upturned wings, so characteristic in exported Dutch illustrations that we might mistake it for a national headgear, is worn only in Volendam, whereas the small, round caps in the photo, on page 361, of the group of little girls walking together by the water, and the wide knee breeches of the lone boy trailing behind them, are worn in Marken.

There is available online a fascinating tabulation, done over fifteen years ago, of the survival of traditional costumes in the Netherlands: for twenty-one different places, we are given the number of women and men still wearing traditional dress year-round and the age of the youngest of the group; if the costume is no longer worn, we are given the year in which it disappeared and often the name and age of the last person to wear it (*draagster*, in Dutch). In some regions, in 2003, there were only a handful still wearing traditional clothing; in others, hundreds. There would be fewer now, and those wearing it would be still older, of course: in one after another of Dutch family group photographs of the twentieth century, we see most of the family in contemporary clothing and the oldest generation, often a single old woman, in traditional dress.

Traditional dress, it should be added, was worn mainly by the working classes—mostly fishermen and farmers and their families—and was common in the country rather than the city. Nicole, the Dutch proprietor of a local bookstore near where I live, and an occasional informant on things Dutch, grew up in a prosperous town near The Hague. She tells me that her great-grandmother, born in the late 1870s, would never have dreamed of wearing the traditional regional costume, but rather, throughout her decades-long widowhood, until she died in 1959, appeared daily in a simple long black dress with a white collar and a brooch at the throat.

It was a chance event one day that led me to become particularly interested in Dutch culture and history—a conversation with a friend in Amsterdam who persuaded me to try my hand at translating some very short texts from the Dutch. Over the years following, as I continued these translations, I learned to read simple Dutch and also learned something about the Netherlands, though there are large gaps in my understanding.

Then, several years later, I was visiting two old friends in Philadelphia, and one evening as we were talking about my Dutch translations, Francie brought out her laptop and showed me some old photos taken in Holland by an ancestor. I was entranced. I did not remember ever having seen historical photos of ordinary Dutch people in the costumes of their place, at work and at play. I was suddenly lifted beyond the endlessly repeated stylized depictions of cute Dutch figures to the everyday working reality of this small, densely populated, complex nation, with its rich history. True, the photos represent some of the same things one sees in those stylized images—the women's caps, the full dresses and aprons and shawls, the men's broad-brimmed hats, the wooden clogs, the canal boats—but here, the traditional dress is simply part of everyday life: women are returning from church, children are playing with toy sailboats in a canal, women in a marketplace are selling fresh fish. Daily life goes on, and the visitors from America who happened to have witnessed it have captured the images on their camera.

Who took these photos, which are, many of them, so harmoniously composed? At first Francie could not remember, then she did: it was her great-great-grandfather

Theo Shaw and his wife, Sarah Van Doren Shaw. Theo was a prosperous dry-goods merchant in Chicago, Sarah a painter of watercolors. They were enthusiastic travelers in general but had two particular reasons for visiting the Netherlands: Sarah's Dutch–New Amsterdam ancestry and her desire to paint scenes of Holland.

What we needed to find out, next, was when the photos were taken and exactly where in Holland.

It is in part the traditional costume, of course, that first attracts the tourist and photographer and now charms the modern viewer—it is the exotic that we hunger for, in the sameness of our own lives. It is the costume, too, that helps to locate the photos: since it is specific to a small area, if we can identify it, then we know where the photos were taken. But the fact that it has persisted with little change even into contemporary times also means that it will not tell us whether the photos were taken in the 1890s, as I first thought, or in the early 1900s, as is more likely. Only the "modern" and cosmopolitan clothing, with its changing fashions, can date the photos more precisely when it is present.

Interestingly, though, the possible dates are limited by several immutable facts: the type of camera most likely used, which I find out was manufactured between 1896 and 1904; the formats of the images, which came into existence in 1903; and the death of Theo, which occurred in 1906.

I thought I had another good clue: the photo of the Middelburg marketplace shows the vast sixteenth-century *stadhuis* in the distance, on the far side of the square, a fantastically ornate structure with a long, steeply sloping roof that accommodates no fewer than three stories of attic windows. Because the left part is covered in scaffolding, I thought the dates of the restoration work might tell me the period in which the photo was taken. But inquiries to the *stadhuis* archivist revealed that one part or another of the building was often covered in scaffolding. His best guess, however, as he looked at the photo, did at least agree with my hypothesis of the early 1900s.

I also learned from a Belgian friend who used to visit the marketplace in his childhood that the building and town have long been a well-known tourist destination. Then I realized what should have been obvious right away: probably our American friends, the Shaws, visited only the better-known spots in Holland, rather than straying too far off the beaten track. This might help to identify the specific places where the photos were taken.

I had had an inkling of this when I did a little research into the head coverings worn in one of the first photos that Francie showed me—the little girls walking together by the water. A Dutch friend, Paul, had immediately speculated: Volendam, Marken, Urk, Stavoren, "*een haven langs de voormalige Zuiderzee* [a harbor along the former Zuiderzee]?"

These are indeed villages and towns to the north of Amsterdam. The old fishing village of Volendam, I now know, is a popular tourist destination because it is not far from Amsterdam and has retained some of its old-fashioned character, especially in the traditional dress still worn by a number of its inhabitants.

It is remarkable that the traditional costume was common so far into the twentieth century and that it persists even now. There were several obvious factors in its gradual disappearance: the changes in geography leading to a decrease in isolation; the changes in work, on the part of both men and women; the cultural penetration of modern life via television and other media. And one not completely negligible factor in its disappearance seems to have been, ironically, the intrusiveness of tourists gaping at people in regional costume—although, paradoxically, it is now the interest of tourists, as well as of the Dutch themselves, that encourages the deliberate cultivation and display of regional customs, including traditional dress.

In examining these photos, of course I think of the invisible other side of the encounter. Observing these native Dutch people from behind the camera were the two rather elderly Americans, in American dress of the time—elaborate and fantastic in its own way. To judge from their expressions, the Dutch subjects do not seem to have warmed to the visitors, and I doubt they were paid for posing—as some were—though we can't be certain. Most of the pictures are not posed: the subjects are often in motion, often captured in the midst of their activities—the boys pushing a younger sibling in a carriage; the old women knitting and chatting. Some don't even seem to notice the camera, like the boys with the cart on the beach; others see it, but with curiosity, indifference, or possibly even hostility, like the father with his infant on his lap; only some, like the girl with the yoke and two baskets, seem frozen in position, waiting for the shutter to click.

One effect of this naturalness is that we intuit some sense of the subjects' real lives, and we feel more present, because less observed by them.

2013

Girl with umbrella, probably Middelburg, Zeeland. This elegant girl with coils at her temples, dressed in clothing typical of the island of Walcheren—like the other girls and women in the photo—has momentarily turned away from the spectacle that has attracted this crowd. Behind her, two women are standing on chairs, the better to see. A painted pattern such as the one on the door is often found on the shutters and/or doors of public and private buildings in Holland (including the Middelburg *stadhuis*). The umbrellas, two more of which are visible, are for protection against the sun, not the rain.

Three boys with baby carriage. Like many others in these photos, the boys are working—in this case, minding a younger sibling—and are apparently taken by surprise, to judge from their expressions and their positions midstride.

Young fish peddler from Arnemuiden: Here is a young version of the *visleursters* seen in the Middelburg marketplace. The pattern on her baskets, checkerboard squares for two rows of weaving (but not usually the third), is typical for the fish peddler, as are her shoes, either men's shoes or low boots, worn by these women for the three-to-five-kilometer-long walk from the coastal fishing village. They might carry as much as eighty kilos of fish suspended from their wooden *juk*, along the path from Arnemuiden. Brick-paved in parts, the path passed through fields, crossed ditches on narrow plank bridges, and was interrupted by at least one canal over which the women were conveyed by a ferry. Each peddler, once she reached town, went off to make the rounds of her own regular customers door-to-door or headed for the marketplace. This young girl is wearing at her temples the typical gold coils that are the end points of the *oorijzer* she wears inside her cap. From these coils, a woman might suspend precious ornaments as a sign of her wealth. This type of wooden yoke was also used to carry cheeses or water. Notice her tight short sleeves, displaying her strong arms—traditionally an attractive attribute. The clean and well-maintained appearance of the building and pavement would seem to be typical, judging from this group of photos.

Boy in typical Volendam dress. This image, given the boy's wide trousers, silver buttons, tilted visored cap, and *klompen* (clogs), may be the most stereotypically Dutch. But one peculiar feature of the photo is that because the brick-paved roadway on which he stands is well above the level of the house behind him, and the photographer is very close to him, he appears to be the "Giant Dutch Boy."

Men, women, and children by harbor, Volendam. In this graceful, atmospheric photo, with its formal, balanced composition, figures stand and sit above something of great interest hidden from our view. Notice the positioning of arms and hands, the combination of intimacy and isolation in the figures, the washy background of sky and water, and in the distance the moored boats used for fishing on the Zuiderzee. The striped skirts on two of the women were typical for this area.

Women crossing square, Volendam. Three women in traditional Volendam dress are clearly shown, and a fourth figure, probably a man, disappears into the darkness of the house in the background. One younger woman, or girl, turns to look at the photographer. Her companion holds a cane and seems to stoop slightly. Because the women are not carrying baskets or any other object associated with work, and because they are all headed toward the little houses in the background, we have the impression that they are returning from some more festive or ceremonious event, perhaps a church service. The small white scarves worn by two of them support that assumption, since they were worn only on special occasions. Their shadows are not long, so we can assume the time is around midday.

Boy with basket. This little boy is leaning back slightly to counter the weight of a basket overflowing with what looks like seaweed or fish packed in seaweed but may simply be vegetables. He stands on cobblestones near the window of a house or shop. Visible below the basket are either his pant legs or his thick socks, almost always worn to cushion the clogs.

Boys with rowboat, Volendam. In the background is what appears to be a row of fishermen's houses with some wash hanging in front. Also hanging to dry, next to the boys (and stretching back far behind them), are many *hoekwant*—a kind of composite fishing line with multiple hooks attached. Given the angle of the photo, it would seem that the photographer crouched down quite low to take the picture. Does this make Sarah more likely as the photographer than the somewhat older (and stouter) Theodore?

Children walking, Marken. These lively girls with their patterned bodices, striding along the waterside roadway, are from Marken: we know this from their clothing and that of the lone boy, his full knee breeches and brimmed hat being typical of that island and quite different, for instance, from the dress of the boys in the preceding photo.

Father with infant and wooden clogs, Volendam. Clogs were left outside the house so as not to dirty the floor. The Dutch, as reputed, were indeed very clean, even to the extent of washing the stoops of their houses and the pavement in front once a week; neighbors might do it at the same time so that the whole street was clean. Clogs were worn beginning early in childhood, and even toddlers had no trouble getting around in them. They seem outsize to us because they were: for comfort, they were worn with one or two (or more) pairs of thick socks, with perhaps the addition of a sheepskin pad or (more recently) newspaper inserted inside. They were and still are very warm and practical, especially in mud and sand, and for dirty work.

Old women knitting. These three old women, not from Holland, though also photographed by the Shaws, found their way in among the Dutch photos, and we have opted to keep them here for their busy hands, expressive faces, and sturdy shoes. They talk as they knit, and if one would perhaps like to be part of their circle, one would not like to be the subject of their talk. Set into the wall is an iron hitching ring, for a horse or other animal. The space has the feel of a barnyard, given the rough ground, the ring, and the ladders or other appurtenances in the background. Or perhaps it is a rough-surfaced alleyway or street. Though the costumes are not Dutch, the same elements figure, including the ever-present cap—here, one is black, while the others are white, surely signifying something.

Ducks and toy boats, Volendam. The children are playing with the toy boats in a canal that runs behind the houses, or perhaps the boys are playing with the boats while the older girl feeds the ducks that swim nearby. Where is the photographer? Assuming it is Sarah, is she on a boat moving down this canal, or is she walking on a path opposite the children? From the lie of the water in front of her, she seems to be on it, and maybe the ripples in the foreground are even caused by the motion of her own boat.

WRITERS (3)

The Problem of Plot Summary
in Blanchot's Fiction

I was once asked to summarize two novels by Maurice Blanchot for two publishers who needed jacket copy or publicity copy—in other words, to produce summaries comprehensible to a larger audience, of writings very hard to comprehend. One summary I did badly, the other better. Being forced to summarize meant I was forced to identify precisely what was happening in the novels and what moved the action forward. This was not easy in the case of Blanchot's fiction. Here is one perfectly accurate summary, though the briefest possible one, of *Celui qui ne m'accompagnait pas* (*The One Who Was Standing Apart from Me*): "In a house in the southern part of some country, a man goes from room to room being asked the question 'Are you writing now?' by another character who may or may not exist."

(This summary would not be suitable for commercial release.)

Another description, longer and more detailed, would be more conventionally acceptable:

In a house in a region identified only as somewhere in the south (of France), during seasons that seem

to change from autumn to winter to summer, a
man moves restlessly, at long intervals, from room
to room: he looks out into a garden he remembers
with pleasure; he goes to the kitchen for a glass
of water; he stands by the staircase; he climbs to
the upstairs room in which he says he lives and
writes; he returns to the large ground-floor room,
which contains a table and suddenly, now, a large
disordered bed, a bed so vast, in the eyes of this
man, the narrator—for whom the things of the
world have an illusory quality that causes them to
shift or disappear constantly—that it might not be a
bed after all, but the ground itself, which is why he
hesitates to lie down on it, though he is exhausted.

He looks out the bay windows of the room into
the garden again, where a man who may or may
not really be there stands looking into the room,
though this man does not seem to see the narrator. When he is not moving about the house, the
narrator is engaging in a dialogue with his "companion," who may or may not be another aspect
of himself, and may or may not exist outside his
imagination, and when he is not moving or speaking, he is thinking.

This novel appeared in 1953 during an extremely
fruitful period in Blanchot's writing life, five years after
his novel *L'Arrêt de mort* (*Death Sentence*) and four years
before his novel *Le Dernier Homme* (*The Last Man*). In
it, almost nothing "happens," in a sense. Yet between
the two characters in the book, and within the mind of
the narrator, a great deal happens, on a mysterious level
where abstractions like immobility and light become

strong concrete presences interacting and effecting emotional changes within the narrator and between the narrator and his companion.

Throughout the novel, this companion presses the narrator with the question "Are you writing now?" and what the novel sets out to explore in the most astounding detail, from within the very center of the narrator's almost desperately heightened consciousness, is his hesitant approach to the idea of writing, his consideration of the possible effects of his writing, and his relationship to his own words, which themselves become active, concrete presences in the novel, sometimes flying gaily and violently through the house, and sometimes closing about the narrator in a suffocating circle.

Thus, yes, there is other action and interaction in the book besides the concrete action of the narrator and the interaction between narrator and a possible other person: for instance, there is also the interaction between the narrator and an abstract actor such as thought; and, climbing to a further, almost vertiginous level of abstraction-made-concrete, between the narrator and the *absence* of the abstract entity. (As in so much of Blanchot's writing, absence is a compelling presence and a compelling character in the work.)

In this narrative, then, in which paradox and impossibility are incorporated as perfectly natural elements of the action, an attempt to identify actors and types of action and to separate out concrete actors from abstract, as well as permutations of both, yields these notations:

1. There are concrete actors, such as the narrator.
2. There are abstract elements that perform as actors, such as the narrator's "desire" or "immobility."

3. There are possibly but not certainly imaginary actors, such as a figure, possibly of the narrator's invention, who may be sitting in the room.

4. There is concrete action in concrete space, and the narrator declares it positively (e.g., "I moved").

5. There is possible concrete action in concrete space; the narrator qualifies it (e.g., "I think I moved").

6. There is a possible concrete situation; the narrator is even more tentative about it (e.g., "I had the feeling someone was sitting in the armchair").

7. There is a concrete interaction, but it takes place between one concrete entity and one abstract entity (e.g., "I was stopped by my own immobility").

8. There is "concrete" interaction between things that do not concretely exist, that exist only in the narrator's mind or imagination—thoughts, sensations, illusions.

9. There is no interaction between the narrator and, say, an imaginary figure; but there is interaction between the narrator and the effect, on the narrator, of that lack of interaction.

The list could go on.

2007

Stendhal's Alter Ego:
The Life of Henry Brulard

The other day I was listening to a program about astronomy on the radio, and in the space of about half an hour I learned at least five or six startling things, among them that most meteors are no larger than a raisin; that a meteor the size of a grape would light up the entire sky as it descended; that if we could see him, a person poised on the edge of a black hole would appear, from the vantage point of the earth, to hover there indefinitely, frozen in time, whereas from the vantage point of the black hole itself he would be swallowed up instantly. Some of this was hard for me to understand, and while I was still agog with it, along came the next and most disturbing comment, one concerning the nature of time: there is, they said, a good deal of evidence suggesting that at the deepest level of reality, time as we are accustomed to imagine it does not actually exist, that we live in an eternal present.

If I can comprehend it at all, this idea is not a very comfortable one. I would prefer to think of objective time as an unbroken stream of equal intervals stretching infinitely far back and far forward; then I may peaceably watch subjective time as it defies measurement by behaving in its usual capricious, elastic, elusive manner, shrinking and expanding unexpectedly or collapsing in on itself. And this was my habit of thought before I heard the radio program and while I was engrossed in reading Stendhal's *Life of Henry Brulard*. For time is very much one of the subjects of this *Life*, which remarkably transfigures or transcends it, as Stendhal looks back at his past and speaks forward in time to his readers of the future, but also, by his manner of writing, brings those readers into what now seems to me, after the radio program, to be an eternal present.

Stendhal wrote this strangely fragmented, digressive, and yet beautifully structured pseudonymous memoir in four quick months over the winter of 1835–1836. He had written *The Red and the Black* five years earlier, in 1830, and he was to write *The Charterhouse of Parma* (another quick book, occupying the seven weeks from early November to late December) less than two years later, in 1838. At the age of fifty-three, he is looking back at the first seventeen years of his life, at the events of what we would call—and what he would recognize as—his "formative" years and subjecting them to a close examination and analysis "so as to work out what sort of man I have been."

Yet he is also looking ahead, contemplating and occasionally addressing the readers who will pick up his book in 1880, readers who, he thinks, may be more sympathetic to him than his contemporaries—though just as often, he frets that they will be intolerably bored by the minutiae of his life. "I have no doubt had great pleasure from writing this past hour, and from trying to describe my feelings of the time *exactly as they were*," he says, "but who on earth will be brave enough to go deeply into it, to read this excessive heap of *I*s and *me*s?"

He occasionally, even, looks beyond the readers of 1880 to those of 1900, 1935, and, surprisingly, our own 2000. He is not sure, he says, if the reader of the future will still be familiar with *Les Liaisons dangereuses* by Choderlos de Laclos—yes, we still know it, we would like to answer him. He believes the reader of 1900 and one hundred years later will certainly have a more enlightened understanding of Racine. Well, there we would probably disappoint him.

Whenever we read a book, of course, time, in a sense, collapses: we feel we are reading in the same moment the writer is writing, or that we cause him to speak, and as he speaks we hear him—there is no interval, and the converse is also true, that we have only to stop reading for a moment, and he stops speaking. What immediate authority the handwritten message of a dead parent still has! Reading is the necessary completion of the act of writing. Yet Stendhal's *Life*, more than most, jumps beyond the bounds of its time and tradition, speaks across nearly two centuries in an intensely personal voice.

How does it achieve such immediacy? And why is this minutely detailed tabulation by this irascible grumbler so appealing?

Certainly it shares some of the qualities of other eccentric autobiographical works that continue to strike us as fresh and new despite the passage of time (if time does indeed pass): Kafka's *Letter to His Father*, Cyril Connolly's *The Unquiet Grave*, J. R. Ackerley's *Hindoo Holiday*, Gertrude Stein's *Autobiography of Alice B. Toklas*, Theresa Hak Kyung Cha's *Dictee*, Michel Leiris's *Rules of the Game*. For one thing, the style of *The Life of Henry*

Brulard is plain and straightforward, conversational and direct. For another, it is full of keenly observed and striking detail—a room so cold the ink freezes on the tip of the pen, a dying man carried home on a ladder, clothes "smelling of the makers."

It is written with passion. Stendhal, like the narrator of a Thomas Bernhard novel, is terribly attached to his every feeling. He is just as furious today (at the time of his writing and our reading) as he was at age fourteen, when his greatest love was mathematics ("I fancy I said to myself: *'True or false, mathematics will get me out of Grenoble*, out of this mire that turns my stomach'") and he was endlessly frustrated by the complacency and hypocrisy of his teachers: what a shock, he says, "when I realized that no one could explain to me how it is that a minus times a minus equals a plus $(- \times - = +)$!" Further rage when no one will resolve another puzzle: Is it or is it not true that parallel lines, when produced to infinity, will eventually meet?

Clear-eyed about his good points and bad, Stendhal aims for accuracy ("I am witty no more than once a week and then only for five minutes," he tells us), and what a complex and interesting person emerges from this self-examination. Stubborn, opinionated, and cantankerous yet brilliant, minutely observant, and appealingly fallible. Not an easy friend; someone in whose company one would be always on edge—he would be sure to pounce on any sign of fatuousness or mental sloth. Intellectually ambitious, and not merely concerning literature and politics: he still thinks he ought to study worms and beetles—"which nauseate me"—as he had intended to do while he was a soldier fighting under Napoleon.

He has much to say about memory because he is relying entirely on that unreliable faculty in his re-creation of his early years. There is a great deal, he tells us, that he had forgotten until the present moment of writing: things come back to him that he has not thought of for decades. He often says that a certain memory is obscured because of the great emotion he experienced at the time: the emotion wiped out the memory. He points out, further, that if he remembers this much of an event, he has also forgotten a great deal more, but that if he were to begin supplementing the truth with his imagination, he would be writing a novel and not a memoir. "I protest once again that I don't claim to be describing things in themselves, but only their effect on me."

Yet *The Life of Henry Brulard* has several even more unusual features. For one thing, there are the aide-mémoire sketches, nearly two hundred of them, thin, spidery diagrams with scribbled explanations showing where young Stendhal was positioned in relation to others, in a room or on a mountainside, in a street or a square ("I clouted him with all my might at O"), and these sketches, minimal, crabbed, and repetitious as they are, oddly enough make his memories more real to us, too.

For another, there is his abiding and multilayered pretense at self-concealment. He not only refers to himself at points as a certain overly loquacious "Dominique," but more significantly titles the book (on the title pages of several sections of the manuscript) as *Life of Henry Brulard written by himself* and then describes it, for the benefit of "Messrs the police," not as an autobiography, but as a novel in imitation of the very bland and innocent *Vicar of Wakefield*. Now, all the layers of the self-concealment are quite transparent: he is not Henry Brulard, he is not writing a novel, and this book does not

in any obvious way resemble Goldsmith's tale. It seems
unlikely that he is making a serious effort to protect himself, or even that this is merely a sustained joke. It seems
more likely that the man we obligingly refer to as Stendhal, but who was of course actually Henri Beyle, and
who made a habit of adopting a variety of pseudonyms in
his published writings, must have been more comfortable erecting a screen of fiction behind which he could
give himself permission to write with utter sincerity.
There is in fact a wonderful moment well into the book
when the real and the fictional names are forcibly melded
in an act of sheer impudence, as Stendhal refers to "the
five letters: B,R,U,L,A,R,D, that form my name."

And then, the book appears to be unfinished. Certainly it is unusually rough. Passages of expansive, fully
developed narrative will be followed by a succession of
terse one-sentence paragraphs, fleeting afterthoughts,
qualifications, or digressions inspired by his narration—
and perhaps such brief paragraphs are a perfect representation of the disconnected way in which our thoughts
sometimes move. Stendhal has left blank spaces in the
text where he has forgotten a name or can't think of the
right adjective. He has abbreviated words freely, moti-
vated sometimes by haste and sometimes by (he says) a
fear of censorship. He includes occasional cryptic private references and secret codes. He inserts reminders
to himself throughout the text, usually in the margins,
or corrects errors as he goes along (below a diagram:
"Entrance steps or rather no entrance steps"). He repeats
himself, twice asserting, for instance, that the only passions that have remained with him throughout his life
(besides the desire to write and to live in Paris) are his love
of Saint-Simon and of spinach. Other marginal notes de-

scribe his present state as he writes: "18 December 1835. At 4.50, not enough daylight. I stop. . . . From 2 to half-past 4, twenty-four pages. I am so absorbed by the memories unveiling themselves to my gaze I can scarcely form my letters."

And so it is a curiosity, an anomaly: the book appears rough, unfinished, and yet there are suggestions throughout that this may be just what its author intended. I would like to know—because if Stendhal meant to leave it as it is, he has in effect written a surprisingly modern book. Did he or didn't he plan to fill in the blank spaces, write out the abbreviated words, delete the notes to himself, and in general revise and rewrite to "smooth it out"? Reading with this question in mind, I came to a clue in a marginal note: "Idea. If I don't correct this first draft, perhaps I shall manage not to tell lies out of vanity." It would seem that this thought came to him only as he was writing. Not far away another clue appeared: "I'm well aware that all of this is too long, but I get amusement from finding these early if unhappy times reappear, and I ask M. Levavasseur to shorten it should he publish. H. Beyle." Apparently, at this point, he did not intend to go back and shorten it himself. Toward the end of the book, I came to another: "I shall perhaps have to reread and emend this passage, contrary to my intentions." (The book ends with seven drafts of "Testaments" bequeathing the manuscript to a host of possible publishers, including the bookseller Levavasseur, with instructions to publish it fifteen years after Stendhal's death with all the women's names changed and none of the men's.)

Why is the fragmented, the rough, sometimes so much more inviting than the seamless, the polished? Because

we are closer to the moment of creation? ("Handwriting," he notes in a margin. "This is how I write when
my thoughts are treading on my heels.") Because we are
intimate witnesses to the formulation of the thought?
Inside the experience of the writer instead of outside?
Because we are closer to the evolution by which an event
of the past, long forgotten—though evidently somewhere
present in the brain cells of the writer—is reawakened,
reimagined, re-presented, put into words? ("My heart
is pounding still as I write this thirty-six years later.
I abandon my paper, I wander round my room and I
come back to writing.") As though we were taking part
ourselves, involved in and identifying with the action, the
action being in this case the re-creation and understanding of a life?

Perhaps, too, a work that comes to us so fresh, so raw,
from the writer's mind is more exciting because we see
how precarious is the writer's control—the material is
almost more powerful than he is. As Stendhal himself
says, it was the material—his ideas, his memories—that
commanded him, not some "literary ideal." And so it is
a work that changes as he writes it, that is full of his own
discovery as he goes along; and for his own purposes, and
to our delight, he notes the elaboration of this memoir
even as he writes it.

At one point in his narration Stendhal refers casually to a moment later in his life when he was in mortal
danger: alone in a Silesian field, he saw coming toward
him a company of Cossacks. He does not go on to tell us
what happened next. I wondered, as I continued reading, whether he was merely being artful and would sat-
isfy my curiosity before the book ended. I suspected he
would not, and he did not. His intention in the book,

after all, is not to tell a dramatic story. Yet a different, and greater, drama unfolds as we read, because of the constant double surprise: being alongside him as he works, rather than being handed the result of a later revision, we surprise him in the very act of writing even as he surprises himself in the act of remembering and understanding. And so we are privileged to watch what is really the very dramatic moment, enacted again and again, of the unremembered or half remembered being fully brought to mind, the unformed being formed, the internal becoming external, the private become public.

2002

Maurice Blanchot Absent

It was with Maurice Blanchot's *Death Sentence* that I had my extended initiation into translating very closely and very exactly, more closely and exactly than ever before—for in the case of his words one would not be willing to paraphrase, or to normalize; every word and its placement in relation to every other word had to be respected. This was in 1974 or so. In the years after, until about 1991, I was often working on M. Blanchot's prose, as I translated three more of his novels and a novella, as well as the selection of literary essays that went to make up what was titled *The Gaze of Orpheus.* During those years, I corresponded with him at intervals, with sometimes a year or more passing between letters, and he became a benign presence abiding near the work. Once, when I was planning to be in Paris, I asked him if we could meet, knowing that he rarely met with anyone anymore, but thinking he might make an exception for me. He declined with a gracious explanation: *I live henceforth altogether in retirement and have put such a distance between myself and the world that . . .*

The experience of translating the essays was the most difficult I had ever had in translating, and almost the most difficult I would ever have. (A poem by Anne-Marie Albiach was equally difficult, but for a different reason, because the words and phrases so often appeared in isolation, or with almost no context.) As though this experience were, in fact, a piece of fiction by Blanchot, the meaning of a difficult phrase or sentence became a physical entity that eluded me, that ran from me, that I nearly overtook, that I failed to overtake, this pursuit being enacted inside the arena of my brain even as my brain was also the pursuer of this fleet, evasive thing, the meaning. Understanding became an intensely physical act.

It was during this translation that I experienced another strange struggle with meaning: although, in a simpler paragraph, I found I could follow the thread of M. Blanchot's argument from one sentence to the next, and that it made sense to me, I could not seem to summarize, at the end of the page or even at the end of the paragraph, what I had just read. I thought that this was my own intellectual weakness; then, when I described this difficulty to others, I found that it was true for them as well: it seemed to be in the nature of M. Blanchot's argument to resist summary, even though resisting summary did not mean resisting understanding. Somehow the experience of reading had to take place moment by moment; one had to remain in the moment and not look back on the whole; or one had to dwell inside the moment and not stand back from it; one's understanding proceeded like the guide's flashlight, which illuminates one by one the animals painted on the wall of the prehistoric cave while all else remains in darkness, or at least dimness.

It is difficult for me here, too, to make a general

or comprehensive statement about M. Blanchot, just as it is not easy to summarize what actually goes on in a novel of his, but one can identify certain recurring themes.

Absence is one of those themes, and it has figured largely not only in the narratives of his fiction, and as an element in his literary criticism, but also in the central biographical conundrum of M. Blanchot's existence—his bodily absence, his unwillingness to present himself to others except in letters and phone calls, his unwillingness to be depicted visually. That this is such a well-known and outstanding fact about him does not diminish the puzzle of it: that a man so warmly connected to his friends should live in such retirement, in such retreat, though after all it is perfectly consistent with what he has written. And so, does it become oxymoronic (or simply somewhat moronic) to say one will miss Maurice Blanchot now that he is truly gone? And yet how much more removed he is, now, than he was already by the increasing weakness of old age, by his habit of invisibility, by the accumulating years of epistolary silence (in my case and that of other correspondents).

He was reputed by those who did see him face-to-face in his less retiring days—in the days, some decades ago, when he would rendezvous with a friend, for example, in a pretty church square (Saint-Sulpice) and repair with him to a nearby café; or meet a friend at a train station at midnight in order to solace this friend's troubles with a late supper—to be, in his humility, generosity, and simplicity, like Dostoevsky's Prince Myshkin. Certainly in the letters that he wrote to me over the years and that I am rereading now, he is always elaborately kind, thoughtful, and without apparent self-interest. When solicited, just once, to express a desire, he is modest, though perfectly clear; when, on another occasion, he voices an objection to a fait accompli (a book cover), he expresses it gently in the perfect conditional—*I would have preferred the face to remain the invisible into which it had faded away*—and then softens it with a most characteristic observation: *But the invisible remains nevertheless.* He replies to some of my news with the gently and quietly effective *Permit me to answer in my thoughts.*

In these letters, he is concerned about what is happening—usually not good—in the world (in 1981, apropos of Ronald Reagan: *Thus far, everything seems to have gone well for him, but a time will come when, without realizing it, he will find himself confronting the abyss*; ten years later came the Gulf War, with *its cruelties, its barbarities*). He offers a gift of sympathy when he calls university teaching a *painful ordeal* (*rude épreuve*). He then goes on to describe Georges Bataille's manner in the classroom: *His lectures were interrupted by long, and by interminable, silences; it was distressing but for that very reason enriching.* He adds, in a subsequent letter, that Bataille *could remain silent as though meditating without his listeners experiencing anything but the sense of the anguish that was his.* There is a constancy, over the years, in his preoccupations, in his memories, in his references to friends, of whom he speaks most warmly, and three of the closest of whom he lost in quick succession in 1990 and 1991—Robert Antelme, Michel Leiris, and Edmond Jabès (*mort inattendu*).

Of course he is to some degree present again, or still, in his writings, and especially so in his letters. The letters spoke, at the time he wrote them, from out of his absence when he was no more than geographically remote, and by habit invisible; they speak as distinctly now that he is truly gone, though what is also gone now, as it was not then, is the possibility of replying to him, except in one's thoughts.

2003

A Farewell to Michel Butor

September 14, 1926–August 24, 2016

When you hear that a writer you first came to know in your youth, decades ago, is still writing in his advanced old age, you are at first surprised, as though he has risen from the tomb to write the poem you are reading. Then, once you absorb this fact, you go on to believe, quite illogically, that he will not die—after all, he has not died thus far. Certainly he will not die soon, in any case.

For me, those two responses happened just this year: in the spring, Michel Butor was asked by the organizers of the Albanian Pavilion of the Venice Architecture Biennale if he would contribute a poem for an album of songs on themes of migration and displacement. After he sent it to them, they asked me if I would translate it. And then, on August 24, just a few months after I sent in my translation, Michel Butor died. I was startled and saddened: How could he leave so abruptly, when for me he had just, in a way, returned?

That Butor would, at the age of nearly ninety, respond to the Biennale's request with a poem so emphatic and moving as "Squandered Bullion," which opens, "The bank has gutted itself / like an old-time samurai / practicing seppuku / and the safes' entrails / spread through the street," should not really come as a surprise, considering his long, productive writing life, his ever-renewed formal innovation, his strong political and social convictions, and his wide-ranging interests.

My own active involvement in his work occurred at three neat points in my life—early, middle, and late (or should I hedge and say, instead: early, middle, and recent).

In college, at the age of twenty or so, I chose as thesis topic the writers of the so-called New Novel (*le nouveau roman*)—a label that Butor himself resisted. In the paper, I discussed Robbe-Grillet, Sarraute, perhaps Duras, and Butor. While the other authors interested me intellectually but did not touch me emotionally, I found Butor's *Degrees* (read in Richard Howard's English translation) entrancing.

Degrees was Butor's fourth novel. His third, *La Modification* (*A Change of Heart*), tightly structured and unusual in form—it is written entirely in the second person, its action confined to a single train compartment—had won him the Prix Renaudot, France's most prestigious prize after the Goncourt. This "fragile and ephemeral notoriety," Butor later wrote, allowed him to settle in Paris and embark on a book that would be still more formally audacious.

A substantial book at 450 pages, *Degrees* recounts the lives and studies of teachers and students in a Paris lycée as told by three different narrators in succession, beginning with a teacher whose ambition it is to bring together into a coherent and rational whole, for the benefit of his nephew, the different courses of study in the upper-grade curriculum. What I appreciated was, for one, the patient and unstinting detail—somewhat akin to the more factual sections of James Agee's *Let Us Now Praise Famous Men* or perhaps *Moby-Dick*'s more technical chapters; the embrace, within a work of fiction, of various bodies of knowledge—which I relished also in Flaubert's *Bouvard and Pécuchet*; the extensive and frequent quotations from the works the children were studying—one critic at the time complained that the reader drowns in a sea of them; and the mathematical fascination of author and narrators (and, of course, reader) with the complex interrelations, familial and other, among the characters (which now remind me of Georges Perec's *Life: A User's Manual*, confined to the population of a single apartment building—as was Butor's first novel, *Passage de Milan*).

I'm sure it also appealed to me because I was still very close, in those years, to my own equivalent of the lycée experience. At the time, I imagined *Degrees* to be an established classic, not realizing that it had first appeared in French only in 1960, some seven or eight years before I read it. (It was published in English the following year, with remarkable promptness, thanks to the translator Howard and the publisher Simon & Schuster.)

While its structure and literary aims are sizable, and its plot will develop to become strangely obsessive, the book opens with a calm familiarity that allows one easy access. Its setting shares that of the opening of *Madame Bovary*—the French schoolroom, teacher presiding, students ranged before him:

> I walk into the classroom, and I step up on to the platform.
> When the bell stops ringing, I take out of the briefcase I have just laid on the desk the

alphabetical list of the students and that other
sheet of white paper, on which they themselves
have indicated their seats in this classroom.

Then I sit down, and when all the talking has
stopped, I begin to call the roll:

"Abel, Armelli, Baron . . . ,"

trying to fix their faces in my memory.

It was a collection of travel essays that next brought me
into a working involvement with Butor's writing, when,
in 1985, the adventurous and discriminating Marlboro
Press (essentially Austryn Wainhouse's one-man opera-
tion) hired me to translate the first volume of Butor's
suite of five "travel autobiographies or geographical
meditations," as he called them, titled *Le Génie du lieu*
(The Spirit of the Place).

This book, which we titled *The Spirit of Mediterranean Places*, opens with an essay on Cordova ("Its net-
work of white streets, . . . its walls the color of sand or
lime . . . the coolness of the precise shadows it cast, tri-
angles or trapezoids changing proportion according to
the day and the hour, the memory of my patient but too
brief efforts to read it"); and continues with Istanbul,
Salonica, and Delphi; Mallia, Mantua, and Ferrara; and,
finally—the entire second half of the book—Egypt, ending with the question "When will I return to Egypt?"

Later volumes of this series became more formally
innovative. Visiting the United States in the 1960s, particularly New York City, Butor was convinced that he was
discovering something that had yet to reach France, that
he was, in a sense, looking into the future. He felt that he
should inform himself as best he could about the country. This led him to write the prose-rhapsody *Mobile*,

subtitled *Study for a Representation of the United States.*
Other travel books included the experimental stereo-
phonic novel called, in English, *Niagara* (the original
French title, more mysterious and eccentric, could be
translated as "6,810,000 Liters of Water per Second"),
using three typefaces and three margins.

In addition to his novels and travel books, Butor wrote
literary criticism and art criticism—he said that he loved
painters' studios and their conversation; poetry, including translations of Friedrich Hölderlin, Lukács, Shakespeare, and others; a work of fiction that incorporated
verse; and a series of collections of invented dreams based
on his own and others' real dreams. He taught in many
institutions, in France but also in Thessaloniki, Egypt;
the United States; Manchester, England—the latter providing him the material for his second novel, *Passing
Time*—and, for many years, Geneva.

Butor was honored during his lifetime with many
prizes besides the Prix Renaudot, among them the Prix
Apollo, the Prix Mallarmé, the Prix Fénéon for *Passing
Time*, and, from the Académie française in 2013, the
Grand Prix for his life's work. He was born in 1926 in
Mons-en-Barœul, near Lille, spent the later part of his
life in the Savoyard village of Lucinges, in southeast-
ern France near Geneva, and died not far from there in
Contamine-sur-Arve. His wife, Marie-Jo Mas, teacher
and photographer, died in 2010; together they had four
daughters. He grew a snowy white beard after he became
a grandfather, and preferred to dress in overalls.

He was not a writer who gradually faded from view,
but one who gave generously to the extent of his capacity right up to the end. The poem that Butor sent earlier
this spring was one he had written in 2014 for his artist

friend Jacques Riby. It ends on a cautiously optimistic note, suggesting the power of the individual to rescue a thing of value, something that could "galvanize" our lives, from the catastrophe of economic corruption and collapse: "The rare pearl ripens / in its wasteland exile / awaiting its discoverer."

2016

Michel Leiris's *Fibrils*, Volume 3 of *The Rules of the Game*

In his massive autobiographical project, *La Règle du jeu* (*The Rules of the Game*), Michel Leiris anticipated certain works very much of the moment in our twenty-first century: this is a writer's ruthlessly honest, multivolume examination of himself that admits into its arena the banal and quotidian as well as the dramatic and rare. But beyond the fact that Leiris's work was begun some seventy-five years ago, there are a couple of other critical considerations: Leiris, by the time he began *La Règle*, had rejected fiction and embraced realism—he called what he was doing not a "novel" but an "autobiographical essay." And, second, the project extended over thirty-five years—begun when he was barely forty and completed when he was in his seventies—so that it had the scope and endurance to contain his reflections and objectives as they changed over time: we are fully brought into his mind, and we accompany his thinking as it matures.

As he was writing volume 1, Leiris evidently foresaw a second volume, but not more. Similarly, in *Fibrilles* (*Fibrils*), the third volume, published in 1966, he appears, from the tone of his conclusion, not to have anticipated

volume 4. After that one, was the work finished? Not
quite, since the fourth was followed by separate but
related work in 1981. He had more to say; he was
speaking in order to speak, he offered, ironically and
not quite truthfully. *Le Ruban au cou d'Olympia* (*The
Ribbon at Olympia's Throat*)—which takes its title, and
one of its continuing subjects, from Manet's painting of
a recumbent prostitute clothed in little else but a black
ribbon—centers on the expressive power of fetishism in
a broader, not merely erotic, sense. (It includes, for example, a brief text on the act of writing as hurling a
lasso, and another about the urgent desire to smoke when
one is already smoking.)

In addition, extending the scope of the project backward in time, the four volumes of *La Règle* were in fact
preceded not by a trial run, but by a first exploration
into the territory of himself, this one concentrating specifically on his sexuality: *L'Âge d'homme* (1939). Published in English, in Richard Howard's translation, as
Manhood in 1968, it depicts the full range of sexual ob-
sessions of a man—or this man, in any case—as he grows
into manhood: daydream, masturbation, impotence, cel-
ibacy, homosexuality, prostitution, marriage.

Michel Leiris was born in 1901, within a comfortable
bourgeois family in Paris. He was educated at the Lycée
Janson de Sailly (in philosophy), the Sorbonne, and the
École pratique des hautes études. After a tentative sortie
into the study of chemistry, he cast his lot in the world
of writing and art, specifically gravitating to poetry and
the idea of becoming a poet, as he describes in the present volume. When he was not yet twenty, he met Max
Jacob, and through him became involved in a circle of

Dadaists and surrealists, identifying himself as a surrealist until he broke with the group in 1929. A somewhat emotional decision, in 1931, to take part, as secretary-archivist, in a two-year ethnographic expedition across sub-Saharan Africa led, after further and extensive study, to a career as professional ethnographer. He continued that career, occupying a post at one division of Paris's natural history museum, the Musée de l'Homme, until late in his working life, pairing it with his equally full career as writer.

Throughout his long life, prolific and productive until close to his death at age eighty-nine, Leiris wrote a variety of works in different genres: essays on jazz, the theater, literature, and art; volumes of poetry and poetic prose; the vast, rich journal that resulted from his African expedition—*L'Afrique fantôme* (*Phantom Africa*); an eccentric dictionary of personal definitions evolving from wordplay and private associations called *Glossaire: J'y serre mes gloses* (a punning title for a punning work—one inventive equivalent in English is James Clifford's *Glossary: My Glosses' Ossuary*); the surrealist novel *Aurora*; a collection of his dreams and his dreamlike waking experiences called *Nuits sans nuit et quelques jours sans jour* (translated by Richard Sieburth into English under the title *Nights as Day, Days as Night*); essays and book-length studies in the field of ethnography; prefaces and catalog texts; book reviews; political texts; and, most regularly, appreciations of artists and writers, particularly within the wide circle of those he knew personally—among them André Masson, Miró, Raymond Roussel, Francis Bacon, Raymond Queneau, Picasso, Michel Butor, Sartre, Duchamp, and Giacometti.

In was in the midst of this other writing activity, in

the early 1940s, that Leiris embarked on what was to be
his masterwork, the work on which his enduring literary
reputation would rest: the autobiographical essay—as he
later described it—called *The Rules of the Game*. Most of
the first volume was written during the German occupa-
tion of France; the final volume was completed in 1975.
He was henceforth to divide his life among his continuing autobiographical project; his multifarious other
writing; his editorial activities; his political activities; his
family and friendships; his travels; and his ethnographic
work.

With *Biffures* (*Scratches*), volume 1 of *La Règle*, Leiris began his extended project, the objectives of which fully
emerge only over the successive volumes—to write in
order to see more clearly into himself, to work out his
personal identity; at the same time to unite the two tendencies in himself between which he felt divided: on the
one hand, poetry, the attraction to the *over-there*, to
myth, to timelessness; and on the other, morality, knowledge, the *right-here*, lived reality; and to formulate a de-
finitive "golden rule," the rule that, he hoped, would
both govern his ars poetica—his poetics—and be a rule
for living, a *savoir-vivre*, an ethics, the code by which he
would live.

He opens the book with one of his continuing central preoccupations, language in all its aspects: language
as the raw material of poetry; the mysteries of language;
the sounds of words, taken in themselves; the elusive and
personal meanings of these sounds and of words themselves; private language versus shared language; language
as connection to others; the discoveries possible through
language; the failure of language. Cataloging, or inven-

torying, his memories from various periods of his life, but especially from his childhood, he begins the book with the mystery he found in language when he was a child, in his misunderstandings of names, songs, scraps of speech—misunderstandings that created for him an alternate universe of things, people, customs, emotions. In this volume, he comes to define the literary use of speech as a way of sharpening one's consciousness "in order to be more—and in a better way—alive." The relationship, then, is reciprocal: the writer lives in order to write, but also writes in order to be more fully alive.

The next volume, *Fourbis* (*Scraps*), continues the inventory, though its preoccupations have inevitably shifted a little with the passing years. Its main themes and subjects of inquiry, as described by Leiris, are now "to trim the claws of death, to behave like a man, to break one's own walls"—in other words, to tame death, to take action, and to break through the circle of the self. This volume begins to reflect the attraction exerted on him by external, historical events, including political activism. It also tells of his continuing preoccupation with the erotic, specifically detailing the story of his liaison with an Algerian prostitute, Khadidja, when he was a soldier stationed near Beni-Ounif during World War II, describing what he saw as her moral as well as physical beauty. In this volume, as in the first, he brings to his method of composition his training as ethnographer, working from slips of paper on which he had previously made notations—of facts, memories, ideas—which he then takes as starting points for his explorations.

In the third, and present, volume, *Fibrilles* (*Fibrils*), though Leiris worries that his objective itself has also shifted with the passing of time, the problem becomes clearer: how to reconcile literary commitment and social commitment. Here, he looks in particular to the example of his close friend, the poet Aimé Césaire, who combines both without compromising either. Having opened the book with an account of his participation in a delegation to China, his attraction to that country, and his hopes for its future, Leiris continues with an exploration, again, of contrasts: his perception of China (representing morality, constraint, reason) as one of two poles between which he is divided, the other represented by the large market town of Kumasi, in Ashanti country (symbolizing sentiment, dilection, imagination), and the thronged Easter service Leiris attended there in its (ugly, he calls it) cathedral. The heart of *Fibrils*, however, the story that dominates this volume, is that of an emotional dilemma and its consequences: his division of loyalties between the woman with whom he has been having an affair, and his wife, called only "Z." He describes his impossible situation—being frank and honorable with either woman would betray the other—and his resultant suicide attempt, as well as its aftermath and the ramifications of both. The associative explorations in this book delve deep into several significant dreams, including some he had while half awake in his hospital room in the days following his suicide attempt, but his discussion of these dreams always circles out to include other narratives from his past, accounts of travels, or of friendships. (Leiris's preoccupation with his erotic life and, more broadly, love, as well as his suicidal tendencies and his avowed cowardice in the face of his own "annihilation," began early, showing up, for instance, in *L'Afrique fantôme*, when he was barely thirty and already married to Louise "Zette" Godon.)

We realize, in the course of this volume, that the subject here is not only Leiris himself, and his actions, feelings, and thoughts, but also Leiris in the act of writing, and the writing of this essay itself. He talks about this book in the act of writing it. He describes the slips of paper, he quotes from them, allowing each to lead by association to more "data" for his explorations. He hopes to establish between them connecting threads, the "fibrils" of the title. His punning and his associative pairing—wordplay was an essential part of Leiris's relationship to language—are never arbitrary, but constitute so many knots where some of the multiple threads of remembrances and ideas come together. In this volume, he fears that he will nearly die of the effort it costs him, even before fate finishes him off. Whereas he had hoped by writing to escape time, he is nevertheless subject to time—the past of his life, his present life in the changing world, and the time of the writing itself. Perhaps, he also realizes, the rules he seeks will be directives implied by the game itself. Perhaps he should settle for a "professional morality" as opposed to a more universal Morality.

In the last volume, *Frêle bruit* (Frail Noise), more ample, at four hundred pages, than the previous, Leiris once again defines the purpose of the whole of *The Rules of the Game* as to "expose as thoroughly as possible the sample of humanity that he is." He describes this volume not as a logical or chronological sequel to the other volumes, but as a peninsula or constellation; it is not a rational construction, but a "florilegium" drawn from all periods of his life. The form of the book, therefore, is unlike that of the previous volumes of *The Rules*: whereas they are continuous, with only a few breaks into separate parts, this last volume includes many very brief sections, some less than a page, as though Leiris were bringing his last, disconnected thoughts together into one place. It contains, for instance, stories, chants, curses, poems, meditations, lists of titles, scraps of memory, and bits of his journal. But there could be no "last thoughts"; the ongoing autobiographical project, which included several more shorter works even after *Le Ruban au cou d'Olympia*, would not be so much ended as finally interrupted by death, since even after his death, his vast, self-reflexive, and self-critical journal was published, at his instruction—more than eight hundred pages.

In the pages of *Frêle bruit*, Leiris is all the more acutely conscious of the passage of time, even more relentlessly haunted than in the other volumes by the fear of his own death; because by now, as he concludes the book, he is, in fact, in his midseventies—an old man. But he has also managed, over the course of the four volumes, to clarify certain things for himself: he has recognized in himself, he says in this volume, a need "to merge the *yes* and the *no*," a need that sometimes seems to denote "a perverse inclination to find enjoyment only in ambiguity and paradox . . . sometimes . . . sanctified by the idea that a marriage of contraries is the highest summit one can metaphysically attain."

Both *Manhood* and *The Rules of the Game* were preoccupied with the horror of his own mortality, the specter of his own death. It is possible to imagine Leiris, even more than most chroniclers of their own lives, wanting to complete the work that can never be completed, by writing about his death. But as the writer can't find a vantage point from which to look upon his death except one that precedes it in time, it seems that Leiris's whole endeavor, in this work, was somehow to get around that difficulty, somehow to comprehend, embrace death beforehand in such a way as to have documented as completely as possible what he might also have liked to document as it was happening or after it had happened. The voice that said this, so lucidly and so frankly, has been silenced by Leiris's actual death in 1990, and, in a way that is not yet clear, this changes the voice one hears in the pages of his work. This voice both does and does not come to us from beyond the grave.

On the other hand, it is also possible that Leiris wished to write in precisely the situation in which he did write: documenting his life in the shadow of his death. For a kind of completeness is certainly achieved here in *The Rules of the Game* through the avoidance of closure, changing the terms of the work so that the motion is infinite insight inward, infinitely continuing investigation. No event is "closed," no thought, no datum. Progress is inward, and circular, rather than forward, involving the close examination of all sides of things: not only people and events but motives, effects, interpretations, and the nuances thereof. And digression, as well as expansion outward, is a natural part of this close examination.

Amplification away from the main narrative track throws light on what is being described, fills in the picture, at least, of how Leiris himself reacted to what went on. Amplification can be infinite, of course, and even infinitely justified. It not only illuminates but also works dramatically to suspend the action, to delay satisfaction. It gives the event, which may be quite banal in itself, an added richness and depth; it may extend its meaning from personal to public. Amplification strays from the point, but it also particularizes and nuances the subject.

In fact, Leiris's close attention to documenting the ordinary elevates it into something so particular that it becomes strange. As he came to distrust the exotic, he found otherness in the familiar, foreignness in the domestic.

Although his main subject is himself writing these works, part of the activity of his exploration is to bring the world into the discussion: it is through oneself that one gains knowledge of the "other" and of the world. His examination of himself is not exclusive but inclusive. He does not reject politics, history, or culture as part of his own self-portrait. Throughout his life, he was fully involved, literarily and politically, in the world outside himself—particularly with his fellow artists and as an activist against the "flagrant" injustices of society and "our Western arrogance," as he put it—and he includes his political activities and his friendships in his account of himself, as well as the non-Western cultures he studies as an ethnographer.

What is our sense of the narrator himself? It is curiously paradoxical. Leiris is rarely brief, rarely plain, in *Fibrils*, since every thought seems to produce a possible counterthought that should be included, and his constant elaboration and qualification, his ruthless honesty, his stated doubts express or imply a certain modesty, self-recrimination, apology. Yet at the same time he effectively and relentlessly commands our steady attention by involving us in his thoughts as they unfold. The play of opposites is active here, too, as it is throughout *The Rules of the Game* and in Leiris's work in general: the pendulum swings between reticence and self-display, private and public, inside and outside, self and other.

Leiris maintained a separation between his work as writer and his work as ethnographer. He constructed his days themselves as alternations between work at home, as writer (in the mornings), and work at his office, as ethnographer (in the afternoons), the two spaces "stirring up different ideas," as he said: he was rarely an ethnologist when at home and rarely a writer when at the museum. The two spaces were connected, physically, by the familiar, daily reiterated path of the number 63 bus.

It was in this office, a small room below ground level at the Musée de l'Homme, that I met Leiris for the only time, on a day probably in the mid-1980s that I can no longer pinpoint. To judge only from appearances, his preoccupation with the erotic, his periodic love affairs at home in Paris, and, even more, his liaison with the Algerian Khadidja, would seem quite incongruous for this cloistered scholar, this awkward, reserved man, in tailored clothing so correct and elegant, with his skin so pale, bony skull so naked, expression so tense and haunted, eyes so fearful: this was how he appeared to me that day. The museum, next to the Trocadéro Gardens and across the Pont d'Iéna from the Eiffel Tower, was surrounded by tourists milling about in the morning sun and by African vendors flying uncannily lifelike mechanical birds. Leiris's voice trembled when he greeted me outside the elevator in the basement corridor. He was shy, as I had been warned, and he fell into silence often. He was deaf in one ear—forewarned of this, also, I probably spoke too loudly. The single window, above some radiator pipes, was now and then filled with the faces of curious tourists shading their eyes to see in. They would have seen a woman sitting nervously erect on her chair across from a thin old man, his bald head slightly bowed.

Khadidja herself had at first mistaken him for a monk. But the opposition between external appearance (tailored, spotless, ascetic) and internal being (emotionally chaotic, uncertain, vulnerable) is inherent to Leiris's central preoccupation, well explored in *Fibrils*, and this apparent contradiction is a part of Leiris's more general complexity, a complexity he was at such pains to try to understand and demonstrate in *The Rules of the Game*.

Leiris wrote me a postcard early in the final year of his life, some three decades ago (on this, there is a date), signed in shaky, spidery script. In it, he offered, most graciously, and with a typical qualification, typically inserted with syntactical elegance into the sentence—*dans la mesure du possible*, "insofar as possible"—to give me whatever assistance I might need from him. I was then completing a translation of his collected occasional writings, *Brisées: Broken Branches* (which includes, among other colorful and beguiling offerings, a brief piece on metaphor, one on human saliva, and a decoding of the captivating, to him, Fred Astaire). I never asked him for help, in the end, but there are a few points in *Fibrils* I would not mind checking with him, now that it is too late. But it is too late.

2017

THE BIBLE, MEMORY,
AND THE PASSAGE
OF TIME

As I Was Reading

Some time ago, I was reading a history of France, beginning, with a misguided zealousness, at the very beginning of this book, three inches thick, with the intention of reading it straight through. I was startled to discover, by page 30, how very little happened in a thousand years, back in the last Ice Age.

Our present millennium, the twentieth century, was creeping and climbing and halting toward its end. Every hundred years of it had been so fought-over, so exceedingly complicated, filling history books. Not only had it been eventful, but each event had given rise to so much interpretation. But back then, it seemed, in what I thought of as those Paleolithic times (I was not really sure what *Paleolithic* meant), very little happened in a millennium.

What about this thing, a millennium? Before I continued reading this 679-page book, I decided to spend a little time investigating. I wanted to find out some things—what other millennia had been like, how long a millennium really was, whether it was longer at different times, how much happened during one, what happened. So I started looking here and there to see what I could find out.

I wanted to start with the word *millenary*. But as I was already slightly befuddled and more familiar with the word *millinery*, I immediately lost my way, and instead of reading about a period of a thousand years I began reading about hats. I already knew that hats used to be important in the United States, or more important than they are now. I did not know that the simplest form of head coverings, in antiquity, were the cap and the hood. Hats developed from these. The first known type of hat (Greek) was distinguished as such by having a brim. (This hat tied under the chin and was worn by travelers.) In the nineteenth century, women's hats increased in size with their coiffures. With the advent of the closed automobile, hats became smaller. I knew that Danbury, Connecticut, had been a center of hatmaking. I remembered this because I had a cousin Louise who lived in Danbury. I thought about it every time I drove near the city. I did not know that its hat industry began all the way back in 1780. In the 1960s, the industry declined. I thought I knew that the decline began with JFK not wearing a hat at his inauguration.

All this was interesting, although I wanted to know when, exactly, the Greek hat was developed. What, exactly, did they mean by *antiquity*? Elsewhere it was defined as "in ancient times." But when was "in ancient times"? Roughly, they said, before the Middle Ages.

Next, I discovered that *the millennium* can refer to the thousand years in which, according to Revelation 20, Christ will reign again gloriously on earth and holiness will prevail. A millennium can also be a period of great happiness or human perfection. The article referred me to "Judgment Day."

I thought I knew what Judgment Day was, but I decided to refresh my memory. On Judgment Day, this world will come to an end, the dead will be raised up in the general resurrection, and Christ will come in glory to judge the living and the dead; then the sinners will be cast into hell, and the righteous will live in heaven forever. *Glory*, specifically, means the splendor and beatific happiness of heaven. It can also mean a ring or spot of light. I did not know which meaning applied to Christ coming in glory—perhaps both. There was apparently no generally accepted teaching among Christians as to when the Second Coming would take place, but many individuals had ventured to prophesy its dates. Those who lay stress on the end of the world are called adventists, chiliasts, or millenarians.

I wanted to know what the word *chiliasm* meant. I thought I could remember this word by thinking of chili and chasm. But instead of *chiliasm*, I looked up *chiasma*, meaning "crossing over." Crossing over occurs in the first division of meiosis. Two chromosomes of a homologous pair exchange equal segments with each other. Crossing over results in recombination of genes found on the same chromosome. Under the microscope, a crossover has the appearance of an *X* and is called a chiasma. *Chiasma* is Greek for "crosspiece" and comes from the Greek *chiazein*, to mark with a *chi*, or *X*.

Once I found *chiliasm*, I learned that it comes from the Greek *chilioi*, meaning "one thousand." Belief in the millennium is called chiliasm by historians of the ancient church. Looking back from *chiliasm* I saw *chiliad*, a period of a thousand years. Looking ahead from *chiliasm* I saw *chili con carne* and *chili sauce*. Before *chiasma* came *chiaroscuro* and before that *chiaroscurist*, before that *chiao*, a Chinese coin, *Chianti*, and *chi*. After *chiasma* came *chiasmatype*, the spiral twisting of homologous chromosomes during zygotene that results in chiasma formation and provides the mechanism for crossing over; *chiaus*, a Turkish messenger; *Chibcha*, a Chibchan people of central Colombia; *chibouk*, a long-stemmed Turkish tobacco pipe with a clay bowl; *chic*; *Chicago*; and *chicalote*, a white-flowered prickly poppy of Mexico.

A few days before, I had heard from a Romanian visitor how the history of his country had been affected by having such neighbors as Turkey and Russia. I also learned that Romania was successively overrun, after the Romans left it in the third century, by the Goths, the Huns, the Avars, the Bulgars, and the Magyars. I was eating in a Salvadoran restaurant. Our waitress was of Swedish descent. Our host was English. His wife, who was American, apologized because she had to leave in the middle of dinner to attend a class in Sanskrit. She explained that the students were taught not just the language but also the concepts behind certain of the words. How interesting, I thought. But what did I know about Sanskrit, really? I knew it was very old. The only other thing I knew was that in the latter half of the nineteenth century, in a work of fiction that was based on a real account, the sixty-seven royal children of the king of Siam were purportedly studying Sanskrit. I learned this from reading *Anna and the King of Siam*.

Some of the oldest surviving Indo-European documents are written in Sanskrit, though Hittite is probably the earliest recorded Indo-European language, with at least one text dated around the seventeenth century B.C. I was surprised that Sanskrit was an Indo-European language. When I said the word to myself, I must have been thinking of *European* more than *Indo*. In fact, I

couldn't remember just what *Indo-European* included.
Now I learned that it included those languages spoken
in most of Europe and in the parts of the world colo-
nized by Europeans since A.D. 1500 and also in Persia,
the subcontinent of India, and some other parts of Asia.
The year 1500 was beginning to seem recent to me, by
now. By now, I had to marvel that only in the past half
millennium or so had Portuguese been spoken in Brazil,
or, for that matter, English in America.

Indo-European includes, for instance, Romany, Kash-
miri, Kurdish, Ukrainian, Czech, Lithuanian, Haitian
Creole, Scotch Gaelic, Welsh, and Frisian, but not, for
instance, Finnish, Hungarian, Lapp, Estonian, Samo-
yed, Turkish, Mongolian, Kalmuck, or Cree (which
belongs to the Algonquian branch of the Algonquian-
Wakashan linguistic stock of American Indian languages). Indo-European is a family of languages that may
have descended from an original parent language called
Proto-Indo-European, which is believed to have been
spoken some time before 2000 B.C. and before writing
was known to its speakers.

"Before 2000 B.C." was vague, I thought. It covered
a very long stretch of time. I had already learned from
the French history book, which had started all this, that
"modern man" had been in existence since 40,000 B.C.

If asked, I realized, I could not have said much about
the Hittites. And yet I thought I should have known
something about them, if theirs was the earliest recorded
Indo-European language.

I learned that the name *Hittite* comes from the Hebrew
Hitti, which in turn comes from the Hittite *Hatti*. The
Hittite language is sometimes considered part of the
Indo-European language family. It is known to us from

hieroglyphic texts. The Hittites were a conquering people of Asia Minor and Syria with an empire in the second millennium B.C. The aboriginal inhabitants of the land were apparently the Khatti, or Hatti. The capital of the Hittite Empire was Hattusas. Hattusas still exists, in Turkey, though now it is only a village and is called Bogazköy. In the ruins were found, in A.D. 1906, ten thousand tablets bearing Hittite inscriptions.

I would not have paid much attention to the fact that the Hittites' neighbors to the southeast, in the Upper Euphrates, were the Khurrites, were it not for the fact that on the page before the entry for *Hittites* was an entry for a Lebanese American professor and scholar named Philip Khuri Hitti, who had taught Oriental languages and Semitic literature at Columbia and Princeton and written at least four books. I was struck by his middle and last names. I also noticed, looking at his birth date, that the Hittite tablets were discovered at about the time he turned twenty-one. Did this discovery come at just the right moment to determine his subsequent career?

I stopped and reflected that only as the last centuries of our millennium have crept and halted along have we even discovered the existence of such earlier civilizations as the Hittites. I remembered hearing it said that at a certain point in the past—a few centuries ago? in the Enlightenment? much earlier?—a single human being could know everything—about history? about science?—that was known. In other words, a great deal less was known then. But I'm not sure how far back that was.

Before *Sanskrit*, in my encyclopedia, came a listing for *San Sebástian*, a city in Northern Spain on the Bay of

Biscay; and before that, *sans-culottides*, the last five days of the year in the French Revolutionary Calendar. The sans-culottides were named in honor of the *sans-culottes* ("without knee breeches"), the lower classes in France during the French Revolution. After *Sanskrit literature* came *Andrea Sansovino*, a Florentine sculptor and architect of the High Renaissance whose real name was Contucci and who took the name of the place where he was born. After him came *Jacopo Sansovino*, an Italian sculptor and architect of the Renaissance whose real name was Tatti and who took the name of his master, Andrea Sansovino.

I was talking to people about my investigation as it went along—about time, history, and dates—and I discovered that not just I, and not just Christians, but most people seemed to take their bearings from the year 0, the year in which Jesus of Nazareth was (mistakenly) supposed to have been born. (Even the actual birth of Jesus, which I think was in 3 B.C., was reckoned from that mistaken year 0, the year of the birth of Christ.) It seemed to me that the reason for this was not just convenience, but a failure of imagination, or the illusion that because of the zero, something had begun then. I said to myself that people who used Fahrenheit also thought of zero degrees Fahrenheit as some kind of absolute, even though it is not any particular point, such as the point at which water freezes. If the year 0 had been the beginning, two thousand would be many years. But it was not the beginning at all, only a point along the way.

What about this? What about years computed from a fixed point (like the birth of Christ)?

I learned that in chronology, an era was a period

reckoned from a fixed point in time. I wanted to know what some other fixed points were. The encyclopedia I happened to be using is Western, so it is biased toward information about the West and therefore limited, but some fixed points in time were the creation of the world (Jewish, equivalent to 3761 B.C.; Byzantine, 5508 B.C.); the founding of the city of Rome (753 B.C.; year designated A.U.C. for *ab urbe condita*, "from the founding of the city"); and the hegira.

But I had to stop. Did I know what the hegira was? The word comes from the Arabic *hijrah*, meaning "breaking off of relations." The hegira was the flight from Mecca of the Prophet Muhammad, driven out by angry businessmen, in September of A.D. 622. The Muslim era is dated from the first day of the lunar year in which the hegira took place (July 16, 622).

I went on: another era was reckoned from the founding of the Olympic Games in ancient Greece (776 B.C.; time in Olympiads); another from the proclamation of the French Republic (September 22, 1792). The French Revolutionary Calendar was divided into twelve months of thirty days each, named after vintage, fog, frost, snow, rain, wind, seed, blossom, pasture, harvest, heat, and fruit. The remaining five days, the sans-culottides, were feast days.

I was confident that I knew what a calendar was, but I looked it up anyway. I discovered one thing, at least, that I had not known. The word *calendar* comes from a Latin word meaning "moneylender's account book."

Before *calendar* came *Robert Calef*, a seventeenth-century Boston cloth merchant known primarily as the author of *More Wonders of the Invisible World*. My amusement turned to respect when I read on and learned that his book attacked Cotton Mather, condemned the view of witchcraft then prevailing, and had a salutary effect throughout New England. After *calendar* came *calendering*, a finishing process for paper, plastics, rubber, and textiles; followed by *calendula*, an annual with flower heads that are yellow to deep orange and a popular garden flower in Shakespeare's time—what he called "marigold."

The term *epoch* was apparently often confused with *era* in writing. I did not know specifically what *epoch* meant, but I was to learn later.

Before *era* came *Er*, Judah's first son; before that, *Er*, the chemical symbol of the element erbium. After *era* came *Eran*, Ephraim's grandson; the *era of good feelings*, a period in U.S. history after the War of 1812 when people were anxious to return to a normal life, forget political issues, and strive for unity as a nation.

I noticed that in my exploration of history, I kept coming up against religion, often the Christian religion but sometimes another religion: Judaism (apropos of the creation of the world), Muhammadanism (apropos of the departure of the Prophet). My encyclopedia was full of names of characters from "our" Bible.

Religion was defined as not only the service and worship of God or the supernatural, or a personal set of religious attitudes, but also a system of beliefs held to with ardor and faith.

I thought: People needed their systems of beliefs in order to make sense of a world of facts? Or what? I was close to a thought but not there yet.

I found myself considering the turn of "our"

millennium with some dread, not because I was a believer in any particular religion or any particular calendar, but because I was afraid of people who believed, certain of whom tended to do insane and violent things in the name of their beliefs.

I began to wonder why I was pursuing this investigation. Maybe I did not really want to find out how long a millennium was. Wasn't that a little too silly? Maybe I did think the world was going to end at the end of this millennium, and these years would be my last chance to study the history of the world. I had never paid enough attention to history. In school, I had never liked the subject history, because it offered no clear answers, as math and the sciences did. I had gotten poor grades in history.

Or was the real goal of my investigation to retreat into the millennia of the past, so as to make the present millennium less present? Was I afraid of the present millennium?

I went back to my history of France, maybe for reassurance. There was a calm and friendly tone to the book. The author was just as amazed as I was by the vast stretches of time he was describing. He kept expressing them in different ways: Neanderthal man remained essentially unchanged for sixty millennia! For six hundred centuries!

Sheep were first domesticated in about 5000 B.C. The first use of their fleece for wool is dated at about 4000 B.C.

Could this really be true? That a thousand years went by—about the same number of centuries as between the Norman Conquest and now—before people understood how they could use sheep's fleece?

I made a short list for myself going up the millennia:

The first signs of the transformation from hunters to farmers (in France): about 7000 B.C.

The first villages and transhumance (in France): about 5000 B.C. (*Transhumance* was, and still is, the movement of sheep up into the mountain pastures for the summer and back down into the valley pastures in the fall.)

The first use of the fleece of sheep for wool: about 4000 B.C.

The beginning of Greece's long Neolithic period: about 4000 B.C.

"Important cultures" had developed in Greece by about 3000 B.C.

The unification of Egypt under one ruler: about 3000 B.C.

The age of the great pyramids in Egypt: about 2500 B.C.

In India, the Indus Valley civilization, one of the earliest, and highly sophisticated, flourished: about 2500–1000 B.C.

The Minoan civilization and the Mycenaean civilization had disappeared by about 2000 B.C.

Was it pure coincidence that so many "great" civilizations began or flourished between 3000 and 2000 B.C.?

The Mayan civilization began about 1500 B.C.

First dynasty (Shang) in documented Chinese history: about 1500–1000 B.C.

Confucius lived around 500 B.C.
The Incan empire began around A.D. 1200.

Apparently Greece's long prehistory, its Neolithic period, began about 4000 B.C. Where, in the course of a Neolithic period or after, would a hat be likely to develop? How would I make an educated guess about the development of that hat? Could I start by supposing that Greek civilization would have to be advanced enough to have "travelers" rather than nomads? But I was not even sure what *Neolithic* meant. At least I was now beyond confusing *Paleolithic* with *Ice Age*, as I had done when I first started my reading.

I had vaguely thought "Paleolithic times" were the same as "the Ice Age." I had also thought there was only one Ice Age. I realized later that perhaps I was confusing *Paleolithic* and *Pleistocene*, because the Ice Age most familiar to us is also called the Pleistocene Epoch. Now I understood that remark about *era* and *epoch* being incorrectly used in writing. *Epoch* was a term belonging to geological time. In geological time, an epoch was a smaller unit within an era.

Paleolithic, on the other hand, meant "ancient stone age" and referred to a stage of civilization, so that one people could be in their Paleolithic stage and another in their Neolithic stage. *Paleolithic* related to the second period of the Stone Age, characterized by rough or chipped stone implements. *Neolithic* was the latest period of the Stone Age, characterized by polished stone implements. Of course, a people could be in their Paleolithic stage during the Pleistocene.

Neolithic was a stage of cultural evolution or technological development also characterized by the existence of settled villages largely dependent on domesticated plants and animals, and by the presence of crafts like pottery and weaving. The termination of the Neolithic period was marked by such innovations as the rise of urban civilization or the introduction of metal tools or writing.

Then I imagined that the Greek hat was developed late in the Greeks' Neolithic period, with the rise of urbanization. I was perhaps wrong, but because I imagined the Greek "traveler" would be going from one urban center to another, I thought the development of cities and the development of *travel* and *travelers*, and the hat, would all have come at the same time.

The earliest known development of Neolithic culture was in Southwest Asia between 8000 B.C. and 6000 B.C.

I was confused. Did this mean the most advanced early culture was in Southwest Asia? Or the earliest known advanced culture? Maybe this would become clear to me with more reading.

Was this earliest known development of Neolithic culture connected to the melting of the ice at the end of the Ice Age?

The ice melted (the last glacial period ended) about eleven millennia ago. The human diet changed to include more plant food. The land, relieved of the weight of the ice, rose in places.

How could the land rise? Was it floating? Or was it not floating but had been compressed by the weight of the ice? Or was it able to rise and fall because the center of the earth is liquid?

I thought: You couldn't form settlements (enter your Neolithic period) unless you could grow crops, could you? Or maybe you could. Would the earliest development of

Neolithic culture have to be after the end of the last Ice Age? You couldn't turn from hunting and gathering to farming until plants began to grow, could you? During the Ice Age, there was only tundra. But I was a little unclear what tundra was, exactly.

I discovered that the word *tundra* comes from Russian and is related to the Lapp word *tundar*, "hill" (not an Indo-European word). A tundra is a level or undulating treeless plain characteristic of arctic and subarctic regions.

But what grew on the "plain"? What grows on tundra now, in summer anyway, is an abundance of mosses and lichens, and some flowering plants. The tundra supports a small human population, including Samoyeds.

So was I right to see a pattern? The ice melted, then within two or three thousand years Neolithic cultures began, then over the next three or four thousand years various different civilizations became highly developed?

I left off thinking about the complexities of the highly sophisticated civilizations and returned to the peace and emptiness of the Ice Age.

During the last Ice Age there were apparently some trees. They grew up only in protected spots. More generally, mammoth bones were burned for winter fires. (The cutting of the Grand Canyon took place chiefly during the Ice Age.) Temperatures in summer averaged 54–59 degrees Fahrenheit, with evening frosts. That seemed to me mild enough, especially on a south-facing slope in the sun.

Many Ice Age human footprints, always of bare feet, have been found in the clay and sand floors of caves. The people must have been walking in mud, since if there had not been mud, there would not be footprints. The floors were wet and the bare feet were walking in the wet.

Maybe I was wrong not to be interested, just then, in the epochs or eras of earth's history before humankind appeared. But, right or wrong, I liked to see the first appearance of humans, and especially the first signs of humans making art. There was something refreshing about this.

The earliest evidence of art-making, I learned, dated from about thirty-two millennia ago. The art-making became increasingly refined over the next twenty thousand years.

I realized that I would not have been able to say, before looking it up, when prehistoric cave painting was being done. I wondered if other people had a more accurate idea, if only my own ignorance was at fault. I asked various people to name a date. I was given a range of answers: "sometime B.C." (from a woman in the health-care field); 2000 B.C. (from two painters, separately); 5000 B.C. (from a writer and teacher); 20,000 B.C. (from a jazz pianist cum astrologer); 50,000 B.C. (from a writer); "oh, hundreds of thousands B.C." (from an English professor). For some of the believing Christians I talked to, it seemed to me, any portion of the time before the year 0 became a murky area mostly filled by stories from the Bible. Even for non-Christians, in many cases. Until they remembered the Egyptians. They knew the Egyptians had been building their pyramids before the birth of Christ.

I would have liked to go back to some of those places on the earth in which *Homo erectus* had lived. Until recently, some of those places remained relatively untouched. Now this was no longer true, I knew, and my only access to them in their original state was through my imagination.

I made another list: *Homo erectus* dated from 1,800,000 B.C., or 1,800 millennia ago (1,802 counting our nearly 2 millennia since the year 0).

I said it to myself again: 1,800 millennia ago. The earliest remains of human culture dated from this time.

I was not even sure how to define *culture*. But there it was, defined for me: *culture* meant tools, language, and social activity.

I went on with my list:

The use of fire began: 500,000 B.C.

Early *Homo sapiens*: 300,000 B.C. Early *Homo sapiens* included Swanscombe man and Steinheim man.

Homo sapiens: 100,000 B.C. Neanderthal man. This species, with its clearly defined characteristics, remained essentially the same for sixty millennia.

I had to say it again: unchanged for sixty thousand years.

Then, "suddenly," this species was wiped out. But "suddenly," in this history, was a period of five thousand years. The *suddenly* was true, and the five thousand years were true. This species gave way to *Homo sapiens sapiens* in about 40,000 B.C., a completely different species morphologically, already virtually indistinguishable from present-day humans, and including Cro-Magnon man, Grimaldi man, Boskop man, and Wadjak man. This was the beginning of the last Ice Age in Europe.

End of the last Ice Age: 10,000 B.C. (twelve millennia ago counting our two millennia since the year 0).

Only at the end of the list, the end of the last Ice Age, did our two millennia become a significant fraction of the number. Through the rest of the list, especially in the beginning, these last two thousand years were so small a part of the number that they really had to be "rounded off."

It felt strange to me, being "rounded off." It was an uncanny sensation to see our two millennia gone, mathematically, in a moment. I already knew that in the universe, spatially, we were small. In time, too, our lives were brief, but it was easy to forget.

I went on reading, about the limestone hills of Southern France, about the Magdalenian cultures.

In that region of the country, the same human profile existed then (it was there in the Ice Age portraits) as now.

Was that possible? The same human profile continuing for twenty thousand years?

More than five hundred pieces of nonutilitarian shale or slate were found on the floor of a number of hilltop huts in Gönnersdorf, Germany, dating from around 10,500 B.C. They are engraved with hundreds of "buttocks" images, marked and overmarked.

Signs and symbols were engraved on stones and bones. Material included stone, bone, ivory, clay, antler, and horn. They painted with fingers, sticks, pads of fur, or moss; they daubed; they dotted; they sketched with colored materials and charcoals; they blew paint from their mouths or through a hollow bird bone. They used mineral "crayons," brushes of hair and fiber. There was both humor and perspective earlier than we once supposed. There was the same outburst of innovative image-making at the same time among different people speaking different languages and having different bone structures. (No visitors from space were required to teach them.)

But what had originally startled me and what continued to surprise me was that this art changed so gradually, over twenty thousand years.

I had to wonder: Were the later millennia, including ours, actually longer, or larger, because more happened than happened in any one millennium between 30,000 B.C. and 10,000 B.C.? Was our millennium less of a negligible fraction than I had thought?

But then I had to ask myself if it was really true that less had happened. Wasn't it just that the farther back we go, the less we know about what happened? But then I remembered that the farther back we go, the fewer people there were in the world, and the fewer people there are, the less that happens—to people, anyway. So it really was true that less happened to people.

What was the population of the globe during the last Ice Age? I wanted to know. But I could not discover this. I could only discover that between the time of the Roman Empire and the colonizing of the New World, the world population increased from a quarter of a billion to half a billion. I could discover that in the "ancient world" the world's population increased by only 0.1 percent a year.

But what I had also learned was that during the Pleistocene, the ice would come and go. Glacial advances would be interrupted by interglacial stages, during which the ice retreated and a comparatively mild climate prevailed. This was not what startled me. What startled me was learning that because the interglacial periods of the Pleistocene lasted longer than the time that has elapsed since the last retreat of the ice, the epoch that is occurring now, our epoch, called the Recent Epoch, may be merely another such interglacial stage and the glaciers may return at some future time.

Because I had not heard this before, I began to worry. Maybe everyone else knew this fact and I simply had not been paying attention. But maybe my reference books were too old, and most of what I thought I was learning had now been proven factually wrong.

I looked at their copyright pages. Yes, it was true that my books were rather out of date. My encyclopedia was about twenty-five years old. My dictionary was also about twenty-five years old. I was forty-eight years old, so when I bought them, I realized, I was young and they were new. I did not notice, as the years passed, that as I grew older they also changed, that my books were gradually becoming wrong about certain things.

Even though twenty-five years was not very long in terms of millennia, in each one of those past twenty-five years, many things happened, and a discovery might have been made that would cause me to have to change what I had thought especially about Paleolithic cultures, or the Ice Age. In fact, the discovery that the Pleistocene began more than 1.8 million years ago was made only five years or so before my encyclopedia was published and nearly missed being included in the book. Before that discovery, it was thought that the Pleistocene began much more recently.

The catalog I had from an exhibit of Ice Age art was about eighteen years old. But now I saw that my history of France was more recent—ten years old—and it confirmed what I was reading elsewhere. Best of all, a friend who read the newspapers every day confirmed, at least, the approximate dates of the prehistoric art-making. I saw that I could consider this friend to be a reference resource that was updated daily.

I was left with no answer to the question I had asked myself along the way: Was the real purpose of my investigation not to find out how long a millennium was and begin to know past millennia, but rather to situate myself further back in the span of time, so that what happened now did not matter as much? Was I, in fact, afraid of the present age, and was I even glad, rather than merely surprised, that the glaciers might return?

1996

Meeting Abraham Lincoln

1.

At a gathering just after Christmas last year, someone brought up the idea of how many handshakes might separate you from a famous person: that is, you might have shaken the hand that shook the hand that shook the hand of Muhammad Ali. It's a nice idea: it makes you feel close to greatness, or close to someone who otherwise would be very distant in time or in personal fame. I then told my story about Abraham Lincoln and shook the hand of each person standing in the small circle near a very broad fireplace with a hearth of worn, uneven bricks. We were in a house whose age is hard to pinpoint exactly because of contradictory architectural features, but that was built sometime between 1790 and 1830. I told them they were shaking the hand that shook the hand that shook the hand that shook the hand of Abraham Lincoln.

I can say that I am only three handshakes away from Lincoln, although it would be more accurate to say one handshake and two handclasps, since I did not shake but clasped my mother's hand for the fifty-seven years that

I knew her and she did not shake but clasped her great-grandfather's hand for the fourteen years that she knew him. He was the one who shook Lincoln's hand, traveling to Springfield, Illinois, to do so. But there are at least four somewhat differing accounts of this event, which makes you wonder about the accuracy of any historical account. Clearly the meeting with Lincoln is something that certain members of my family have been proud of ever since it happened, but no one has it quite the same. Even old Grandpa Bent, the man who shook the great hand, may have had some of it wrong.

My mother's was probably the hand I held most often, during certain years of my life, first when my hand was small and hers was larger, and last when she was often lying on her bed and I was sitting beside her, her hand softer and weaker and more crooked than mine. She herself held many hands when she was a little girl, because she was born into a family of three older brothers and an older sister as well as her widowed mother, many aunts and uncles, two grandparents, and two great-grandparents. Upon the death of her great-grandmother, when my mother was three years old, her family moved into the large house of her great-grandfather Bent, and beginning at that time, the old man, though he could be hard-hearted and mean-spirited, no doubt often held her hand, even kindly.

Clinton DeWitt Bent was named for DeWitt Clinton, governor of New York State in 1817, the year he was born in Sterling, New York. At the time of his birth— as his newspaper obituary pointed out—"Monroe was president of the United States, Napoleon Bonaparte was spending his days at St. Helena and Abraham Lincoln was a boy eight years of age." The population of the entire United States was less than nine million. (Thus, the year 1817, though it is some two hundred years in the past, is only two handclasps away from me, even though I am only just leaving late middle age.)

Clinton Bent grew up in Sterling, married, and had three daughters. When the daughters were adolescents, the family went by train and covered wagon out to Iowa, where, two generations and some forty-seven years later, my mother was born. "He didn't talk much about the trip out here," said another of his great-grandchildren, "except that Grandma was afraid of the wolves." In Iowa he planted orchards of fruit trees and became known as a highly skilled fruit grower.

The house was a good-sized brick one of two stories with central halls upstairs and down and a tall Scotch pine by the front windows. In the front yard, also, grew a cherry tree that bore white cherries, and on the south wall a special variety of apricot. The orchard contained peach and apple trees.

When my mother was four years old, her mother went back to work teaching in the local public school, and my mother was left in the care of the old man, who was known by all the family as Grandpa Bent, though he was grandfather only to some of them. At the time, he would have been eighty-nine or ninety. He was a teetotaler, a staunch Episcopalian, and tightfisted, driving hard bargains even with his own family. His great interests, besides the raising and breeding of fruit, seem to have been politics, education, religion, and managing his money.

Some of his and my mother's activities during their days together we know about, and some we can guess.

They walked every morning to the post office, half a mile or so away, probably often hand in hand, to collect his mail, including his copy of the *Congressional Record*. He spent some part of each day tending his orchard, with my mother tagging along behind. He would wheel out a large, heavy wheelbarrow to collect broken or trimmed branches for the fireplace. He had made the wheelbarrow himself out of the wood from an oak cask. He would sometimes wheel my mother in it as they went through the orchard.

Sometimes he did complicated work on the trees, once grafting multiple kinds of the best peaches onto one good trunk, thereby creating a single tree that bore several varieties. He would gather honey from his hives, a black veil hanging from his straw hat, his cuffs buttoned over his gloves, operating a bellows-like "smoker." The cellar of the house was used for storing fruit and vegetables, and for the extra equipment of the beekeeping activities. It smelled of apples in the fall and winter, and decaying potatoes in the spring and early summer, overlaid with beeswax and bee smoke.

Outdoors and in, his little great-granddaughter would help the old man in small ways. When he was chilly, he would ask her to bring his sweater, saying, "Fetch my wampus!" He was a man of few words, a frequent admonition being "Take care!" We know that he spent a good deal of time in his room, reading his *Congressional Record* and the Bible, as well as another publication he subscribed to, *The Prohibitionist*. The old man consistently voted for the candidate of that party, when there was one, and when he died, he left most of his money to the cause. For decades, beginning in the mid-nineteenth century—a time when the citizens of the young nation were attempting to reconsider and refine its character—the temperance movement was strong: upright citizens were supposed to be teetotalers, and Iowa was a dry state.

Grandpa Bent's room was the former parlor, off the dining room. It contained a massive four-poster spool bed, a hard-coal stove, and a screen before the fireplace depicting a boy in a yachting cap and short jacket helping his mother wind wool. Some of the pictures on the wall were framed with pine cones, others with carved wood. There was a cherry highboy and a corner whatnot with souvenirs from far-off places given to him by another of his granddaughters, who was a missionary in the Philippines.

In this parlor at four o'clock every afternoon he would peel and eat an apple, an unvarying habit even when, by late spring, before the early summer crop came in, the apples were small and wrinkled. He attributed his longevity in part to his daily apple and in part to his meager diet.

When my mother's family first moved in with him, he ate dinner in the dining room with the five children and their mother, but he was not always pleased with the children's manners. My mother's mother liked them to be sociable and talkative at dinner, and she had also elicited a promise from him that only she would "speak to" the children. And so he would sit in silence glowering at them when they committed a breach of manners. Eventually his dinners were brought to him on a tray in his own room, whether by his choice or hers is not clear.

One could say that an interest in politics must have run in his family, to judge by his parents' naming him after Governor Clinton. On the other hand, the country itself was so young in 1817—only about forty years old—that a lively concern with the government of the country would most likely have been deeply inherent in everyday life. The first five presidents of the United States, after all, had been Revolutionary Patriots. Still, he seems, on the evidence of his subscription to the *Congressional Record* and his unfailing habit of voting in presidential elections, to have been particularly keen or dedicated. By the time he died, at age ninety-nine and a half, he had voted in twenty presidential elections. This was a record in those days, and would be hard to surpass even now, of course. He was taken by carriage to the polling place for the last time just nine days before his death. In this election he voted for the Prohibition candidate, declaring that he wanted to cast his twentieth vote for president against the whiskey evil. (Three years after his death, Prohibition was enacted.)

It was his keen interest in the business of government that led him to seek out Abraham Lincoln. Although, in each election, he favored the temperance candidate in any case, he had heard good reports of Lincoln and wished to meet him face-to-face in order to form his own opinion of him. This much, at least, seems clear. In our family lore, however, there are at least four different accounts of this meeting, which is where the writing of history reveals itself to be so complicated.

The briefest comes in a letter dating back forty years or so, from the same great-grandson who had heard about Grandma Bent and the wolves during the journey out west by covered wagon:

> Grandfather Bent told me the story of how he happened to vote for Abe Lincoln. He went to

Springfield and spent the afternoon visiting with
Mr. Lincoln. He came away convinced that he
would vote for him. They really valued their voting rights in those days.

This account, since it is the sparest, is also generally
in agreement with the others, except that afternoon becomes evening in the expanded versions. My mother's
mother tells a longer version that does not contradict
this brief version, but we can't be sure how reliable she
was. Her reports of her life, in the pages she left behind,
are sometimes colored with a positive view that my
mother found false, saying: "I have wished that Mother
had been more realistic in her account." My mother's
mother, for example, says that her grandfather Bent
was "the sunniest, dearest old man that could be desired. 'He was no more trouble than a canary-bird,' I
used often to tell people, and it was true. He was a fine-
looking old gentleman with regular features and a full
white beard. With kindly blue eyes that twinkled with
fun most times when he looked at you." My mother
says: "How can she describe her grandfather Bent as always full of fun? When he was my babysitter I remember
him as laconic, to say the least." We know from other
sources about the glowering at the dinner table, the
hard bargain over a land rental with a certain nephew,
the intolerance when it came to drinking liquor. With
due skepticism, then, here is account number 2, by my
mother's mother:

> Grandpa loved to tell us of the time that he had
> gone to see Abraham Lincoln in Springfield Illi-
> nois. He went to the house and Mrs. Lincoln let

him in, he said. Lincoln was out but she invited Grandpa to come in and wait till he returned.

The story was quite a long one as Grandpa told it. He had heard and read much of this great man, he said, but wanted to talk with him personally before voting for him.

But after this visit and the conversation he had with Lincoln, he told us that he was convinced that his vote would be well cast for "Honest Abe." Then Grandpa finished the story, always exactly the same way:

"I looked up at the tall man, I had to look way up to him, and I said, 'Well, Mr. Lincoln, I hope you get to be president, and that you will be as much better than the rest of us as you are taller.' He laffed, and thanked me, and—"

Now, my mother herself has a different account of the meeting. She was a smart woman and had a gift for telling anecdotes and great consistency from one telling to the next. But she was also a romantic, and a proficient short-story writer accustomed to condensing and reshaping and adding the occasional flourish. She may have been tempted to alter and embroider in this case, too. Her account includes afternoon and evening both:

Before the 1860 election he was undecided, so hitched up his horse and traveled to Springfield, Illinois. There he waited all afternoon in the outer office while pleaders for appointments made their pitch. Then Lincoln, learning how far he had traveled just to give disinterested thought to his vote, invited him home to spend the evening. At the end of the visit Grandpa stood below his tall host on the porch steps saying goodbye. Looking up at Lincoln he said, according to the story, "I hope you will stand as far above the other presidents in history as you stand above the common man in stature."

She goes on to comment, "I myself never heard any such eloquence from Grandpa. By the time I knew him he was as economical with his words as with his money."

The last version comes from the newspaper obituary published at the time of his death. This is perhaps the most dependable version, since the writer was a trained journalist who had interviewed Bent directly. But perhaps it is not, since that interview had taken place a few years before, and the writer was remembering the facts as best he could. The journalist places the meeting with Lincoln before the date that my mother gives, at a time when, according to him, Bent was still living in New York State:

Owing to the death of his father and the poor health of his eldest brother, Clinton DeWitt was early called upon to manage the home farm in New York. During this period he came to Chicago to attend a political convention and went from there to Springfield, Illinois, where he also attended a convention. After the convention he was invited by Mr. Abe Lincoln to go home with him for supper and he was entertained for several hours by Mr. and Mrs. Lincoln. In speaking of this visit a few years ago to the writer, Mr. Bent said that at that time he was greatly impressed by

> Mr. Lincoln and after enjoying his hospitality for
> several hours he bade him good bye with words
> something like this as nearly as he can remember:
> "Mr. Lincoln I thank you for your kindness and
> some day this nation is going to hear from you."

In this version, the rhetorical flourish at the end is reduced to a plain understatement, more in keeping with
the character of the man as my mother remembered him.
But there is no question of simply "hitching up his horse"
to go this distance. In fact, when I imagine it, I wonder
that a busy farmer and father of three children would
travel from New York State all the way to Illinois to
attend a political convention.

I had thought there was a fifth version, but then my
own memory is not entirely reliable. I may be imagining a fifth, or it may exist and I may still come across it.
In fact, a fifth version is the one produced by my own
faulty memory. After only a few months without looking
at the other versions, my memory had already worked its
own changes, and my story was that Bent had traveled
not from New York State, but from his home in Iowa,
and that he had looked in on Lincoln in Springfield
because he happened to be nearby at a livestock market.
Why I supplied a livestock market in place of a political
convention I don't know, unless it seemed more likely—
perhaps by then I knew that he had also at one time
raised animals, before specializing in fruit.

2.

On the other side of my family there is another chain
reaching back to Lincoln, this time via three handclasps

and the touch of Lincoln's hand, not upon an ancestor's hand but upon his own hat brim as his eyes rested, at least, on the eyes of that admiring ancestor. The ancestor leaves behind two descriptions of what amount to sightings of the president.

Sidney Brooks was my father's great-great-uncle, or, to give the links of the generations as they more naturally came together, my father's grandfather's uncle. He was born in 1813, four years before Grandpa Bent. A tall man with a pleasant face and a more agreeable personality than Grandpa Bent, he was described by friends, in tributes paid after his death, as modest, diffident, cordial, full of intellectual and natural curiosity, entertaining, and a fine and dedicated teacher. Although his family, which lived in the town of Harwich on Cape Cod, was more inclined toward mercantile and banking concerns than education, he himself felt a strong compulsion to go on with his schooling, and his father agreed to support him in his desire, though ready cash for such a thing was scarce. And so, at the age of twenty—not so unusual in those days—Sidney enrolled in Phillips Academy at Andover. To get there from his home in Harwich, he had to go either by fishing boat or by the "Brewster Packet" around the Cape to Boston and then by stagecoach overland. After completing his studies at Andover, he went on to Amherst College, graduating in the class of 1841 at the rather advanced age (by our standards, probably not theirs) of twenty-eight. (The last part of his trip to Amherst, later, was also by stagecoach, in this case from Worcester.)

After he graduated, Sidney returned to the Cape and worked for three years as a schoolteacher, then founded and built his own seminary in Harwich. After twenty successful and fulfilling years directing the school and teaching, he was forced, for financial reasons that have not been explained, to leave the seminary, selling it to the town. With his wife and fellow teacher he went off to take charge of a school ship anchored in Boston Harbor called the *George M. Barnard*, on which the pupils learned the arts of navigation and the handling of a ship. School ships at the time could function either as reformatories for juvenile delinquents or simply as secure training institutions for poor boys who would otherwise roam the streets. It is not clear which sort Sidney's ship was. His friends variously refer to the pupils as "rough boys" and "waifs." Sidney calls them "bad boys," but we don't know how seriously he means it. Certainly he misses his seminary and refers to himself as being "imprisoned" in the school ship.

Before occupying his new position, however, he had a brief experience of the Civil War. Being fifty-one years old, he was exempt from military duty but wished to give more personal service in the defense of "our Country's rights and human emancipation." He therefore joined, in July 1864, the U.S. Christian Commission, a northern civilian organization of volunteers funded mainly by donations from local church congregations and providing the soldiers with food, clothing, medicines, and bandages as well as spiritual sustenance. Communications being what they were, he and his group of fifteen or twenty journeyed all the way to the Gettysburg area by train and wagon before finding out that not all of them were needed there. Most of the wounded soldiers, besides, were Confederate, and Sidney evidently hoped to have a chance to tend his own townsmen. He therefore joined a contingent that went on, or back, to Washington, D.C., where they were needed. This is where he had the good fortune, as he clearly regarded it, of seeing Lincoln at first hand, though from a distance.

His opinion of Lincoln, and that of most of his fellow townsmen, may be inferred from one of his descriptions, in the memoir he left, of the years leading up to the war:

> And now the thrilling events of '61 drew crowds to the Post Office at every arrival of the mail, and now the newspaper was sought at the close of school and the evenings consumed in reading and telling the news. Then our Sabbath day services and our Fast Day services were more solemn and fervent than usual, then the heaven-directed acts of President Lincoln began to be admired and discussed and his noble qualities to shine forth.

It surely would have appealed to Sidney that Lincoln was a man of simple habits. It would have appealed to both Grandpa Bent and Sidney that the president was a devout Christian and supporter of the cause of temperance, rarely touching alcohol himself—since Sidney, like Bent, was to become a committed advocate of temperance and eventually a prohibitionist.

While in Washington, Sidney wrote home regularly to his wife, sometimes using a barrel head as a desk. His letters would have been of interest to all his family and shared among them—his wife, his older brother, his four sisters, three of whom still lived at home (only one, Sarah, did not approve of Lincoln, whose religious beliefs differed from hers in what she felt were important respects). A series of these letters was also published in

the local *Harwich Republican*. He reported both encounters with Lincoln in the same letter, dated July 25,
1864. (A barouche was a four-wheeled, horse-drawn carriage; horse cars were streetcars pulled by horses; and
the platform on which he stepped out was the open-air
platform at the back of the streetcar.)

The first encounter:

> July 25. I had been seeking an opportunity to see
> the President. He goes out to his country resi-
> dence every night, and the road that he takes is the
> same by which I go to my hospital. He was some-
> times too fast and sometimes too slow for me.
> He rides in a barouche, escorted by 20 men finely
> mounted on black horses. Riding home in the
> horse cars one night some little frolicsome girls in
> the car exclaimed, "Uncle Abe." I roused up just
> in time to see the tail end of his cavalcade. The
> next time I did better, saw him coming, stepped
> out upon the rear platform, looked straight into
> the barouche where were both the President and
> his wife. He touched his hat to me, but I was so
> intent on my object that I forgot all propriety and
> did nothing but gaze. He is as thin as a hatchet,
> but really a good looking man.

Since Sidney was, to judge from his own narration
of his life and from the testimonials offered by friends,
conscientious and naturally courteous, his forgetting his
manners on this occasion shows the extent to which a famous or prominent figure ceases to be entirely a human
being, but is reduced to something of an object, even to
a person of sensitivity. Also striking, of course, are Lin-

coln's accessibility and the affection of the "frolicsome girls" who call him Uncle Abe.

His accessibility and that of the White House are even more startling in Sidney's second account, in which he sees the president leave the White House to set off with his cavalcade. Sidney's word *piazzi* is one he uses elsewhere, too, eccentrically, for what we call a portico or colonnade. His description of the "negro" should be seen in the following context: he and his fellow Harwich townspeople were generally abolitionist and for the previous nearly twenty years had been holding lively debates about the slavery issue. Sidney himself called slavery a "disgrace" and described enjoying the company of one Mr. Jones, "a colored man of the deepest hue and a noble Christian" who "lectured in the Church and enlightened us much on the cruelties of the system." He speaks with respect of Mr. Jones, though with high awareness of the unresolved issues of a black man's acceptance into white society: "Mr. Jones was more than once a guest of ours, nor did my wife object to his sitting at our table and at receiving his benediction." The black man in the following passage, as he depicts him, is presented as more picturesque. As for the White House, it was an earlier, far more modest version of the present building, and was described by a contemporary journalist, Noah Brooks (no relation to Sidney), as being open to "the multitude, washed or unwashed" for their "free egress and ingress"—in fact, certain members of the public, on visits to the place, were so bold as to snip off bits of curtains, curtain pulls, and even carpet in order to carry them home as souvenirs. Sidney writes:

Last Saturday I took it more leisurely. Leaving my hospital at 4 o'clock I visited the White House.

Went into the "East Room" which is always accessible and the "Green Room" which leads out of it. The East Room is very magnificent. Very rich looking paper covers the walls. Eight or ten very large mirrors, three splendid chandeliers and a carpet, patterned expressly for the room, are the prominent features in the picture of it now in my mind's eye. I was very much pleased with the White House. From the avenue it appears like a plain moderate size mansion. It was not until I had paced it in front that I could form a correct idea of its size. It is 180 feet in the main body. Shrubbery and trees of most graceful form crowd close around the front side which faces a beautiful lawn sloping and undulating to the Potomac.

While I was there the escort of cavalry arrived. The President's carriage was brought up under the lofty piazzi and quite a crowd of persons with the same object that I had gathered around.

A pleasant episode to the main performance occurred, which, as it shows so plainly the character of President Lincoln I will describe. A very tall and intelligent looking negro[,] very black, with large and dusty feet, supporting himself with a very long walking stick, an excellent model as I thought for a painter or sculptor, walked up the steps, across the spacious area under the piazzi to the door and wished an interview with the President. The porter haughtily turned him off, stating the utter impossibility of his seeing him at that time. Apparently pacified, he sat down in a distant corner. The horsemen were drawn up, the Captain, ready to give the word of command, the President took his seat in the carriage. To the surprise of all, at that instant the tall negro was on the opposite side[,] his arm already around the back of the seat[,] leaning over in the most familiar manner. The President told the driver to hold on, gave the negro a moment of patient attention[,] smiled and replied in a gracious manner. The negro seemed to urge his case, the President began to gesture with one hand as he spoke as if to convince the applicant that he could do nothing in the matter, then he raised both hands and very emphatically but very kindly repeated his gesture with both hands, ordered his man to drive on, saluted the crowd and was off. A burst of admiration arose from the company, [the negro] appeared greatly pleased, and we all retired feeling, I am sure, that another good lesson had been learnt.

It is not perfectly clear what lesson Sidney believed had been learned from this episode—perhaps something more about Lincoln's patience or evenhandedness. It is interesting that what moved the spectators, evidently, was Lincoln's manner of refusing a petition and dismissing the petitioner, and that even the disappointed petitioner appeared pleased.

Sidney evidently wrote both descriptions down almost immediately, or at least within a few days. He is so particular about the details that it is hard not to believe they are correct. What they add to our knowledge of Abe Lincoln is another matter.

The two men from the two sides of the family, Grandpa Bent and Sidney, were both intent on meeting or seeing

President Lincoln, but their motives, springing directly from their different characters, were not the same. Grandpa Bent had a certain righteous sense of his own position and power as an informed citizen and voter and wished to interview Lincoln to see whether Lincoln met his standards of probity and integrity. His persistence was rewarded by a visit of several hours in Lincoln's home, which satisfied him. Sidney was more modest in his sense of himself and his rights and already convinced of Lincoln's worth; he wished only to lay eyes directly on a man he admired as a leader of strength and conviction whose beliefs coincided with his own. There is always a fascination exerted by the physical person of a prominent political figure, especially a U.S. president, even if he is a mediocre or bad one. In this case the president was a great or at least a good one (except in the opinion of some, including Sidney's sister Sarah).

2006

"Paring Off the Amphibologisms":
Jesus Recovered by the Jesus Seminar

The beginning of the path that led me to *The Five Gospels* is as hard to discover as the beginning of a goat or cow path in a meadow, but somewhere along the way was a reading of Ben Franklin's *Autobiography* and then William Cobbett's utopian descriptions of self-sufficient farming, eventually a videotape in the BBC series *Civilisation* about the eighteenth century and the Enlightenment, specifically the figure of the inventor, the revolutionary, the independent thinker (including the unaccredited amateur versus the professional and academic), and Thomas Jefferson. There was Monticello, which he designed himself, inspired by a French model, the Hôtel de Salm in Paris, and excited particularly by the idea of the one-story facade concealing two stories. There were the farm implements he modernized (he won a gold medal from the Société d'agriculture du département de la Seine at Paris for his improved moldboard plow). There was his seven-field crop rotation system. His botanical experiments. His design for his bedroom and study suite, with his bed in the middle so that he could get out on either side. What characterized him through most of his projects, much of the time, it would seem, was confidence in his own abilities and independence of thinking, independence from the norm, the accepted, a readiness to question the received, the conventional. He must have been moved by some dissatisfaction, nonacceptance—dissatisfaction with this conventional desk, with this grand staircase—and also by the pure pleasure in doing the thing himself, in *poiein*, "making." His house was always in progress, with piles of wood around, treacherous catwalks, and half-lit narrow stairs. It was this spirit that put him at the center of the declaration of a radical break from England, though it took Thomas Paine's *Common Sense* to convince him, among others, to make the move.

It was in the same spirit that he approached the Bible. Dissatisfied with it as it read, he decided to reduce it "to the simple Evangelists" and even from them to select "the very words only of Jesus," those parts that seemed to him the true teachings of Jesus. He cut passages out of his Bible and pasted them into a blank book to form a coherent work, *The Life and Morals of Jesus of Nazareth*, for his own use. This project he carried out while he was president, in the evenings before he went to sleep, and worked on further at Monticello. He was pleased with the result, though reluctant to advertise very widely what he had done. (The Federalists already viewed him as irreligious.) He wrote to a friend, "I am . . . averse to the communication of my religious tenets to the public, because it would countenance the presumption of those who have endeavoured to draw them before that tribunal, and to seduce public opinion to erect itself into that inquest over the rights of conscience, which the laws have so justly proscribed."

Thomas Paine, whose path crossed that of Benjamin

Franklin early in his career (Franklin, who met him in London, advised him to seek his fortune in America) and that of William Cobbett late, became a hero in the United States because of his pamphlet, for which, although he was always out of pocket, he accepted no profits so that cheap editions might be widely circulated. He was another independent thinker drawn to invention, like Jefferson and Franklin, and after the war was over, he settled down for a while to design a smokeless candle and an iron bridge without piers. Then (to abbreviate the story), whereas he had been regarded as a hero for speaking his mind, he began getting into trouble for the same tendency. In England, in 1791, he published *Rights of Man*, this time voicing support for the French Revolution and also for republicanism, outlining a plan for popular education, relief of the poor, pensions for aged people, and public works for the unemployed, all to be financed by the levying of a progressive income tax. The ruling classes found these ideas menacing and indicted him for treason, but he was already on his way to France. There, he became involved in the revolution and put himself at risk once again by saying what he thought, this time opposing the execution of the monarch, thereby antagonizing Robespierre's radicals and causing himself to be thrown into prison.

It was in prison that he wrote the first volume of *The Age of Reason*, an exposition of the place of religion in society and in part a critique of the Bible. He believed in a Supreme Being but did not think Jesus Christ had any divine origin. He did not think the story of Mary and the Holy Ghost was believable. He objected to the barbarity of the Old Testament and questioned the authenticity of the New Testament. He said that "if Christ had

meant to establish a new religion, he would have written it down himself." He said in his introduction to the
book that he had intended this one to be his last writing because he knew it would make him unpopular but
had started it earlier in his life than intended because of
finding himself in prison. He wrote in the preface, "It
contains my opinions upon religion. You will do me the
justice to remember that I have always strenuously supported the right of every man to his own opinion, however different that opinion might be to mine."

The book did indeed make him very unpopular. He
returned to the United States to find that he was widely
regarded as the world's greatest infidel. Though he was
poor, ill, and given to bouts of drinking, he continued
to attack privilege and religious superstitions. (While still
in France, he had published another pamphlet, "Agrar-
ian Justice," that protested inequalities in property own-
ership and added to his enemies in establishment circles.)
He died lonely and without funds in 1809. Six people
attended his funeral. (His bones were later exhumed by
William Cobbett, in fact, who took them to England
with the intention of giving them a proper funeral, but
on the way lost them.) For more than a century following his death, he continued to be thought of in the
terms of his obituary—as one who "did some good and
much harm."

*The Five Gospels: The Search for the Authentic Words
of Jesus*, by Robert W. Funk, Roy W. Hoover, and the
Jesus Seminar, is dedicated to Thomas Jefferson, among
others. As Jefferson and Paine did, it takes a fresh look
at the Bible, specifically the four gospels of the New Testament along with a fifth, the Gospel of Thomas. (Like
Jefferson's and Paine's works, it also takes a risk thereby—

laying itself open to a negative reaction from public opinion and the establishment. In fact, at least one of the scholars in the Jesus Seminar lost his university position as a result of this work, and others were forced to withdraw from the project as a consequence of institutional pressure.) One difference, however, is that this is a work of critical scholarship and at various times has involved between thirty and two hundred scholars (seventy-four are listed in the roster at the back of the book).

Along with the commentated and color-coded gospels of Mark, Matthew, Luke, John, and Thomas, *The Five Gospels* contains various front and back matter, including an "Index of Red & Pink Letter Sayings," and is supplemented throughout with other matter, including chronologies, figures, and "cameo essays" in boxes clarifying certain points or issues. One, for instance, compares versions of the Lord's Prayer with interesting results.

As described in its preface, this is the collective report of gospel scholars working together on a common question: What did Jesus really say? The scholars "first of all inventoried all the surviving ancient texts for words attributed to Jesus. They then examined those words in the several ancient languages in which they have been preserved. They produced a translation of all the gospels, known as the Scholars Version. And, finally, they studied, debated, and voted on each of the more than 1,500 sayings of Jesus in the inventory."

A number of different factors, or "rules of evidence," as the Seminar calls them, come into play in determining which words in all likelihood originated with Jesus himself and were handed down from the time of the oral tradition into the written tradition and which words were editorial or storytellers' additions contributed by the evangelists themselves.

Nothing extant was written down during Jesus's lifetime. Thus, only what could have been transmitted orally from Jesus's time, only what was memorable for one reason or another, easily memorized, can be proved to have been Jesus's words or close to them. "Only sayings and parables that can be traced back to the oral period, 30–50 C.E. [i.e., A.D. 30–50], can possibly have originated with Jesus." For this reason, when there are many versions of a saying or parable, usually the briefest and simplest will be the oldest one, the one closest to the original. Also, a parable may reveal evidence of mnemonic techniques common in oral literature—triadic structures and the repetition of catchwords—and thus be more likely to have been handed down from the oral period.

A storyteller will tend to supply dialogue appropriate to the occasion, putting words in Jesus's mouth that would not have been handed down independently from the oral period, and those additions can be spotted and identified as the contributions of the storyteller. The first narrative gospel, the Gospel of Mark, was not written until about A.D. 70. It was preceded (A.D. 50–60) by "sayings" gospels—that is, gospels that did not embed sayings and parables within a narrative. The names of the authors of the four gospels in the New Testament are names made up and assigned to them. It is not known what their actual names were. Surviving fragments of other, unknown gospels indicate that there were once many gospels. About twenty are known, and there may be many more.

A comparison of gospel texts in which parables are recounted will reveal a core parable that may have been handed down from the oral period. Likewise, similar material coming from different sources will imply that the material existed independently at an earlier time. Stylistic analysis of a single gospel will reveal habits of thought or flourishes characteristic of one evangelist (e.g., Mark's attitude toward Jesus's disciples, Matthew's fondness for the phrase "in the heavens"), which can then be pared away.

An example of a comparison of texts would be setting side by side the two accounts of Jesus's dictation of the Lord's Prayer, one in Matthew and one in Luke. When we take away editorial emendations by the evangelists, such as "who art in heaven," which was one of Matthew's favorite phrases and one that does not appear in Luke, we are left with a form of four petitions that Jesus probably did address to God, though not assembled into a single prayer: that the name of the Father be revered, that he impose his imperial rule, that he provide daily bread, and that he forgive debts. The only word, however, that we can be certain Jesus spoke is the opening word *Father*, or *Abba* in Aramaic. Curiously, because of what we cannot be sure he said, the one word he surely said, *Abba*, assumes great force.

A consideration of the historical context in which the gospels were written—the early years of the evolving Christian movement—will reveal still more about the ideological bias or proselytizing tendency of the evangelist and influence our reading of a gospel. For instance, Luke, unlike Matthew, omits Jesus's admonition "When anyone conscripts you for one mile, go an extra mile." Since his gospel was a defense of the Christian movement for Roman consumption, Luke may have omitted the admonition for fear that it would offend the Romans, who were probably the ones doing the conscripting. Another instance: Parables involving masters leaving and returning were especially popular with the evangelists because they foreshadowed the later accounts of Jesus leaving and returning, and so have to be examined with particular vigilance.

As they searched for the authentic words of Jesus, members of the Seminar had to proceed on the assumption that his voice was distinctive in a crowd of Galileans that included other sages. A sage was a repository for received wisdom, free-floating proverbs, witticisms of the time. Some of this commonly accepted wisdom of the time may have been attributed to Jesus by the evangelists, and some of it may in fact have been repeated by him. Since it is not distinctive, we can't know. For instance, one of the evangelists has Jesus say, "Be at peace with one another," but this was a common sentiment that nearly everyone uttered at one time or another, so one can't say these were Jesus's words.

The Five Gospels is a color-coded report of the results of those deliberations. In red are printed "words that were most probably spoken by Jesus in a form close to the one preserved for us." Bold black signals that "Jesus did not say this; it represents the perspective or content of a later or different tradition." The remaining two colors, pink and blue-gray, signal positions in between the two extremes: "Jesus probably said something like this" and "Jesus did not say this, but the ideas contained in it are close to his own." The color-coded gospels "answer the question 'What did Jesus really say?' within a narrow range of historical probabilities."

The book does not specifically promise that a portrait of Jesus will emerge, but of course it does, through the sifting of texts to discover what Jesus probably said, because the more we learn about his style of speaking and thinking, the more we learn about his personality and character.

Until just a few months ago, for me the figure of Jesus had been so painted and repainted with layers of dogma, sentimentality, hypocrisy, hyperbole, prejudice, deception, and illusion that what might or might not lie beneath—the historical figure, the sage of Nazareth—was for the most part obscured. The very words traditionally associated with Jesus, including most of all the name "Jesus" itself, carried a burden of association that tended to close my ears before speech began. I see this in some others, still, if I mention Jesus or the words of Jesus—or perhaps it is not that their ears are closed but rather what is expressed by the Mandarin verb construction *ting bu jian*, "one listens but fails to hear." ("Anyone here with two good ears had better listen!" is a traditional refrain that appears regularly in the gospels, especially following parables and sayings that were difficult to understand. It cannot be proven that Jesus himself actually said it.)

The words of Jesus appear everywhere, all the time, in this culture: a reference to "turning the other cheek" (which it seems Jesus probably did advise) on a poster in a veterinarian's examining room showing a kitten being licked by a puppy, a reference to shaking the dust from one's feet in a comic strip in the Sunday paper ("And whatever place does not welcome you or listen to you, get out of there and shake the dust off your feet in witness against them" [Mark 6:11] is concluded by the Jesus Seminar not to have originated with Jesus but to have been a vindictive response by early missionaries). But the figure of Jesus that keeps appearing to us in this culture turns out to be in certain of its aspects unlike the historical Jesus, or unlike the Jesus that emerges in *The Five Gospels* "within a narrow range of historical probabilities."

Jesus wrote nothing, so far as we know. We do not know for certain that he could write; we are not even positive that he could read. His native tongue was Aramaic. We do not know whether he could speak Hebrew as well. His words have been preserved only in Greek, the original language of all the surviving gospels. However, it is possible that Jesus also spoke Greek, in which case some parts of the oral tradition preserved in the gospels may have originated with him. (Sometimes, as in Mark's account of the raising of Jairus's daughter, Jesus's purported words were quoted, within the Greek gospel, in the original Aramaic, possibly for the reason that to readers of the Greek, the Aramaic *Talitha koum* would sound like a magic formula, whereas it simply means "Little girl, get up!")

Jesus was a carpenter.

Jesus was probably a disciple of John the Baptist.

Jesus was a sage, a wandering sage, a wandering charismatic. In his wanderings he was frequently accompanied by followers.

Many of Jesus's followers started as disciples of John the Baptist.

He apparently abided by these rules while traveling: Not to carry a bag on his back, bread (food), a purse (money), or a second shirt (change of clothes). Not to move around town once he arrived, but to stay under one roof. He may have worn sandals and carried a staff. The staff and sandals would have been a concession to road conditions. More stringent would have been no staff and no sandals. (Another clue in the detective work of the Jesus Seminar was that early followers of Jesus were likely to be more severe in their asceticism than either Jesus himself or later followers.) But the guiding principle, in any case, was to trust in the provisions of providence.

He paid little attention to food and clothing, except what was required for the day. His petition in the Lord's Prayer—"Provide us with the bread we need for the day" (Matthew 6:11)—would therefore have been characteristic. (Luke expanded this from the single day to a more extended future by adding "day by day.") He advised that others disregard food and clothing, as other sages also advised.

But he and his disciples did not fast. On the contrary, he apparently liked to eat and drink, and probably enjoyed weddings. Among some people, he had a reputation as a "glutton and a drunk" (Luke 7:34).

He probably did exorcise what were thought to be demons. But like other sages of the time, he did not offer to cure people. People seeking his help either petitioned in person or had someone petition for them.

He rarely initiated dialogue or debate. Rather, he responded. (This sometimes provides another clue in the search: when he is shown, by the writer of the gospel, initiating a dialogue, these were probably not his words.)

He was, like other sages of the ancient Near East, laconic, slow to speak, a person of few words.

He was self-effacing, modest, unostentatious. He urged humility as the cardinal virtue by both word and example. He admonished his followers to be self-effacing.

He tended to focus attention away from himself and on God instead.

He rarely made pronouncements or spoke about himself in the first person.

He made no claim to be the Anointed, the Messiah. He probably did not think of his work as a program he was carrying out. He was not an institution builder. (He was not a Christian, of course, but he was made to talk like a Christian by the evangelists.)

He taught on his own authority, characteristically making his points by parables and aphorisms, not apparently invoking scripture.

Jesus's public discourse was remembered to have consisted primarily of aphorisms, parables, and retorts to challenges.

The flat refusal, the unqualified statement, was characteristic of Jesus.

Jesus frequently indulged in repartee. He was a master of enigmatic repartee. For instance, when asked by some Pharisees and Herodians whether they should pay a poll tax to the Roman emperor, he does not advise them either way but says simply: "Pay the emperor what belongs to the emperor, and God what belongs to God!" (Mark 12:17).

His enigmatic sayings and stories were readily misunderstood and often provoked a strong negative response.

He challenged the everyday, the inherited, the established. He undermined a whole way of life. He endorsed countermovements and ridiculed established traditions.

He was antisocial. (I'm not sure how this fits in with his possible enjoyment of weddings.) He erased social boundaries taken to be sacrosanct. He was sympathetic to outcasts and those who were marginal to society. He associated freely with outcasts (e.g., sinners—meaning nonobservant Judeans—and toll collectors).

He rejected the notion that ritual impurity could result from contact with lepers, the dead, or gentiles. (The rabbis held that heathen dust was polluting and therefore made Judeans ritually unclean.) He felt that impurity could come only from within. "Listen to me, all of you, and try to understand! It's not what goes into a person from the outside that can defile; rather, it's what comes out of the person that defiles" (Mark 7:14–15). (King James Version: "Hearken unto me every one of you, and understand: There is nothing from without a man, that entering into him can defile him: but the things which come out of him, those are they that defile the man.") He had in general a relaxed attitude toward the law.

He deliberately confused the distinction between insiders and outsiders. He believed that God's domain belonged to the poor. (The early, Palestinian Christian community was essentially a movement of poor peasants. Many abandoned family ties, property, and social position in response to his summons.) He took a more liberal view of women and the status of women than was usual in the patriarchal society of the time.

Jesus's sayings and parables went against the social and religious grain—as, for instance, "Love your enemies" (Luke 6:27). They surprised and shocked: they characteristically called for a reversal of roles or frustrated ordinary, everyday expectations.

He turned expectations on their head: "What does God's imperial rule remind me of? It is like leaven which a woman took and concealed in fifty pounds of flour until it was all leavened" (Luke 13:20–21). Shocking, because leaven at that time was customarily regarded as a symbol of corruption and evil.

He spoke often about God's imperial rule. But he spoke of it as already present, not in apocalyptic terms. (It was Mark's habit to speak in apocalyptic terms.) He conceived of it as all around but difficult to discern, close or already present but unobserved. (Evidence of this lies in Jesus's major parables, which do not reflect an apocalyptic view of history: e.g., Samaritan, prodigal son, dinner party, vineyard laborers, shrewd manager, unforgiving slave, corrupt judge, leaven, mustard seed, pearl, treasure.)

God was so real for him that he could not distinguish God's present activity from any future activity. He had a sense of time in which the future and the present merged, in the intensity of his vision.

Jesus's sayings and parables are often characterized by paradox, as in, again, "Love your enemies." Those who love their enemies have no enemies. Or: "Do good, and lend, expecting nothing in return" (Luke 6:35). Lending without expectation of repayment is not lending. Or: "You must be as sly as a snake and as simple as a dove" (Matthew 10:16). To adopt the posture of the snake and the dove at the same time is a contradiction.

Whereas his followers were more serious-minded, Jesus tended to employ comic hyperbole and graphic exaggeration, as in the following: "It's easier for a camel to squeeze through a needle's eye than for a wealthy person to get into God's domain!" (Mark 10:25). As *The Five Gospels* explains, "This saying presented difficulties to the Christian community from the very beginning. Some Greek scribes substituted the Greek word [for] rope (*kamilon*) for the term [for] camel (*kamelon*) to reduce the contrast, while some modern but misguided interpreters have claimed that the 'needle's eye' was the name of a narrow gate or pass, which a camel would find difficult, but not impossible, to pass through."

Jesus's sayings and parables are often characterized by humor, paradox, and exaggeration combined. In the parable of the mustard seed, for instance, he compares God's domain to the lowly mustard weed. He uses the image of the mustard weed as a parody of Ezekiel's mighty cedar of Lebanon and the apocalyptic tree of Daniel, traditional images for God's domain at that time. Jesus is poking fun at the symbol of the mighty tree that prevailed. But the evangelists were swayed by that same symbol to try to bring Jesus's metaphor closer to it. "What is God's imperial rule like? What does it remind me of? It is like a mustard seed which a man took and tossed into his garden. It grew and became a tree, and the birds of the sky roosted in its branches" (Luke 13:18–19). (King James Version: "Unto what is the kingdom of God like? and whereunto shall I resemble it? It is like a grain of mustard seed, which a man took, and cast into his garden; and it grew, and waxed a great tree; and the fowls of the air lodged in the branches of it.")

Many of Jesus's sayings and parables employ a concrete natural image, as, for instance: locust, rooster, snake, fish, dove, sparrow, crow, fox, camel, shirt, coat, belt, hand, foot, cheek, hair, eye, city, marketplace, synagogue, house, lamp, lampstand, jar, couch, seat, needle, bushel basket, grape, wine, wineskin, vineyard, salt, leaven, dough, bread, meal, seed, grain, sickle, harvest, sun, rain, dust, mountain, stone, pearl, coin, timber, splinter, bramble, thorn, thistle, reed, slave, master, doctor, beggar, bailiff, judge, emperor, bridegroom, toll collector. The concrete image is exploited in a surprising and unusual way, as for instance: "Figs are not gathered from thorns, nor are grapes picked from brambles" (Luke 6:44).

Jesus often raised questions from a literal to a metaphorical level. His sayings and parables were customarily metaphorical and without explicit application. Because his parables were told in figurative language, because the figures could not be taken literally, because the application of the saying was left ambiguous, what he said was difficult to understand, and the disciples often did not know what he was saying. (Mark made the disciples out to be stupid; this was one of his particular biases, and it is he who has Jesus say such things to his disciples as "Are you as dim-witted as the rest?") But Jesus did not explain. Instead, he gave them more questions, more stories with unclear references. The answer shifted the decision back onto his listeners. Jesus's style was to refuse to give straightforward answers.

Jesus emphasized reciprocity: "Forgive and you'll be forgiven" (Luke 6:37).

Jesus spoke out against divorce.

Jesus gave injunctions difficult for early communities to practice (such as "Love your enemies" and the injunction against divorce).

He may have realized the potential danger he incurred by challenging the status quo.

During a meal, Jesus might very likely have engaged in some symbolic acts. He probably made use of bread or fish and wine. (Bread and fish were the staples of the Galilean diet.)

It is possible that one of the disciples betrayed Jesus and that Jesus may have become aware of that betrayal.

Jesus did not speculate about the appearance of the

Messiah in the last days or about counterfeit messiahs and false prophets.

Another saying or parable characterized by exaggeration or hyperbole is the following: "That's why I tell you: don't fret about life—what you're going to eat—or about your body—what you're going to wear. Remember, there is more to living than food and clothing. . . . Think about how the lilies grow: they don't slave and they never spin. Yet let me tell you, even Solomon at the height of his glory was never decked out like one of these" (Luke 12:22–28). The exaggeration: Human beings are not given clothing by God in the same way that lilies are clothed.

The King James Version of this passage reads: "Therefore I say unto you, Take no thought for your life, what ye shall eat; neither for the body, what ye shall put on. The life is more than meat, and the body is more than raiment. . . . Consider the lilies how they grow: they toil not, they spin not; and yet I say unto you, that Solomon in all his glory was not arrayed like one of these."

The Scholars Version has the ring of "translationese" to it, an effect partly of colliding dictions (the slangy "decked out" sits unhappily in the same sentence as the more formal and archaic "one of these"—and numerous other examples of these unhappy marriages can be found throughout the translation); and partly of "wooden-ear" choices such as the pairing of "Yet let." There are, further, rhythmical deficiencies that make it far less generally euphonious than the King James Version, though it is undoubtedly more accurate and based on a more accurate version of the original text.

"Consider the lilies how they grow" sings to us

more than "Think about how the lilies grow" for several reasons having to do with rhythm: in the first line, the scansion of the three-syllable "Consider," accent on the second syllable, propels the line forward and the three-syllable "the lilies," accent again on the second syllable, continues the momentum, whereas "Think about" causes the line to stutter; we stumble over the awkward rhymed pair of "about how"; and the monosyllables "how the" slow the motion further, so that the concluding "lilies grow" sounds flat and unexciting. The sentence as a whole is rhythmically disorganized. In the King James Version the line is divided by a perceptible caesura into two three-word phrases with alliterated middle words, "Consider the lilies" and "how they grow," that could conceivably stand alone, which creates a pleasing balance, the caesura giving a gentle emphasis to the word "lilies." This balance of paired phrases is echoed in the more closely parallel pair that immediately follows—"they toil not, they spin not"—and in fact maintained through the entire passage quoted above, from just after the opening "Therefore I say unto you" until the concluding "and yet I say unto you," when the departure from the pattern heightens the eloquence of the closing declaration. But in the Scholars Version the balanced structures so precisely maintained in the King James Version are often either slightly lopsided—"they toil not, they spin not" becomes "they don't slave and they never spin"—or abandoned altogether—"The life is more than meat, and the body is more than raiment" becomes "there is more to living than food and clothing." Other rhetorical devices—repetition, alliteration, assonance—that are deployed in the King James Version to further tie the passage together may be absent or seem almost accidental in the Scholars Version.

But I find that when I turn to the King James Version for comparison, beautiful though it is, my ears often cease to hear. It is hard to tell what it is that closes my ears: whether it is the familiarity of the King James Version, or its association with an inaccessible Jesus figure, or its lyricism. It may be that the words of this translation are so well-known by now that they cease to convey anything; certainly they convey nothing fresh coming from a newly perceived Jesus. It may be that the somewhat antique flavor of the language (the translation was done by a group of forty-seven scholars in the early seventeenth century, relying heavily on earlier work by William Tyndall) further distances the thoughts from us. It is hard to measure just how much attention the very beauty of the language attracts to itself and distracts from the thoughts it expresses. In any case, my attention is in fact turned less effectively to the substance of Jesus's thought in the King James Version than in the more modest Scholars Version—just as the modest (and terse) Jesus tended to direct attention away from himself and toward God (unlike some of his proselytizers). So that, oddly, the unlyrical style of the Scholars Version—the constant jolts, the rockiness—has a tonic effect: it keeps me awake, or keeps the text awake, it refreshes it, allows me to hear it.

The paradoxical effect of putting Jesus back into his historical context, the context of his time, among other sages of his time, other wandering charismatics, is that he, through the style of his language, and through what it reveals of his character and his thought, becomes newly outstanding. The effect of the Jesus Seminar's patient, "critical" detective work in what Thomas Jefferson called "paring off the amphibologisms," is to reveal Jesus more fully than he was revealed before. In this case, anyway, where skepticism clears the way, there is room for belief.

The "final general rule of evidence" of the Jesus Seminar is this: beware of finding a Jesus entirely congenial to you.

"Finding him congenial," here, would mean "seeing him as you want to see him," "seeing him as your preconceived notions would have you see him," "distorting or skewing what you see into what you want to see."

This was their protective amulet against bias, against obfuscation, against muddy thinking. It's a wonderful recommendation in general, one that one might advisedly adopt as one's own guiding principle in life, with certain substitutions: Beware of seeing your native land the way you want to see it rather than the way it is. Beware of seeing a favored ideology the way you want to see it rather than the way it is. Beware of seeing your leaders, political or otherwise, the way you want to see them rather than the way they are.

It occurred to me as I made my way here and there along these paths of history that there is a joy in independence, in the risk of independence in one's thinking and making, and there is joy even in contemplating the works of the independent thinker. But what also occurred to me is that there is a feeling of safety, a reassurance, in being an uncritical follower, especially of an independent thinker, a revolutionary, especially of a newly discovered independent thinker or revolutionary, and that the challenge to the follower, consequently, is to remain independent in turn—even of those we admire, of those who are themselves independent. In other words, to continue to look with clear eyes, with the eyes of the "critical scholar," at Jefferson, at Paine, at Jesus, at the Jesus Seminar, for fear that otherwise we have eyes but do not look. Or maybe that we look but do not see.

1997

A Reading of the Shepherd's Psalm

Once you have heard the Psalm of David a few times—
or, more likely, many times, since this very popular and
moving poem, or fragments of it, regularly recurs in movies, TV shows, songs—you tend to remember it, or at
least isolated lines from it. Of all the many translations
that exist, however, it is the King James Version that is
so memorable and so often quoted. The very first line,
with its four strong beats, is the first that remains engraved on our memory:

> *The Lórd is my shépherd; I sháll not wánt.*

One source of its power is probably the immediate
homely domestic or animal imagery—the introduction
of the extended analogy that will follow: the Lord compared to the shepherd, and the "I" of the psalm compared
to a sheep within a flock. Another source of the power
of the line is its mostly monosyllabic, Anglo-Saxon vocabulary: lord, shepherd, want. Every word, in fact, is
Anglo-Saxon, and every word is monosyllabic except for
"shepherd." The meter is initially the dancing amphi-
brachic (unstressed, stressed, unstressed; unstressed,

stressed, unstressed). This is the meter of the classic limerick: "There once was / a girl from / Nantucket"; as well as other kinds of poems: "How dear to / this heart are / the scenes of / my childhood" (Samuel Woodworth, "The Old Oaken Bucket"). The line then slows to the walking iambic.

"Want" is a strong word, though with a different meaning from the one we usually give it today, the same meaning as in the sensible alliterative maxim "Waste not, want not"—if you are careful with what you have, you will never lack for what you need.

The plainness of the statement is further strengthened by the four-monosyllable negative statement: *I shall not want*. Contrast this KJV version with the Good News Translation: "The Lord is my shepherd; I have everything I need." The meanings are not quite the same, for one thing, but for another, whereas "I shall not want" suggests a modest sufficiency, "I have everything I need" carries a slight suggestion of covetousness, a desire for material things, a tendency to appraise one's possessions, and (in the repetition of "I") a preoccupation with self. The emphasis in this version is on "have" and "need," "I" and "I," as opposed to the KJV double negative meaning "not lack."

The extended metaphor of shepherd and flock continues in the second line:

He maketh me to lie down in green pastures: he leadeth me beside the still waters.

This line, too, is pleasingly constructed, almost perfectly symmetrical—in fact, the beginning and end of each of the parts is symmetrical: "He maketh me . . . green pastures," "he leadeth me . . . still waters."

In this line, I puzzle over a couple of things: the many flocks of sheep I have seen over the years grazing in various pastures, here in upstate New York, or across the road from where my old school friend lives in the Cotswolds outside Bath, England, or as seen from the train in the Scottish countryside, seem to decide when they wish to lie down and when they prefer to be up on their feet grazing. They are without a shepherd, but I know that not so long ago, relatively, a shepherd did often accompany a flock of sheep. I cannot imagine, though, that a shepherd could make them lie down.

One of the many impassioned, anonymous commentators on the various websites that invite reactions to this psalm says, many times over, that sheep are stupid, and, further, that they need to be made to lie down. (Contrast this with the clear declaration of an online sheepherding manual, which implies at least one kind of intelligence: "Sheep have excellent memories." I have read elsewhere—where and when I no longer remember—that a sheep can recognize the face of another sheep for as long as two years.) Perhaps one of the other translations, the nineteenth-century Young's Literal, employing a gentler or more indirect verb, is closer to the reality of sheep behavior, or to the original text, here: "He causeth me to lie down"—in other words, the shepherd brings it about indirectly, by simply providing the pasture.

On the other hand, another of these website commentators offers—whether from personal experience or sound scholarship, or neither—the startling idea that if a lamb strayed too often from a flock, the shepherd might break one of its legs so that it would remain lying down in the pasture. I have not heard of this before, and of course I can't imagine that the psalmist had this in mind.

Yet another commentator asserts that sheep are afraid of moving water and will drink only from quiet water. A picture I have in my mind, from a farm not far from where I live, is of a small, still pond with a single file of six or eight sheep on the far side of it walking calmly, as though in a dream, along the water's edge toward another field. The water was still. They were not being led, or driven, as it happened; they were walking past it of their own accord.

Certainly it is true, however, that green pastures and still waters together create the image of a harmonious, fertile, and safe landscape in which sheep may flourish.

The parallel structure is continued in the next line, which has two parts, like the preceding line and the first line, and each of the two parts opens with "he" and a verb.

He restoreth my soul: he leadeth me in the paths of righteousness for his name's sake.

The second verb, "leadeth," is in fact the same as the second verb in the preceding line, and this repetition reinforces for us the idea of the shepherd as guide: first leading the sheep beside the still waters, now leading the sheep in the paths of righteousness. The interaction between "he"—the Lord—and "I"—the sheep—continues, though the sheep-ness of the I is abandoned in the first part—"He restoreth my soul"—and in the second part is sustained only by two words, "leadeth" and the strong and important (in sheep-rearing) "paths."

In this line, the two parts of the sentence are separated by a colon rather than a period or a semicolon, and this change of punctuation creates a change of relationship between the two parts. Whereas the period and the semicolon signal that the two parts of the line are equal, syntactically, the colon signals to us that the second part follows from the first and explains or expands upon it: evidently, what the author of this psalm *means* by "He restoreth my soul" is that "he leadeth me in the paths of righteousness for his name's sake."

With the third line, then, we are moving away from the shepherd-sheep metaphor and into the more explicit message concerning the Lord's spiritual guidance and our salvation.

Now, in the fourth stanza, we come to another very famous part of the psalm and also to an interesting shift in person. The psalm up to this point has been narrated in the third and first persons: "The Lord" and "he" interact with "me" and "my." Now, although the "I" is retained, the "he" is addressed directly and personally as "you," or, in the KJV, the familiar "thou."

> *Yea, though I walk through the valley of the*
> *shadow of death, I will fear no evil: for thou art*
> *with me; thy rod and thy staff they comfort me.*

This shift could be read as an emotional one: the speaker has been objectively describing a situation, how the Lord interacts with him; now, overcome by the emotion of this relationship, he, or she—but, although I don't know what the latest scholarship has decided about the authorship of the psalms, it would be convenient here to assume the psalm was written by King David—directly addresses the Lord, in gratitude, perhaps.

The explanation could also be that the two parts of the psalm—the first three stanzas and the last three—were composed by different hands.

This fourth stanza is perhaps the emotional heart of the psalm, strong though the first line is; longer, more dramatic than the other lines, it is certainly climactic both rhetorically and imagistically. It may be this part that has made the psalm so memorable to so many believers, as well as nonbelievers, especially in times of fear or crisis, its phrases being so charged with emotion, even including the intimate "thou": "the valley of the shadow of death"; "fear no evil"; "thou art with me"; "comfort me."

It is this stanza that I think about when I am contemplating the effect of translation, and, more generally, the importance of the effect of the beauty of the King James Version in conveying the spiritual messages contained within many of the most eloquent passages of the Bible.

Would this line have had the same emotional effect if it had been known first, or only, in any of the other available translations?

Even when I walk through a valley of deep
   darkness;
even though I walk through the darkest valley;
even when I go through the darkest valley;
even when I must walk through the darkest valley;
even if I shall walk in the valleys of the shadows of
   death;

Maybe. And then there is also Young's Literal, which claims to be the closest to the original—though it does not claim to be the most eloquent and is sometimes impossible to understand:

also—when I walk in a valley of death-shade.

I can't compare any of these to the original Hebrew, although evidently Young's Literal should be reasonably close, but I do prefer the KJV, again. Is this merely because of long familiarity?

It is rhetorically, or stylistically, different from the preceding lines: it begins with an exclamation—"Yea"—followed by a dependent clause—"though I walk," in contrast to all the other sentences so far, which have employed a plainer, more direct subject-verb construction.

"Yea" is not the same in meaning as "even," the favorite choice of the other translations. Although the word, or at least this spelling, often appears incorrectly in student writing when the author really intends "Yeah," or even the cheer "Yay," it actually means, most simply, "Yes," as in the phrase "yea or nay." But in some contexts, including this one, it means "indeed" or "truly": "Indeed, though I walk in the valley." And since "though," here, is ambiguous, meaning either "although" or "even when," the line may be understood to begin: "Truly, even when I walk in the valley." And notice the comma after "Yea," an important pause. The translator is writing "Indeed" or "Truly" and asking us to pause and prepare ourselves for what will follow. And what will follow is highly dramatic: we are very concretely and suddenly walking through a valley—to continue the sheep and sheepherding imagery—and it lies in shadow, and the shadow is cast by death itself.

Now, this is a phrase I have always found very powerful: "in the valley of the shadow of death." Is it awkward, or not? Is it more, or less, effective writing to repeat the "of"? I vote for more effective, for reasons of both imagery and rhythm: in this translation, the line unfolds part by part to reveal the image, the valley coming first, the shadow second, and death, climactically, last. Any compression, or economy, I think, takes away from this gradually developing image—any compression such as "darkest valley," "valley of deep darkness" (which, besides the compression, contains an awkward alliteration), or even "valley of death's shadow"—which is also hard to say. To my ear, the repetition of the two "of" phrases creates a strong and pleasing rhythm—and an accumulation of menace, "shadow" being followed by "death."

The image of the valley, with its unfolding darkness and its repeated phrases, is then followed by the very brief and succinct statement, especially strong by contrast: "I will fear no evil." This phrase, in turn, is followed by a colon, again signaling that what follows will explain or interpret what came before—"I will fear no evil" *because* "thou art with me" and, after the semicolon—indicating an equivalent statement—"thy rod and thy staff they comfort me." Here, we return to the sheepherding imagery, though it is not at first apparent to me why the shepherd's traditional single staff has been doubled by the rod.

Shepherds have traditionally carried what we normally call crooks—they are staffs, or staves, that serve as walking sticks but also have a hooked end useful for catching hold of the neck or leg of a lamb or ewe or ram that has gotten caught in an inaccessible place, perhaps a thicket of brambles, or simply for guiding it into the correct path or direction, or restraining it for any one of many purposes. The crooked end, I learned at one point, is also useful for hurling clods of earth at recalcitrant sheep to get them moving. But perhaps the ancient biblical shepherds, and others, too, carried a rod as well as a staff. In some early medieval illustrations, shepherds are depicted carrying only a sort of cudgel. Perhaps the rod referred to in this psalm was a stout stick or club for fending off predators or even disciplining wayward sheep.

In this context, however, since both the rod and the staff "comfort" the sheep, the rod would be for protecting, not disciplining, the sheep and the staff for gently guiding it.

The penultimate stanza seems to desert the sheepherding metaphor:

> *Thou preparest a table before me in the presence of mine enemies: thou anointest my head with oil; my cup runneth over.*

One commentator, however, ingeniously defends the idea that the metaphor has not actually been abandoned, since, he maintains, it was an ancient practice, in at least one sheepherding culture, to lay out feed for the sheep on low stone tables. Similarly, the anointing of the head, he posits, was possibly the administering of a protective medical treatment to the sheep.

Structurally, the elegance of the prose style is maintained with the alliteration of the *pr*'s in the first clause—"preparest" and "presence"; the parallel structure of "Thou preparest" and "thou anointest"; and the harmony of the set of three clauses—three statements—

within the one sentence, the clauses becoming progressively shorter.

The colon suggests that the second and third statements, the anointing and the cup overflowing, describe events that take place as part of the dinner.

The last clause returns us from the second person address ("thou") to the third-person narration ("the Lord"):

> *Surely goodness and mercy shall follow me all the*
> *days of my life: and I will dwell in the house of*
> *the Lord for ever.*

Here, the opening "Surely" echoes the earlier opening "Yea," creating another parallel within the six stanzas of the psalm—both "Yea" and "Surely" being adverbs of intensification, as opposed to the openings of the first three lines and the fifth, which are subject-verb pairs. Adding to the eloquence of this final stanza, I hear the double alliteration in "follow" and "life," though it is subtle; I hear the alliteration also in "dwell" and "Lord," and "Surely" and "shall," and the assonance in "life" and "I." Quiet though these echoes are, they effectively bind these closing statements together and strengthen their emotional impact.

Besides the positive emphasis of the opening "Surely," and the alliteration and assonance, this last stanza gains further force from its return to a mainly Anglo-Saxon vocabulary, as in the opening line. (Only "surely" and "mercy" are Latinate.)

Here, the colon is ambiguous, because of the "and" that follows it: the colon appears to introduce what follows, as an extension of the statement, but the "and" implies something else—that the second part of the sentence provides new and different material.

As for the extended sheepherding metaphor, though it would seem to have been definitively left behind in this final sentence, the same determined commentator who found a husbandry reference in "preparing a table" made an interpretive reach and chose to see "goodness" and "mercy" as, just possibly, two kindly and watchful sheepdogs.

2015

Remember the Van Wagenens

The age of fifty, whether it is or not, looks very much like a halfway point. So this may be why—imagining rightly or wrongly that we are *nel mezzo del cammin di nostra vita*—we find ourselves reconsidering our life to come (looking forward) and our life past (looking back).

I quote this Italian not to show off my familiarity with foreign languages, but because these are some of the few "memorized" words that tend to float into the forefront of my mind quite regularly, if not necessarily accurately. These particular words are sometimes followed by others no doubt even less accurate: *mi ritrovai in un' selva oscura*.

Dream about Mademoiselle Roser: She was in a small-town library, probably this one here in my town but not resembling it. She had short, straight white hair (she did not, in life), and she was very kempt and fashionable, and rather small (she was large, in life). I was very happy to see her there. At last I could tell her that I had grown up to be a translator, and was now in fact translating Proust, which would have to appear to her as a sort of pinnacle of a translator's career, whether it really is or not (the real pinnacle being, perhaps, the less popular Leiris, who may be, in fact, stylistically more intricate and daunting than Proust, and doesn't a translator test her mettle on style more immediately, at least, than on other aspects of the work, on its larger conception or form?). I realized that she might not remember me, but she would still be pleased that a pupil of hers was now translating French. She was an emphatic, exuberant, and generous person, with severe, high standards. I was very happy. Then I remembered that she had died.

I tell my mother I think Mlle Roser, though dead, can still see me and understand. She is shocked. "You don't really believe that!" But I do. I did not use to believe the dead lived on, but I have changed my thinking about that.

There was a hunt, last month, at my old school, for evidence of Mlle Roser. We went down into the basement, even into certain locked inner rooms behind the utility or shop rooms. There were no old boxes of that particular textbook. But back upstairs there were some letters and a few photographs. She was an impressive-looking woman. The photographs seemed to confirm my memory of her, but once I had seen them, I had to work hard to remember what it was I actually did remember, without the influence of the photographs.

When you think you will not remember something, you write it down, either in a notebook or on a handy piece of paper. You have many pieces of paper all over the house and in all sorts of pockets and bags with things written on them that you either don't remember or do, also, remember—either do not have in your mind also or do have in your mind also. So the pieces of paper with writing on them supplement the living tissue of your memory, as though your usable, active memory goes beyond the bounds of your head out onto these pieces of paper.

Could one say that, in outward-moving circles (or planes—rectangles or squares), not only does the notebook supplement and represent the mind, but the desk also, and then the study, the house, and the grounds of the house? (Stopping at the fence: The street beyond it and then the neighborhood and the town are no longer private spaces.)

Gaston Bachelard's *The Poetics of Space* is of course very important to think of (though the translation is in spots unnecessarily abstract and obtuse) when we are talking about the identification of the mind and physical space. The verticality of the house; the rationality, the intellectuality of the attic; the darkness, the subterranean, the unconscious of the cellar.

Where would your oldest friend, Mary, your oldest childhood friend, be, after forty years of disappearance? When you locate her again, where is she? To your surprise, in Africa. But then you see the naturalness of it: Where else would the material of the most essential old memories retreat, but to the continent that has always been so mysterious to you?

Her last name, too, is one that shines, so now there is a light shining in the place that harbors the old memories.

Her two younger sisters, being less essential, have receded only as far as Massachusetts and Philadelphia.

The difference between the thing remembered (the landscape of memory) and the thing as it continues to exist in present-day reality—both of them existing. The difference between the street of the childhood memory, and the street now. The house then, and the house now. Mary and her sisters then, on Crescent Street, and now: in Massachusetts, Philadelphia, and . . . Nigeria. Their grandmother's Whately farmhouse then—surrounded on three sides by vast fields—and now: crowded by other houses. My other earliest childhood friend, Marilyn, next door, then—eating a lamb chop at her kitchen table (clear as day in my mind)—and now, living with her husband and children in Paris (less clear). The thing remembered and what there is now both exist. But one exists only in my brain and the other out there for other people to see, too.

The memories exist physically in the brain cells. A smell opens a pathway to the memory of a canvas book bag that I haven't remembered for years. At least I don't remember that I have remembered it, and yet the cells containing the memory, the memory of the smell, have sat there in my brain for years.

Why is there any need to find them again (childhood friend and grammar book)? To tie together that past and this present, but also that self that I was then with this self now? Is it once again a question of saying, Yes, I do exist, and Yes, I did exist all along? This self that must somehow be dealt with—reaffirmed, subdued, or merely ignored and taken for granted.

———

Trying out the idea that this particular past does not matter anyway. Another person has another past that matters to her. But that doesn't matter in any absolute way, any more than mine absolutely matters. She also wants to find her childhood friends. But I could exchange mine for hers; mine have no more weight than hers. It is all circumstantial and accidental. Which is why other people's "earliest" memories are so often banal: they have no objective interest, and yet their authors are bent on "truthfully" reporting them.

William Bronk writing it over and over again: that we are each only temporary manifestations of Life. Or at least, this is what I want to think he is writing, and so this is how I remember it.

That the dead are still "with us": it started, anyway, with Mlle Roser. I say to my mother, quite sincerely (I am trying again to remember it correctly), that I believe Mlle Roser, whose company my mother remembers sharing more than once for dinner and once for some sort of theatrical performance in Paris, and who died some years ago, is still alive in some form and taking an interest in what I may write about her and in what I may "do" with my French. I say to my mother that I believe Mlle Roser is still aware of some things, and she says in a shocked tone, "Are you serious?" In her tone is not mere interest or curiosity, as I would prefer, but incredulity and a hint of scorn—this notion of mine, if sincere, is ridiculous, even hysterical. (Or am I misreading her tone? Is this really, instead, the urgency of an old woman who can't afford to waste precious minutes of her remaining life reacting to insincere or foolish statements?)

———

What is certain, in any case, is that the dead do live on in memory, in the recesses of the mind of the living. But seem to be outside the mind. Just as a childhood landscape remembered seems to be outside, as it was really outside at the time. That landscape was outside me at the time, but is inside me now. No one sees it but I. Others see what is there now instead of that landscape (what is there being usually a more crowded landscape).

The dead living on, "really": in the case of Mlle Roser, is this impression stronger because she was a teacher, and a teacher of young children, therefore someone overseeing, someone taking command and assuming responsibility for the many young lives who passed through her hands? So that even "up there" she would still feel somehow responsible?

Or is this impression produced by the force of my desire, now that it is too late, to tell her what those early days of her teaching now mean to me? Including the textbook, which I can't find anywhere?

Or is it that when one reaches a certain age of being older than so many people (becoming an elder), instead of being younger than so many (having so many elders), one wishes to bring back a figure who was not only much older but also a teacher, therefore an appointed guide and guardian, in at least one area (the French language)? Is it because, at the age I am now, one's guides and teachers, one's guardians, appointed and unappointed, are dropping away, every day?

The French grammar is called *Le Français par la méthode directe* by Robin and Bergeaud. It is a slim book with a red cover, published back in 1941 by Librairie Hachette, and I have been looking everywhere for a copy, even in poor condition.

We focus always, and over and over each day, on the details of our particularity (I love his particular handwriting whenever I see it) when we (and it all) are really just happenstantial (we love what we come to love, but we might easily never have come to it: I would love his Bronx accent, but he doesn't have one). Am I more lovable, objectively, than that young Hasidic woman standing in the subway car? If I were objectively more lovable, then that young Hasidic man gazing at her so raptly would love me instead. No, even that statement is not true: I could be objectively more lovable and he could still love her instead.

My impression is that almost any one poem of William Bronk's that I could find would say what I am thinking so many of his poems say—what I prefer to remember and think they say—but that is not quite true.

LIVING INSTEAD

*Nothing much we can do about it so we live
the way old bones and fossils lived, the way
long-buried cities lived: we live instead
—just as if and even believing that here
and finally now, ours could be the real world.*

This is not quite the thought I was after: I quote it "instead."

There are certain things I think I "ought to" remember, if I am to be a responsible representative of my time and generation, but where there should be a memory there is often a blank. Commonest example I keep returning to: the Bay of Pigs. I never wanted to remember anything about it. The Cuban Missile Crisis. I erased understanding of these "current" events even as I learned about them. I wanted to wipe the slate clean. To have a "clear mind"? How to have a clean slate and still have a reliable memory bank for reference, and be responsible to succeeding generations?

Hypogeum: the subterranean part of an ancient building. The doubled remove in that idea.

One who shares a past with you loses his memory entirely: What happens to you, the you that he held in his memory? That past is suddenly wiped out, or in danger of being wiped out, or rendered meaningless, or less meaningful, or even more accidental (unnecessary) than it was. If suddenly only you remember it, because Father does not (Father sitting there in his plastic chair with his mouth open). As though it were a geometrical figure that has lost its depth, its third dimension, the legs it stood on.

This memory of mine could be exchanged for any other memory of mine. Any other person's memory, even. Let me tell you something I remember from my childhood: and this is not true, it is someone else's memory, or a story I read that someone else made up. It is fiction. You hear it as my memory. That does not matter; you take it as my memory. Even I may not know it is not mine.

Past gone, like a building gone, or a tree.
   A building is gone, leaving no trace on the ground,

especially no trace in the air—of course—and yet up there, in the air, many lives unfolded.

And then with a certain belief in magic, we think lives that unfolded within walls have left physical traces on those stones, and is that why we pick up a shard of stone from a ruin, or a handful of soil from Greece, and take it away in our pocket? Is it just a belief in magic, or a superstition? Is it laughable?

What about the man who has a fireplace he has built himself incorporating a stone from every state in the continental United States? It is in some sense magical for him, full of potency—those stones are more than ordinary stones in a "fieldstone" fireplace. But they have no intrinsic value, and to someone who doesn't know, they have no value: here comes the wrecker and scatters and shatters the stones, the one from Arizona over there and the one from South Dakota here, gone. They have value only for the builder, who knows them, who has invested them with value. The way we invest our pets with personality, character, with a larger personality and character than a stranger can see, upon first meeting our pet.

A tree is taken down. It leaves no trace in the air, though it was up there in that air for so many years, often a hundred or more.

The vegetable garden that was planted in the same place by this roadside every year is not planted anymore because the gardener grew too old and too feeble. So there is just another twelve-foot square of lawn now, along with the rest of the lawn. The third dimension—the growth several feet up into the air—and the complexity, the tangle and chaos, the richness, the sumptuousness, is gone now.

On the top floor, this time, a floor with lower ceilings, the servants' floor, of a house on Gardner Street in Providence: open the doors of a cabinet, pull out a drawer, lift the cover from a box, and there you see stones labeled as coming from places in Egypt, in Greece, other countries (Persia?), collected many decades ago, even a century ago, by this monied family traveling abroad.

But having said this, I am not sure the house was on Gardner Street after all, or even if there is such a street. I am sure, though, of the cabinet and the stones and the wealthy family.

Was that top floor the part of the house equivalent to rationality, or to memory?

If you don't know that this house here was Mozart's birthplace, you are not interested, even though you, a great lover of Mozart, walk right past it.

If you do know, you stand before it filled with a number of emotions and thoughts, including awe.

On the other hand, if you have made a mistake and are standing in front of the wrong house thinking it was Mozart's house, your thoughts and emotions are exactly the same as if you stood in front of the correct house. Are they just as valuable? You will come back from your trip abroad and tell someone about the experience—your thoughts and emotions included—and that experience will make a difference to you as your life goes on, and will perhaps make a difference to the person or the many people you tell about your experience in front of Mozart's house, and it won't matter that it was the wrong house. It won't matter unless you find out it was the wrong house. Then, in your own eyes, you will feel you did not really have the experience you thought you had. Your experience was false, and had no value.

The example of Mozart's house is not a good example, because it must have a plaque on it, and even perhaps colorful banners, and crowds going in and out. But there are other houses that are unmarked, the former habitations of other much-loved people. And there are other places in front of which we have stood, feeling awe, that will never be given plaques, such as the stationery shop in Paris where Samuel Beckett used to buy his note cards. "That man put his foot on this very threshold, at one time," you say to yourself.

Not only that the dead are still alive, but also, sometimes, the conviction that the past still exists. But I can't tell if this is because I am so fully imagining it (and have returned so often in my imagination to the same place and time) or because it "really" still exists—not in "our" space and time, but in some other dimension.

It has been quite a few years that I have been looking, sporadically, for my early friend Mary and for that grammar book with the red cover. Now I have found out where both of them are, though I haven't yet contacted my friend and do not yet have the grammar book in my possession. I have the address of one, and, of the other, the many pages constituting a xeroxed copy. Paper, again, is replacing or standing in for the real thing, or signaling the real thing, or providing me with a handy reminder of the real thing. Though of course one of the real things, in this case, is itself largely paper.

———

Why do I want the past (the material contained in my memory) to live on in the present? Why do I want evidence of it now? And why do I want someone else to know, too? Why am I not content to leave it where it is and remember it in solitude? Revisit it from time to time? This time it is a dining room with massive dark furniture in Vienna, and there is a block puzzle on the dining room table, brought out for my benefit, as I was then, a seven-year-old? It could also be the ripe cherries from the cherry trees in the enclosed back garden of a house in Graz, and the garden itself. Are the memories of "foreign" experiences more concentrated and more potent for me because these experiences were so unlike what I grew up with before and after, or because they were so much richer, sensually and maybe also emotionally? And if you give a child a certain experience (as of the desert in the American Southwest) that he can't repeat every day (living in the East in a town with lush vegetation in the summer), do you create something inside him (in the form of a memory but also, perhaps, of an unsatisfied desire) that he will want to return to the rest of his life?

The carton I happen to rest my feet on, under my desk, could also be considered to contain a thick pile of thin sheets of memory—since each piece of paper (a miscellany thrown in there and not examined for years), or almost each one, yields a bit of memory or large piece of memory and along with the memory an emotion—a faint emotion or a stronger emotion. But unexamined, it is (in the carton) all potential—like potential energy (the ball at the top of the incline, if I am remembering correctly the physics lesson) as opposed to kinetic energy, as I studied this, with difficulty, in the very large, light-filled classroom on a hilltop in Vermont, under the guidance of a physics and chemistry teacher whom I remember well, though he does not remember me. (And he said something about me at the time that I have kept in mind and returned to regularly all these years, and that helps me to define myself, and yet he does not know who this woman in front of him is, and cannot, even with all the help in the world, revive any image of her as a girl.)

From all the sheets of paper—so thin as to be virtually two-dimensional—arise three-dimensional scenes visible only to me.

Speak, Memory, by Nabokov, in which the raw matter of his memory was developed and refined by the efflorescence of his language into more than it ever was in itself. He did not remember as much as he said. The memories grew in his language.

I go to a place—to Montaillou, for instance—and I am going "back" there, even though I have never been there before, because I have been there so often in imagination. I find only momentary, and tiny, traces of the past I am looking for. I find a treeless hillside with cow paths or sheep paths worn on it, as so often imagined by me while I read the book I so love, about Montaillou, but at the next turn there is a development of modern "villas." There is no abundance, no richness, of remnants of the past but only remnants so nearly crowded out or extinguished by the present, by constructions of the present, that they have no more life in them, or almost none; they are defeated and nearly dead.

A certain life force prevails that can be destroyed, extinguished, by encroachment. On a hillside not far from here, a small treeless cemetery outlined in stone, within an irregular rectangular stone wall, had kept its life force, its magic, until a car wash (though such a relatively tasteful one) was built a little too close to it—not right up against it, but within the same purview. Magic gone. As though the cemetery had been fatally "insulted." Degradation.

A thing can be killed by its very preservation. Killed by the care to preserve it. Interruption, forever, of its growth, its coming into being, its death, in other words its own and owned life cycle. Preservation implying that it has no life force of its own any longer but needs outside help to remain in existence, to remain in the world (not "alive," though). So that even if a bit of preserved "forest" remains here, something very important to it has died: its own force of being, its own insistence, without help.

Similarly, that those pieces of stone or wall, labeled with handwritten labels as coming from this or that particular place along the tour, should remain in the cupboard or cabinet on the top floor of the house of the wealthy old family, though the family no longer lives there but has donated the house to the university, rather than in a museum or other place of formal exhibit, allows them to keep their life: that there is no rope around them, that they are still resting in a place that was natural for them to remain in, at the top of the house, in a drawer, carefully preserved but only as the family would preserve them, not the museum, allows them to continue the natural cycle or progression of their life.

There is an old woman in black, in long skirts, sitting in the sun in a doorway in a small hilltop village in France.

You are almost embarrassed to see her there as you pass the bottom of the street and look up at the sunny house-fronts, because she seems to be an imitation of an old woman in black in a hilltop village; there are no more women like that now, knitting in the sun, as there were for hundreds of years, as well as women in black skirts sweeping their front steps; by now they have all been so depicted and overdepicted, so memorialized, that surely they do not exist any longer, so where did this one come from?

Memories creating three-dimensional space—recent memories shallow space, older memories deeper space, oldest memories deepest space—(and there is Mary in most mysterious Africa). The mind like a house—or an apartment, to a city dweller. In the house, there is attic and basement, in the apartment there are the farthest—most remote—rooms, unsuspected, around corners, down hallways, always another where you thought the apartment ended: this being a recurring dream for years, I thought due to my (real) frustration wanting at last an apartment large enough, now (the dream still recurring) having a house, but wanting a larger house, large enough, at last; but "large enough," I realize now, meaning containing rooms that stay empty, that are not used and not even furnished; but perhaps, all this time, that dream not reflecting any reality but only symbolizing the mind, the mind needing another room and yet another, rooms scarcely known, rooms mostly empty, filled mostly as yet with light and air and some dust (dust being their own sign of a naturally continuing life, a too-clean room having its own natural life interrupted).

The apartment has depth on a single level, horizontally (two-dimensional), while the house has depth vertically (three-dimensional). The mind in fact more like the apartment because I am reaching out for things horizontally.

"Remember the Van Wagenens." Father's memory is mostly gone. Mother is still alive, with a good memory, but someday, only my brother, besides me, will know what this phrase means.

The Van Wagenens lived below us in that apartment building. We stamped and stomped, and were reminded that we were not alone in the building. I want to say to someone else, now, when he stamps and stomps, "Remember the Van Wagenens!" and I am sad that he won't understand. But why am I sad? Why do I want him to know about the Van Wagenens? And why couldn't I say "Remember the Harrises" or "Remember the Smiths" and give it the same meaning? Say that the Harrises or Smiths were our neighbors downstairs. Only my brother, eventually, would know I was not telling the truth. But why does the truth matter?

When we did not stomp, but only shouted, we were reminded to remember the old woman next door; in an earlier building, it was the old couple next door. Now I have forgotten their names. My brother will probably remember. He does not often—though he does sometimes, to my keen pleasure—reveal new memories, when I apply to him for memories of our family life, but he also does not usually forget old ones.

On television, someone says, approximately (I do not remember the exact words), "As we grow older, we can't help but believe that the dead, in some way, live on." This was in the movie made from E. M. Forster's *A Passage to India*, though it has taken me a moment to remember that.

Odorous early-morning fogs—in Graz or in Nottingham. I experience something like it today, or rather the two elements separately but simultaneously—mist in the hills out the window of the bus and at the same time a smell of some sort of fuel burning—and there is a deep physical desire in me to leap back into that fog, especially the fog of the Austrian early-morning streets with trolley tracks running through them. Wanting to go back into that past and into the past more generally, why? Because it is not full of the unknown, as the future is? Or because it is richer, sensually richer, as each succeeding year, in these times, in this country anyway, becomes poorer, sensually? More uniformity (less variety); cleaner people (fewer smells); more plastic surgery and better health (fewer physical deformities and "imperfections"); more television (less singing, dancing, playing on musical instruments, storytelling, communal cooking, gossiping); more "conveniences" (less labor of certain kinds, including cooking with its smells and tastes); more uniformity of speech (less dialect, less eccentricity of thought and behavior, fewer family expressions); more paving and construction (less wildlife, less wilderness, less vegetation); fewer kitchen gardens (neater properties, more clipping and cutting, less planting and growing); less backyard raising of poultry (fewer stinks and squawks, less mud); fewer backyard clotheslines (less flapping and snapping of large white sheets).

Memory as distortion—I read something and remember it slightly wrong because what it actually said suggested a certain thought, somewhat related but not the same, something I wanted it to say, something I had been thinking, or wanted to think.

Then there is the memory of a thought or sequence of thoughts: as I walked past this particular spot two weeks ago, this thought unfolded—it was moderately interesting at the time (kept me mildly entertained or occupied for the twenty seconds it took to unfold as I walked past this building), but not interesting at all, now, the second time; there is nothing left to do with it. Walking past the same spot again now, as the same sequence begins its procession, I forcibly stop it. The most interesting thoughts (or thoughts that continue to be interesting) turn out to be the tricky problems that are not solved after only one or two ruminations (why did Layman P'ang put his head on the knee of his disciple when it came time for P'ang to die?).

(Another puzzle: the case of the man I read about in the newspaper who took a vow not to speak on Sundays—the fact that his perceptions were so much clearer. Was this because his "self" did not get in the way of his perceptions? Our speech so often bringing our intruding selves into the scene. *Open Mouth Already a Mistake.* A title enjoyed in itself over and over again, but also a good book, and also a good thing to remember.)

What was misheard, at a meeting: "breadth and depth" mistaken for another pair of contrasts or contrasting dimensions, "breath and death." But the question is: When we do not mis-hear, when we *correctly* understand, do we not still hear the other words at the same time, though we may not consciously acknowledge this?

Memory: When you have a chance to compare, as you don't always, or very often, what you remember with the actual thing itself, there are almost always differences, some vast, some small—the very distinctly visualized page of that grammar book, with the lovely simple illustration at the top and the paragraph of simple narrative text below, and then below that the lovely simple double list of vocabulary, including, in the first lesson, *pupitre*, *cahier*, and *crayon*, is not after all quite the same as the actual page of the actual grammar book when I finally see it. Close, but not exactly the same, as Mlle Roser's face and figure are close but not exactly the same. (As our memory of a sentence of something read—so important to us that we refer to it in our own thinking quite often—may be close but not the same as the actual sentence, and sometimes crucially different, not the same thought at all.) And this necessarily means that we live closeted with, hedged in by, hosts and scores, sequences, chains, lines of memories all inaccurate.

We are excited by the stone—the shard from Hadrian's Wall—that we carry away in our pocket. As though we need physical proof that something happened. Otherwise, history told in the past tense may seem like a tall tale told in the past tense also, just as the tall tale told in the past tense pretends to be true, fact, history. For "true" history, we have the stories of historians, many accounts slightly different, maybe and maybe not true. Then we have what we are told are stones from Hadrian's wall. We are excited, even if we never cared about Hadrian or his wall. We are excited that many different things happened on this same spot of ground, layers of stories overlapping and covering the many spots of the one earth. As though, again, the past were a space that we could go back into. The past another space, one to enter to get away from this present.

A person stands before the rubble of Hadrian's Wall imagining what occurred and unfolded when the wall still stood, and imagining what has occurred since. For that person, the air is thick with forms, colors. But to the person standing five feet behind the one imagining, to the person who does not know that these stones have any historical significance, the air is clear, the stones are only stones. All that activity is in the force of the imagining of the person five feet in front of him.

I do not know where Hadrian's Wall is, or if it still exists in any form. It is just a name that springs into my mind. I cannot even remember who Hadrian was, exactly.

The stones, the grammar book, the official document, the personal letter, the voice of a person who had been "lost" ("lost" as in the alumnae magazine listings of "lost" alumnae, as for instance the early friend Mary): when we bring them in front of us, they suddenly have a present presence—they belong to the present, have a life in the present alongside their life in the past. Is that why we want to find them? To give them a life in the present in order to make their life in the past more real?

Sometimes, I can't bear it that someone like Mlle Roser isn't still here—and this force of desire is what brings her back into the present in some other way, as: her life story written now, in the present, as I would like to write it; or as: a strong imagining that she still has consciousness in some form (with a willful disregard on my part of actual fact or possibility). The *not being able to bear it* is the *missing*. You want everything you want to be present all the time, or at least present whenever you will it to be present. What do we do about all these missing pieces?

Who is that woman talking to, who sits by her husband's grave and talks to him? She is not "pretending" to talk to him. She is "really" talking to him. She is really talking to someone who is not there, or does not seem to anyone but her to be there. Because of the force of her imagining.

In the brain cells, the old reality coexists with the new reality (the old reality being the training of memory, what memory, consistent over a long time, has trained into those brain cells). For example, the new reality is this feeble old man who doesn't know where his mouth is when he puts up his hand to eat, but the old reality is still there in this old woman's brain cells, so that in times of stress, exhaustion, and confusion (having fallen in the dark in the middle of the night on her way to the bathroom, sick to her stomach) she calls out: "Robert! Robert!" as though he would come help her from his bed in the next room, as though he were not half a mile away in the nursing home. And the old reality probably continues to be there, engraved on brain cells that do not die, but are simply now accessible by routes different from the ones we use in waking, commonsensical life, accessible by routes that become smooth and easy in sleep, exhaustion, panic, when we are less "in control." And so, our childishness, at times of emotional stress, may be simply the brain bypassing the more adult, controlled, later-learned behavior, opening pathways to earlier reactions that are still engraved in us, not erased.

I see that I speculate, but do not want to go and read.

I do not want to go and find out how the brain "really" works, according to someone who "knows." Maybe I don't want to admit that someone else may know more about my brain than I do.

Oh, yes, though. I do believe everything has to be physical, all our emotions, even our "spiritual" life. What else can it be but physical?

Those vast apartments of the dreams—whatever they may symbolize, exactly (their symbolic character being just as "real" as their nonsymbolic character), whether it is in fact the mind, in which case the mind dreams of the mind, or something else—may be so often dreamed that now they are present in waking life, too, their presence felt constantly. Another place (like the past) to go to in the imagination: cease to see what is in front of us, bulletin board or window filled with traffic, and now see that apartment, spacious as we always desired so greatly but never had, or pasture with cow path leading up to Alpine higher pasture that feels essential to us, though exactly why? In what way essential?

This woman reports to me what I had reported to her once, many years ago, and then forgotten: that in the south of France, men who worked all day in the lavender fields would gather in the evenings in the bars, smelling of lavender. This was "my" piece of information, but I forgot it, and she remembered it all these years. After she tells it to me now, I seem to remember it; it seems familiar. Had it been engraved in my mind also, but in a place where I did not have any access to it until now? Am I recalling it now, or learning it afresh? How can I tell?

———

In the pharmacy, family-owned, with a good, steady stream of customers, several of whom are now waiting by the counter holding a prescription or some items they are about to purchase, an old Englishman in a zippered, cream-colored cardigan with remarkably frayed elbows, a scarf at the neck (perhaps an ascot), long silky white hair, an ear plug (or hearing aid), thick glasses, etc., stands at the counter writing a check in a large ledger, and over and over again he looks up and straightens up to reminisce to the pharmacist about his service in South Africa piloting a plane during the war. His daughter or granddaughter, behind him and to one side, holding his "stick," smiles. "He's ninety-two," she says eventually, quietly. "He remembers everything." She radiates generosity and unambivalent love. She does not try to hurry him along, even gently; she is not worried that he keeps some customers waiting by the counter.

Maybe what she said was "He does not forget anything."

I want to remember exactly what she said, but someone reading this does not mind if it is not exact: Please, says that someone, just choose one or the other and get on with the story. Give me fiction, if you have to—the approximation. Not the truth, along with your doubt.

You have no separable *memory* of having learned that word, but you understand that word or at least have a better sense of it than you could if you hadn't learned it at some point.

You pass a house in a strange town and it gives you a peculiar feeling—you know that something about it touches some memory, and although you don't have access to the memory, the feeling comes to you, sometimes lightly, sometimes heavily. Houses in your own town, too familiar to you, may not trigger this same feeling because they are not fresh: the fresh house belongs to a certain type of house that triggers this feeling, but it is a fresh example because it has a color, setting, ornamentation, light, etc., that you have not seen before.

And then: What about houses or other objects that do not explicitly call up a feeling? Can it be that just under the surface, a memory and a feeling are touched and influence your mood in a way beyond your grasp?

What about the "stimulating" effect of travel? Does travel provide not only a succession of new images and thoughts but also a stream of fresh reawakenings of liminal or subliminal memories and feelings?

You see a paper case of sewing and mending needles, arranged in a neat pattern by the manufacturer—it could be anywhere, in a store, in your own sewing basket—and *every time* you see this, it gives you a peculiar feeling. *What is it about those needles? What happened, all those many years ago?* You think it must have been in that sunny back bedroom upstairs where the old sewing machine was, with its wooden case, and where you think sewing and mending went on. But did something happen, or was it just that you, a child, were suddenly struck by the beauty of those arranged needles?

The various stimuli of a given day produce dreams that are either remembered or not remembered. If not remembered, then they are a part of our life in which we were actors but are unaware of our actions, the "lost night" being like the "lost weekend," night after night "lost."

But if you have nurtured, deep in your mind, an equivalency between house and mind or head, eyes and windows, when you look at house after house are you always, on another level, on a less accessible level, seeing mind after mind, or head after head, eyes all around, on either side of the street?

The mind's inevitable habit of making metaphors: in Chinese calligraphy, *tiger + pig = wild boar*. When we come upon an unfamiliar thing, we compare it to something familiar (book reviewers also do this).

And possibly all elements of landscape affect us all the time metaphorically as well as really: he wants to live by water not only because of its real beauties—space, light, reflection, color, constant change and motion—but also its positive metaphorical properties, whatever they may be to him—cradling, nurturing, supporting?—whereas she is afraid of living by water, despite its real beauties, because of its negative metaphorical associations for her—submersion, suffocation, the fact of being overwhelmed by a vastly greater presence than herself. She is more comfortable in a high place: a slight rise or prominence is good, a good place to put a house, for instance; but a mountaintop, even Alpine, is what she craves to experience at least periodically, not just for its real beneficial properties—fine view, spaciousness, good muscular ache in the legs getting up there, good cleansing of the lungs—but also for its metaphorical properties—being "on top of" things, not letting things "get her down," having a "broad outlook," and a "sense of perspective."

She cringes from cramped valleys, narrow declivities, and craves the security of a high place, especially one bare of trees, open, preferably with meadows—and a cow or two, or a few goats would not be unwelcome, the meadows being tamed or domesticated by the presence of assenting cows or goats (judgments made by animals being reassuring, even if often made in ignorance of facts beyond their comprehension).

But is the craving for the Alpine meadow also conditioned or developed by early experiences that laid down a deposit of memories that in turn continue to affect development? (Though this is perhaps beside the point, experiences of sheer beauty may train a child to a certain appreciation of beauty.)

The child is taken to a mountain. Because there is already something in the child that craves a high place (up and well away from a submersive presence), this experience of the mountain is doubly moving and satisfying to the child. Then, the memory of that doubly satisfying experience of the mountain is added to the need that has always been present for what the mountain offers metaphorically, reinforcing the compelling pull of the mountain.

Do chronic mountain climbers always resume this quest for what the mountain offers really and metaphorically? As certain writers always write the same stories, or the same poems? As though certain things can be visited over and over but never quite said in such a way that they are over and done with? The mountain has been climbed, but it is still there.

Another possibility concerning what it means to climb a mountain: When so many difficulties in our lives seem mountainous, it is satisfying to climb an actual mountain. Unlike a difficulty, the mountain is not only *like* a mountain, it *is* a mountain; and it is also easier to climb, or at least simpler.

The Poetics of Space by Gaston Bachelard (though the translation could be improved, so that it would not seem so strange and difficult in places), and *Metaphors We Live By* by George Lakoff and Mark Johnson (though it does not go far enough or have enough in it).

Mrs. Palfrey at the Claremont by Elizabeth Taylor: Reading this for me is a retreat into a depiction of an earlier reality—England in the 1960s in this case, but a very old-fashioned corner of it. And it is comforting because it is earlier, it is England, it was once real, England and English life were once reassuring to me. And if you grant that earlier ("past") realities have the same power as present ones, you feel you can choose to be elsewhere for a time and you will feel safe from this possibly destructive present.

Curiously, when I actually lived in England in the 1960s, I was not in the least comforted or reassured. If, however, living there then, I had read a novel about England in the 1920s, I probably would have been comforted and reassured.

If stress, or an excess or deficiency of certain chemicals, changes the pathways in your brain, and you believe in the past reality and not the present one, or believe in your own created version of the present one, you really will be safe from this possibly destructive present, since this present is pervasively destructive not so much physically—though it is destructive to much and to many physically—as psychically, to humans anyway.

———————

I turn on the television in the middle of a difficult day, for distraction, and happen to encounter again the movie made from Forster's novel, and I watch it for a few minutes, and soon, though in a setting different from the one I had remembered, the words are spoken that I had been so surprised and glad to hear because I had been thinking the same thing, though they are not quite the words I had remembered. They are (preserved correctly because this time I wrote them down immediately):

It's difficult, as we get older, not to believe that the dead live again.

What I had remembered, though still a double negative, was a slightly more positive double negative than what was actually said. In memory, I had altered the statement in a couple of ways to bring it closer to what I myself preferred to think: "As we grow older, we can't help but believe that the dead, in some way, live on."

1998

Acknowledgments and Notes

A BELOVED DUCK GETS COOKED: FORMS AND INFLUENCES I
This essay was written as a talk for NYU's Master Class series given in 2012–2013. An adapted version appeared in *The Virginia Quarterly Review* 95, no. 2 (Summer 2019).

COMMENTARY ON ONE VERY SHORT STORY ("IN A HOUSE BESIEGED")
Previously published in *The Atlantic*, July/August 2014.

FROM RAW MATERIAL TO FINISHED WORK: FORMS AND INFLUENCES II
This was the second Master Class for NYU.

A NOTE ON THE WORD *GUBERNATORIAL*
Previously published in the *Oxford American Writer's Thesaurus* (Oxford University Press, 2012).

JOAN MITCHELL AND *LES BLUETS*, 1973
This essay combines a memoir written for *Artforum International* 34, no. 5 (January 1996), and reprinted in *Poetry Magazine* 201, no. 5 (February 2013), with extracts from a review of Klaus Kertess's *Joan Mitchell* published in *Bookforum*, Summer 1997.

JOHN ASHBERY'S TRANSLATION OF RIMBAUD'S *ILLUMINATIONS*
This review was first published in *The New York Times Book Review*, June 9, 2011.

YOUNG PYNCHON
This essay was a contribution to a Thomas Pynchon issue of *Bookforum* published Summer 2005.

THE STORY IS THE THING: LUCIA BERLIN'S *A MANUAL FOR CLEANING WOMEN*
This essay was written as a foreword for Berlin's story collection published in 2015 by Farrar, Straus and Giroux.

A CLOSE LOOK AT TWO BOOKS BY RAE ARMANTROUT
These two reviews were first published as, respectively, "Some Notes on Armantrout's Precedence," *Poetics Journal* 6 (Spring 1986), and "Why Stop with a Barnacle?" in *A Wild Salience: The Writing of Rae Armantrout*, ed. Tom Beckett (Burning Press, 1999).

SMALL BUT PERFECTLY FORMED: FIVE FAVORITE SHORT STORIES
This piece was written to accompany a review of my *Collected Stories* in *Metro* (UK), August 4, 2010.

THE IMPETUS WAS DELIGHT: A RESPONSE BY ANALOGY TO THE WORK OF JOSEPH CORNELL
First published in *A Convergence of Birds: On Joseph Cornell*, ed. Jonathan Safran Foer (D.A.P., 2001).

SOURCES, REVISION, ORDER, AND ENDINGS: FORMS AND INFLUENCES III
The third of the five Master Classes at NYU in 2012–2013. One section was previously published in *Because You Asked: A Book of*

Answers on the Art & Craft of the Writing Life, ed. Katrina Roberts (Lost Horse Press, 2015). An adapted version was published in *The Yale Review*, Fall 2019.

REVISING ONE SENTENCE
First published in *The Paris Review* 229 (Summer 2019).

FOUND MATERIAL, SYNTAX, BREVITY, AND THE BEAUTY OF AWKWARD PROSE: FORMS AND INFLUENCES IV
The fourth of the NYU Master Classes in 2012–2013. Originally published in *The Columbia Review*, Spring 2019.

FRAGMENTARY OR UNFINISHED: BARTHES, JOUBERT, HÖLDERLIN, MALLARMÉ, FLAUBERT
An earlier version of this piece was originally composed as a talk given at the New Langton Arts Center in San Francisco in 1986. Part of it was subsequently published in *HOW(ever)* 4, no. 2 (October 1987), under the title "Form as a Response to Doubt."

THIRTY RECOMMENDATIONS FOR GOOD WRITING HABITS
The fifth of the NYU Master Classes in 2012–2013. An adapted version was published on the Literary Hub website.

ENERGY IN COLOR: ALAN COTE'S RECENT PAINTINGS
Previously published in *Tweed's* 2 (2014).

"EMMY MOORE'S JOURNAL" BY JANE BOWLES
Previously published in *Object Lessons:* The Paris Review *Presents the Art of the Short Story*, ed. Lorin Stein and Sadie Stein (Picador, 2012).

OSAMA ALOMAR'S VERY SHORT TALES IN *FULLBLOOD ARABIAN*
Previously published as a preface to this collection of Alomar's sto-

ries in New Directions' poetry pamphlet series, 2013; also published in *The New Yorker* online, December 16, 2013, as "Osama Alomar's Very Short Tales."

HAUNTING THE FLEA MARKET: ROGER LEWINTER'S *THE ATTRACTION OF THINGS*
This was a talk given at the Albertine Bookshop on December 2, 2016, to celebrate the New Directions publication of two books by Lewinter translated by Rachel Careau.

RED MITTENS: ANSELM HOLLO'S TRANSLATION FROM THE CHEREMISS
Originally published in *Poems That Make Grown Women Cry*, eds. Anthony Holden and Ben Holden (Simon & Schuster, 2016).

IN SEARCH OF DIFFICULT EDWARD DAHLBERG
Originally published in *Conjunctions* 29 (Fall 1997).

GUSTAVE FLAUBERT'S *MADAME BOVARY*
Previously published, in slightly different form, as the introduction to my translation of *Madame Bovary* (Viking Penguin, 2010).

DUTCH SCENES: A PORTFOLIO OF EARLY TWENTIETH-CENTURY TOURIST PHOTOGRAPHS
First published in *The Paris Review* 206 (Fall 2013).

THE PROBLEM OF PLOT SUMMARY IN BLANCHOT'S FICTION
First published as a section of *Proust, Blanchot and a Woman in Red* (Cahier #5, Sylph Editions/AUP, 2007).

STENDHAL'S ALTER EGO: *THE LIFE OF HENRY BRULARD*
Preface to Stendhal's *The Life of Henry Brulard*, tr. John Sturrock

(New York Review Books, 2002); reprinted in *Brick* 69, Spring 2002, and in *Unknown Masterpieces*, ed. Edwin Frank (New York Review Books, 2003).

MAURICE BLANCHOT ABSENT
Previously published in *Nowhere Without No: In Memory of Maurice Blanchot*, ed. Kevin Hart (Vagabond Press, 2003).

A FAREWELL TO MICHEL BUTOR
Previously published in *The New York Times Magazine*, December 25, 2016.

MICHEL LEIRIS'S *FIBRILS*, VOLUME 3 OF *THE RULES OF THE GAME*
Originally published, in slightly different form, as the introduction to my translation of *Fibrils* (Yale University Press, 2017).

AS I WAS READING
Previously published in *2000andWhat?: Stories About the Turn of the Millennium*, ed. Karl Roeseler and David Gilbert (Trip Street Press, 1996).

MEETING ABRAHAM LINCOLN
First published in *The Harvard Review* 31 (Fall 2006); also posted on the *Harvard Review* online archive feature, 2015.

"PARING OFF THE AMPHIBOLOGISMS": JESUS RECOVERED BY THE JESUS SEMINAR
First published in *Joyful Noise: The New Testament Revisited*, eds. Rick Moody and Darcey Steinke (Little, Brown & Co., 1997).

A READING OF THE SHEPHERD'S PSALM
First published in *The Good Book: Writers Reflect on Favorite Passages from the Bible*, ed. Andrew Blauner (Simon & Schuster, 2015).

REMEMBER THE VAN WAGENENS
Previously published in *The Business of Memory: The Art of Remembering in an Age of Forgetting*, Graywolf Forum Three, ed. Charles Baxter (Graywolf Press, 1999); first published in *Southern Humanities Review* 33, no. 1 (Winter 1999).

ILLUSTRATION CREDITS